TOTAL
COMPETITION

TOTAL COMPETITION

Lessons in Strategy from Formula One

ROSS BRAWN

ADAM PARR

**SIMON &
SCHUSTER**

London · New York · Sydney · Toronto · New Delhi

A CBS COMPANY

First published in Great Britain by Simon & Schuster UK Ltd, 2016
A CBS COMPANY

5 7 9 10 8 6 4

Simon & Schuster UK Ltd
1st Floor
222 Gray's Inn Road
London WC1X 8HB

www.simonandschuster.co.uk
www.simonandschuster.com.au
www.simonandschuster.co.in

Simon & Schuster Australia, Sydney
Simon & Schuster India, New Delhi

The author and publishers have made all reasonable efforts
to contact copyright-holders for permission, and apologise
for any omissions or errors in the form of credits given.
Corrections may be made to future printings.

A CIP catalogue record for this book
is available from the British Library

Hardback ISBN: 978-1-4711-6235-0
Trade paperback ISBN: 978-1-4711-6236-7
eBook ISBN: 978-1-4711-6237-4

Typeset in Stone by M Rules
Printed and bound by CPI Group (UK) Ltd, Croydon, CR0 4YY

MIX
Paper from
responsible sources
FSC® C020471

Simon & Schuster UK Ltd are committed to sourcing paper
that is made from wood grown in sustainable forests and support the Forest
Stewardship Council, the leading international forest certification organisation.
Our books displaying the FSC logo are printed on FSC certified paper.

To Jean Brawn and Emmanuelle Parr

CONTENTS

GLOSSARY OF KEY NAMES AND TERMS

Bernie Ecclestone Chief Executive of the Commercial Rights Holder since 1978.

Charlie Whiting Officially, FIA Race Director and Safety Delegate since 1997; in effect, the Chief Technical Officer of Formula One.

Christian Horner Team Principal of the Red Bull F1 team.

Clarifications A process by which F1 teams seek confidential guidance from the FIA concerning the legality of a design under the Technical Regulations.

Colin Kolles Former Team Principal of the F1 team that competed as Jordan, Midland, Spyker and Force India from 2005 to 2008.

Commercial Rights Holder The owner of the commercial rights in Formula One, variously known as the Formula One Group, of which Bernie Ecclestone is Chief Executive.

Concorde Agreements
The name given to the three-way contracts between the F1 teams, the Commercial Rights Holder and the FIA. These agreements determine how revenues are shared and rules made. They also determine what components of a car must be designed by each Constructor. Until the end of 2012, there was one agreement signed by all the parties. The current agreements began on 1 January 2013 and expire on 31 December 2020.

CVC
The private equity group that acquired Formula One in 2006 and remains the controlling shareholder. The managing partner of CVC is Donald Mackenzie.

Dietrich Mateschitz
Co-founder and Chairman of Red Bull.

Dieter Zetsche
Chairman of the Board of Directors of Daimler AG and Head of Mercedes-Benz Cars since 2006.

Downforce
The force produced when an F1 car moves through the air, forcing the car into the ground. The opposite of lift produced by an aircraft. The penalty of downforce is energy-sapping drag so the holy grail of F1 aerodynamics is to maximize downforce and minimize drag, enabling the car to corner faster with high straight line speed.

FIA
The Fédération Internationale de l'Automobile, owner and regulator of Formula One.

Flavio Briatore
Team Principal of the Benetton and then Renault F1 teams from 1994 until 2009.

FOTA   The Formula One Teams Association, which represented all the teams between 2009 and its collapse in 2013.

Frank Williams Founder and Team Principal of the Williams F1 team.

Jean Todt   President of the FIA since 2009. Formerly, Team Principal of the Scuderia Ferrari from 1994 to 2006, and CEO of Ferrari from 2006 to 2009.

John Barnard F1 designer and technical director whose career overlapped with Ross Brawn's at Benetton and then Ferrari. During his second stint at Ferrari in the mid-1990s, Barnard's design office was located in Surrey, England.

Luca di Montezemolo President and then Chairman of Ferrari between 1991 and 2014.

Martin Whitmarsh Team Principal of the McLaren F1 team from 2009 to 2014, where he was Managing Director from 1997.

Max Mosley   President of the FIA between 1993 and 2009.

Nick Fry   Chief executive of the Brackley-based F1 team that went through several incarnations as BAR, Honda, Brawn and Mercedes. Commercial partner, and fellow shareholder, with Ross Brawn of the Brawn GP team.

Niki Lauda   Chairman of the Mercedes F1 team and former F1 World Champion.

Pat Symonds   Chief Technical Officer of the Williams F1
                       team. Formerly Michael Schumacher's race
                       engineer at the Benetton F1 team and then
                       technical director at Benetton, which became
                       the Renault F1, where Symonds served as
                       Director of Engineering until 2009.

Patrick Head   Co-founder and Director of Engineering of the
                       Williams F1 Team.

Ron Dennis   Shareholder, CEO and chairman of the
                       McLaren Technology Group which includes
                       the F1 team and McLaren roadcars.

Rory Byrne   Chief Designer at Benetton between 1991 and
                       1996 and Ferrari between 1997 and 2006.

RRA   The Resource Restriction Agreement, a cost
                       control measure introduced by FOTA in 2009
                       and which collapsed in 2013.

Sporting   The FIA's rules that govern the Grand Prix
Regulations   events.

Technical   The FIA's technical rules that govern the
Regulations   design of F1 cars.

Toto Wolff   Head of Mercedes Motorsport since 2013.
                       Investor in Williams F1 2009 to 2013.

SOME KEY MOMENTS IN FORMULA ONE DURING THE BRAWN ERA

The 1970s

- Formula One in the 1970s is a battle primarily between Ferrari and the British *garagiste* teams: Lotus, Tyrrell, Brabham, McLaren and later Williams. The multiple championship winning drivers of this decade are Jackie Stewart, Emerson Fittipaldi and Niki Lauda.
- James Hunt, in a McLaren, defeats Ferrari's Niki Lauda by one point to win the politically charged and competitive 1976 season.
- In 1974, Bernie Ecclestone, owner of the Brabham team, sets up the Formula One Constructors' Association to represent and negotiate on behalf of the Formula One teams. This entity will become in due course the Commercial Rights Holder for Formula One.

- In 1977, Max Mosley leaves the March team he has co-founded in order to become FOCA's legal advisor. Mosley and Ecclestone would dominate the sport until 2009.
- Frank Williams sets up Williams Grand Prix Engineering in 1977. Powered by a Cosworth DFV engine, Williams F1 wins its first race at the British Grand Prix at Silverstone in the summer of 1979. At the end of this era the significance of aerodynamically generated downforce from the underside of the cars is discovered and cornering speeds escalate.

The 1980s

- The 1980s start with the new Williams team winning with drivers Alan Jones and Keke Rosberg. Then, after an appearance by Ferrari and Brabham's Nelson Piquet, there follows a period of dominance for the McLaren team, with drivers Niki Lauda, Ayrton Senna and Alain Prost taking titles.
- Concern about high cornering speeds means a regulatory flat bottom to the cars is introduced for 1983, but the genie is out of the lamp and the designers continue to find ways to recover downforce from ground effect.
- Just before the start of the 1986 season, Frank Williams suffers paraplegic injuries in a road accident in the South of France. The Williams team goes on to win the Constructors' titles in 1986 and 1987.
- During this era, turbocharged engines dominate and more manufacturers enter the sport. Both McLaren

and Williams are powered by Honda turbo engines that produced some 1,300 hp in qualifying trim. At this time, engines were replaced after qualifying.

- The 1980s see some dramatic duels between team mates: Prost against Senna in the McLaren, Nigel Mansell against Nelson Piquet in the Williams.

- In August 1988, Enzo Ferrari dies at the age of 90 at Maranello, the home of the Ferrari sports car and racing team – known as the Scuderia – that he founded in 1939.

- The escalating cost and power of turbocharged engines causes a ban from 1989 and a reversion to 3.5 litre normal aspirated engines.

The 1990s

- On the track, the 1990s begin as the 1980s ended, with McLaren out in front, and two championship titles for their driver Ayrton Senna. For the rest of the decade it is Williams – who now have the genius designer Adrian Newey on board – and Benetton who have recruited the young Michael Schumacher. Again there are some notable battles on track: Williams drivers Damon Hill and Jacques Villeneuve taking on Michael Schumacher at Benetton and then Ferrari in 1994 and 1997 respectively. At the end of the 1990s McLaren recruit Newey and enjoy a resurgence with Mika Hakkinen at the wheel – but come up against the powerful new Ferrari organization which includes Michael Schumacher and a new technical team led by Brawn.

- Off the track, the sport's regulator undergoes a generational change. In 1991, Mosley becomes president of the Fédération Internationale du Sport Automobile (FISA), then an independent commission of the FIA. In 1993, Mosley becomes president of the FIA.
- In May 1994, at the San Marino Grand Prix at Imola, Roland Ratzenberger and Ayrton Senna are killed in separate incidents over the weekend.
- The FIA takes measures to improve safety in Formula One. There are no fatal accidents in the sport until the death of Jules Bianchi 20 years later.
- The FIA also takes an active role in road car safety, ultimately succeeding in launching the transformational Euro NCAP safety assessment for new vehicles.
- 'Active' hydraulically controlled suspension, designed to optimise the cars running heights, is banned for the 1994 season.
- The normally aspirated engines are reduced from 3.5 litres to 3 litres for 1995.

2000–2007

- Ferrari and Michael Schumacher dominate on the track for the first five years of the new millennium. Renault and Fernando Alonso then win in 2005 and 2006. In 2007, McLaren's driver Lewis Hamilton comes second in his rookie season, one point behind Ferrari's Kimi Raikkonen and on the same points as Fernando Alonso, now his team mate at McLaren.

McLaren is, however, stripped of its position in the Constructors' World Championship and fined $100 million by the FIA for obtaining confidential technical data about Ferrari's car.

- The first years of the century see a rise in car manufacturers racing in F1. By 2007, Renault, Honda, Toyota, BMW join Ferrari with their own teams. From 2006, the Red Bull drinks company also fields two teams. As these teams are funded from vast marketing budgets, costs escalate.

- For 2006 the normally aspirated engines are reduced from 3 litres to 2.4 litres and a compulsory V8 configuration. For 2007 their specification is frozen, curtailing all engine development unless for reliability or cost reduction.

- Off the track, the German Kirch media group takes a 75 per cent stake in Formula One before going bankrupt in 2002. In 2005, the private equity firm CVC Capital Partners acquires Kirch's stake from Kirch's creditors led by the German Bayerische Landesbank. BLB's representative in Formula One is Gerhard Gribkowsky, who is jailed in 2012 for tax evasion, breach of duty and accepting $44 million in bribes in relation to this transaction.

2008–2013

- The 2008 season sees Lewis Hamilton win his first championship title, taking it from Ferrari's Felipe Massa at the last corner of the last race in Brazil. By then, the Global Financial Crisis has set in. The F1 teams establish the Formula One Teams Association

(FOTA) to negotiate for more revenues and to reduce costs. FOTA is chaired first by Luca di Montezemolo of Ferrari and then by Martin Whitmarsh of McLaren.

- In 2008, the teams and the FIA agreed to work together to introduce a cap on costs. These efforts are side-tracked when the English tabloid *News of the World* publishes an article and video footage that illegally breaches the privacy of Max Mosley.

- At the Singapore Grand Prix in 2008, Nelson Piquet Jnr crashes in circumstances that allow his Renault team-mate, Fernando Alonso, to win the race – and raise suspicions about the incident. A year later, an FIA investigation establishes that the crash was indeed deliberate.

- At the end of 2008, Honda announces it is leaving Formula One. The team is acquired by Ross Brawn and Nick Fry. It goes on to win the World Championships in 2009, powered by Mercedes engines.

- In 2009, the sport adopts its first hybrid engines following pressure from the FIA. The Kinetic Energy Recovery System (KERS) collects energy from braking, stores it in batteries and provides a 100hp boost to the 750 hp engines.

- The Brawn GP cars, along with those of Williams and Toyota, sport an aerodynamic design feature known as a double diffuser. This design increases the surface area of the floor of the car and generates extra aerodynamic downforce. The double diffuser concept is bitterly contested by the other teams who allege that it is not consistent with the intention of the rules. The 2009 rules had been amended in order to reduce aerodynamic downforce and therefore make the cars less sensitive to the turbulence caused by the car in front. It had been hoped that this would make for closer racing and more overtaking. Ultimately, the double diffuser teams win their case in the FIA's International Court of Appeal who rejected the idea that there is an 'intention' in Formula One's technical rules.

- In 2009, Mosley returns to the offensive on costs, proposing a twin-track championship from 2010, in which teams that agree to limit expenditure will have certain technical advantages. The large teams object and FOTA threatens to form a breakaway series. The Williams team is expelled from FOTA for supporting the FIA's proposals. The crisis comes to a head at the British Grand Prix in the summer of 2009 when the teams and the FIA agree a Resource Restriction Agreement to control costs.

- Max Mosley stands down as president of the FIA in 2009 and Jean Todt is elected president.

- Renault, BMW and Toyota leave Formula One at the end of 2009.

- At the end of 2012, the Concorde Agreement (see glossary) expires. Bernie Ecclestone negotiates new contracts with the teams that will take effect from January 2013. The new contracts significantly change the way the revenues are divided and the rules made, with a small group of teams enjoying both a greater share of the money and a bigger say in how the sport is run.

- FOTA collapses in 2013.
- From 2010 to 2013, the Red Bull team and its driver Sebastian Vettel dominate the sport, winning four back-to-back double titles. By 2013, however, the Mercedes team is beginning to be competitive.
- The 2013 season is the last to feature the normally aspirated 2.4 litre V8 engine. From 2014 it is replaced with a new 1.6 litre turbocharged V6 engine, with an expanded energy recovery system. During 2014 and 2015 it is clear that Mercedes have produced the best engine and energy recovery system and their car dominates. During 2016 some progress is made by Ferrari, Renault and Honda but Mercedes still dominate with their engine and car.

Substantial changes to the car technical regulations are to be introduced for 2017, increasing grip and cornering speeds with an objective to improve the racing and reducing the significance of the engine advantage Mercedes have enjoyed. The jury is out ...

INTRODUCTION
Adam Parr

While the battle that is seen on the Formula One track between the drivers – the gladiators of the sport – is the public face, behind them is a billion-dollar engineering war. Formula One requires the teams, around twelve, to design and build their own cars to a set of technical regulations that change almost every year. The technical changes come about to reduce the speed of the cars for safety reasons, to try to improve the spectacle of the sport and sometimes to encourage innovation relevant to road cars. The cars are designed to minimize lap times around twenty-one vastly different circuits: from Australia to Abu Dhabi, Japan to Russia, the United States to Monte Carlo. The top teams can consist of over a thousand people, comprising engineers, designers, scientists, aerodynamicists and highly skilled craftsmen and women. Most of the 10,000 components that go into the chassis and power train are manufactured by the teams themselves to achieve ultimate performance. These components are developed and improved many times during the racing year, culminating in cars often being effectively one to two seconds faster at the last race than they were at the first. It is winning this engineering war that is the foundation of winning a World Championship. Sometimes, an exceptional driver will compensate for a car's weakness, but it is rare. No Championship has ever been won with a poor car.

The overall performance of a modern Formula One car is truly astonishing. The acceleration time from zero to 60 mph is a 'modest' 2.4 seconds, but this is because the car cannot put enough power down through the tyres. In reality the car's acceleration accelerates: the next 60 mph to 120 mph requires only an extra two seconds. And the braking is astonishing: from 200 mph to a standstill in 3.5 seconds. The forces experienced by the drivers are also impressive, 5g in braking and 4g in cornering. By comparison, a high-performance road car might achieve 1g braking and cornering. The excessive g-forces explain why the drivers have to be superb athletes, comparable with any Olympian.

The reason for the impressive performance is largely down to the aerodynamic 'downforce' the cars can generate. They are upside-down jet fighters, with the downforce pushing the car into the ground, through the tyres and increasing grip – hence the reason for the high levels of cornering, braking and acceleration performance. The cars can generate downforce equivalent to their mass, ¾ of a tonne at 110 mph, which means theoretically that, at that speed, they could drive along upside down and stick to the ceiling. At top speed, the cars generate 2.5 tonnes of downforce. The drag is so high that just lifting off the throttle at maximum speed will give over 1g of deceleration – the same level as a performance road car braking hard. In other words, an F1 driver who lifts his foot off the throttle will decelerate as quickly as a Porsche 911 driver doing an emergency brake.

The engines and gearboxes are also impressive engineering achievements. The 8-speed gearbox is highly efficient and changes gear in less than 40 milliseconds. It is also a fully structural part of the car, carrying all the rear suspension components and loads, and the casing is normally made from carbon fibre composite. The power unit consists of a 1.6 litre turbocharged internal combustion engine and an Energy Recovery System (ERS) that captures the kinetic energy of the car and the exhaust energy of the engine through the turbocharger. This energy is stored in a battery pack, and re-applied through two electrical motor-generators installed in the engine. One electrical motor is coupled directly to the power train, providing up to 160 hp for limited periods (in total about 30–40 per cent of the lap) and the other electrical motor is coupled to the turbocharger/compressor to both recover energy and to provide drive to the compressor to optimize the inlet boost profile and eliminate turbo lag. The power unit, internal combustion engine and ERS together can deliver more peak power, in excess of 800 hp, than the previous normally aspirated 2.4 litre V8 power plant. More impressively still, they can do so with less than two-thirds of the fuel used in a race, averaging around 6 mpg at most circuits. This may sound like a gas guzzling engine, but in fact it is perhaps the most efficient use of petrol yet created. In 2015, a single 30 British gallon (100kg) tank of fuel powered Lewis Hamilton's Mercedes car to victory at Monza, a race of 192 miles which he completed in 78 minutes, at an average speed of 147 mph (236 kph).

I have called this book *Total Competition* for two reasons.

First, as we will explore, winning in Formula One requires mastery not only of many technical disciplines but also the economics and politics that are critical to each team's competitive position. As Ross would put it, the goal is completeness. Second, it is a recognition that Ross's success was also derived from his willingness to take every aspect of the sport to the ultimate limit, in the way perhaps that Jack Reynolds conceived what became known as Total Football, and Johan Cruyff became its most celebrated exponent. If anyone can claim to have created and mastered 'Total Formula One', it is Ross Brawn.

Most of this book is, therefore, an exploration of the career and thinking of Ross Brawn. I would like to begin, however, with a brief account of how I came to work with Ross on this project. Unusually for someone writing a book like this, I had the luck – or misfortune – to compete with Ross for several years while I was chief executive and then chairman of one of the oldest teams, the Williams Formula One Team. By coincidence, this was also the team where Ross began his career, 40 years ago this year. I hope to set the context and explain why this book might be of interest to an audience wider than those who follow and are interested in Formula One.

In March 2012, I stood down as chairman of Williams. I had lost a five-year long struggle with the man who controls the sport, Bernie Ecclestone. I described these events in the light-hearted *manga* format of a book I called *The Art of War – Five Years in Formula One*. But these events also prompted me to think about how I had come to lose this struggle, how I had failed in the mission I had set myself – a mission which appeared, then and now, to be entirely rational and beneficial not only for the Williams team, but for Formula One and, indeed, for Ecclestone.

Some people might say that I was ill-prepared for the world of Formula One. I had joined Williams as chief executive in 2006. My career before that had been very different. I had a classical English education at school and Cambridge and in 1987 became an investment banker, working in Tokyo and London. My work brought me into contact with a great British mining company called Rio Tinto and I managed to get myself seconded to them to do some acquisitions. Rio Tinto offered me a job and between then and 2006 I spent eleven years in the mining industry, in South Africa, Europe and Australia. Somewhere in the middle I took a sabbatical to study law and ended up spending a few years as a barrister. But Rio Tinto called me back and I couldn't resist.

My last job at Rio Tinto was head of planning. This was a new position, as the group had never done any form of central planning before. Each of the subsidiary businesses used to do their own plans and then the numbers would be added up. So, I decided to find out first of all, what other ways were there of planning. I went to see some other companies to find out how they did things. This led me to the conclusion that you can't have a plan unless you have a strategy. But Rio Tinto didn't 'do' strategy. In fact, the chairman, Sir Robert Wilson, was, I believe, the person who coined the expression, 'Strategy means paying too much.' By which he meant that if you couldn't justify an acquisition or investment on the basis of a simple financial evaluation, you resorted to 'strategy' to support a case for over-paying. Taken to its extreme, our decentralized and opportunistic business model left no place for planning. Nonetheless, once you have decided you want a plan, then you need to answer the question – a plan to do what? So, I asked myself the question, 'What is strategy?'

Like most people, I was aware that the word strategy comes from the military world, so I made an appointment to visit the Royal Military Academy at Sandhurst, where I met some of the people who teach history to British army officers. This was an important moment for me, as I realized that some of the questions in my mind could be explored through history and specifically military history and the development of military theory. At this stage, my conversations at Sandhurst and subsequent reading led to two fundamental ideas about strategy.

The first was that strategy has three perspectives – political, economic and technical. *Battles* are won on the field through the military superiority of one side. But *wars* are won through a combination of factors, of which military superiority may be the least significant. It is famously said that after World War II the Americans wanted to learn from the German army how to fight outnumbered and win – until someone observed that they had *not* won. Indeed, most great military commanders and armies are ultimately defeated by adversaries who are inferior on the battlefield. So strategy has to look at something broader than *technical* capability. It has to look at the *political* and *economic* resources available to each side and ensure that these are deployed effectively.

The second idea was that strategy is but one level of a hierarchy. I think a lot of people would intuitively recognize that tactics is in some way 'below' strategy. But military theory has evolved a hierarchy that acknowledges four levels: policy; strategy; the operational level (discussed further below as operational art); and the tactical level. This hierarchy matters because people tend to get fixated with the tactical level just as they focus on the technical perspective. I found that these two ideas fitted very well with my experiences as a banker, lawyer and businessman.

I arrived in the world of Formula One at the end of the 2006 season. The fundamental problem for my team – Williams – was that we were up against much richer teams funded by Ferrari, Toyota, Honda, Mercedes, Renault, BMW and Red Bull. These guys were in it for marketing and they were spending as much as ten times what we could afford. Not only that, but the revenues generated by the sport were distributed very unfairly. Ferrari even had a veto over rule changes.

It was not surprising that Williams was on its knees both on the track – our worst season ever – and off the track, with debts of about £35 million. We were close to bankruptcy and, worse still, Ecclestone was pushing for a change in the rules that would have obliterated us. Formula One consists of two World Championships – for Drivers and the Constructors. The Drivers' World Championship obviously goes to the driver who wins the most points during the season. The Constructors' Championship goes to the team whose drivers together have the most points. It is called a Constructors' Championship because under the modern rules, each team has to build its own unique chassis: pretty much everything except the power unit and the gearbox, which they can buy from an engine manufacturer or another team, and some parts, like the tyres, which are now provided by a single supplier in identical form to all teams. So what is different about Formula One compared with most other motor sports, is that the cars are all built to one set of technical regulations, but they are all different. How each constructor interprets the rules is part of the sport. It is also what allows for technical innovation.

But Ecclestone wanted – and this remains the case – teams to be able to buy a *complete* car from another team. This would create customer cars and customer teams. This would have been a disaster for independent teams like Williams. Imagine if you are the fifth fastest runner in the world and someone comes up with the idea of cloning Usain Bolt a few times. You get pushed down the field, your sponsors move to Bolt (or his clones) and you are finished. In Formula One, the car is everything. Look at the career results of Fernando Alonso (see below), undoubtedly a Bolt in his field. Alonso has won two World Championships, and been in the top three in four other years. But he has also finished well down the rankings when his car has been uncompetitive. In the past two seasons he has been racing close to the bottom – but put him in a Mercedes today and he would be racing for the World Championship.

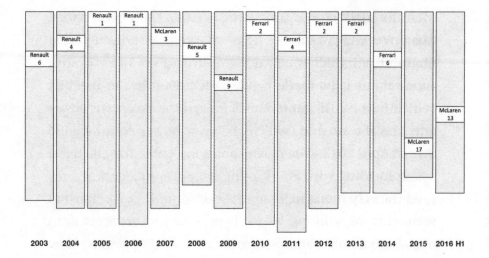

So, we had a few challenges and I devised a reasonably good strategy to strengthen the team financially and to make the playing field more even. The key components were as follows. First, we had to put Williams on a firm financial footing by repaying our debt, diversifying our sources of revenue, and making up for poor on-track performance by being the kind of team that companies would like to be associated with. This meant, for example, being a pioneer in hybrid technology, having high standards of governance and making sure that women were in leadership positions. Second, we had to change the industry structure. This meant fewer car manufacturers, lower costs, a fairer share of the revenues and no customer cars. Third, we needed to rebuild our technical capabilities.

Over the following five years we put this strategy into action, and in some ways it worked better than I could have expected. By March 2012, we had made a profit four years in a row; we had paid off all debts and had some £30 million in the bank. We had floated on the Frankfurt Stock Exchange. We had created Williams Hybrid Power whose flywheel technology had powered Audi to the first hybrid wins at Le Mans for 2012 (and 2013 and 2014). Two out of four board executives were women. We had created Williams Advanced Engineering, which was building the world's most innovative supercar for Jaguar, the C-X75, which starred as Spectre's vehicle in the 2015 James Bond film. And we had put together a technical team and car that would win the Spanish Grand Prix in April 2012 – the first race win for Williams since 2004 and coinciding with Frank Williams' 70th birthday.

At the very moment when the team's strategy for recovery seemed to be working, and our prospects were better than ever, I was forced out of Williams. How this happened I have written about elsewhere, but in many ways it was the same as how Ross Brawn came to leave the Mercedes team the following year. From my perspective, this was unquestionably a failure. From the perspective of Formula One, the absence of any challenge to Ecclestone has already resulted in the reversal of almost every positive reform achieved in the previous decade. The concentration of power in the hands of one man, especially given his long and consistent track record, is unlikely to be beneficial for any sport.

While the fate of Formula One, a sport I love, is of concern to me, my more immediate and personal challenge was to understand why I had failed and whether I – and perhaps others – could learn from this experience. Consequently, I went back to the drawing board. My failure had to be put down to either one or both of two factors: first, that my framework was wrong – or insufficient; and/or, secondly, that I had implemented it badly. It was time to undertake some root cause analysis. In April 2012, I exiled myself to rural France, and began to analyse what had happened. During that summer, I was on a Skype call with Professor Lisa Jardine, who had been my tutor when I was a Cambridge undergraduate. Lisa and I were discussing my interest in doing a PhD and also the subject of my comic book. Lisa mentioned that the library at our old college – Jesus College, Cambridge – had a collection of books on the art of war. She suggested I go and look at it. From this emerged the idea of a PhD thesis, which has, as it turned out, given me the opportunity to look at the very same problem of strategy from a more rigorous and academic perspective.

I will not trouble you with a detailed account of my thesis: it is gathering dust on a library shelf at University College for anyone who wants to track it down. But Ross and I reviewed one aspect of it for this book. This is a section on the first book on strategy, the *Sunzi bingfa* (*'Sun Tzu's Art of War'*). For many people today, this is the work that they think of, if you ask them about 'the art of war'. The *Sunzi* was written 2,300 years ago and argued for a systematic approach to strategy at a time when China was in the midst of a period of incessant competition between many different states fighting for survival and struggling to be the one that would unite China under a single emperor. The final centuries of this competition saw 148 states undertake 256 major wars, until just one state was left standing. This was the state of Qin, from which we get the name China. The *Sunzi* is about what a state needs to do to survive such competition, and about what a person needs to do to be a great strategist. One of its most powerful observations is that a strategist must understand his adversaries and understand himself: 'He who knows the enemy and himself will never in a hundred battles be at risk.'

The *Sunzi* also makes the point that a state can only be completely defeated through internal division, not through external force. And that, of course, is exactly how Bernie Ecclestone controls Formula One and how he defeated me in the non-lethal but nonetheless competitive world that is F1 racing. Bernie knew himself, he knew me and he knew the people around me and he was able to undermine my position to the point where it was untenable.

The process of studying strategy allowed me to understand better where I had gone wrong: quite simply, I had overestimated myself and underestimated my adversary. While my thesis had helped me to come to this realization, I felt that these lessons would be more interesting and accessible if they were presented in a different way. In particular, many people who do not necessarily love motor sport are fascinated by Formula One, precisely because it is almost an intense version of the 'real' world. The competition, the pace of innovation, the two-second pit stops choreographed by twenty or so people, the money, the politics and the sport – these create an environment in which you learn quickly. But I didn't want to write again about my experience of Formula One. I wanted to work with someone who had really nailed it – unequivocally. I chose Ross Brawn.

I chose Ross for two reasons: first, Ross is (to my mind) the most successful competitor in the history of Formula One to date. Ross is famous for his achievements at Ferrari where he was technical director from 1996 to 2006. When Ross led Ferrari to the Constructors' World Championship in 1999, it was the first they had won since 1983, and when Michael Schumacher won the Drivers' World Championship the following year, he was the first Ferrari driver to do so for 21 years. In the six years from 1999 to 2004, Ferrari won six consecutive Constructors' titles and five consecutive Drivers' titles. But that is not the extent of what Ross has achieved. He won World Championships at Williams in the 1980s, with Jaguar (in the World Sports Car Championship and at the Le Mans 24hr Race) at the turn of the 1990s, then at Benetton in the mid-1990s, Ferrari through the early 2000s and finally with his own team, Brawn GP, in 2009. So, Ross has won 24 Drivers' and Constructors' titles in three racing formulae, across five teams and four decades. This is what Ross's career looks like, showing the top placed driver and position in the Constructors' Championship each year:

Year	Team	Best Placed Driver	Constructors
1976	Wolf-Williams (F1)	18 (Chris Amon)	Not placed
1977	Formula 3	—	—
1978	Williams (F1)	11 (Alan Jones)	9
1979	Williams (F1)	3 (Alan Jones	2
1980	Williams (F1)	1 (Alan Jones)	1
1981	Williams (F1)	2 (Carlos Reutemann)	1
1982	Williams (F1)	1 (Keke Rosberg)	4
1983	Williams (F1)	5 (Keke Rosberg)	4
1984	Williams (F1)	8 (Keke Rosberg)	6
1985	Haas (F1)	Not placed	33
1986	Haas (F1)	12 (Alan Jones)	8
1987	Arrows (F1)	10 (Eddie Cheever)	7
1988	Arrows (F1)	8 (Derek Warwick)	5
1989	Arrows (F1)	10 (Derek Warwick)	7
1990	Jaguar (Sportscar)	4 (Andy Wallace)	2
	Jaguar (Le Mans 24 hours)	1 (John Nielsen, Price Cobb, Martin Brundle)	1
1991	Jaguar (Sportscars)	1 (Teo Fabi)	1
1992	Benetton (F1)	3 (Michael Schumacher)	3
1993	Benetton (F1)	4 (Michael Schumacher)	3

Year	Team	Best Placed Driver	Constructors
1994	Benetton (F1)	1 (Michael Schumacher)	2
1995	Benetton (F1)	1 (Michael Schumacher)	1
1996	Benetton (F1)	4 (Jean Alesi)	3
1997	Ferrari (F1)	7 (Eddie Irvine)	2
1998	Ferrari (F1)	2 (Michael Schumacher)	2
1999	Ferrari (F1)	2 (Eddie Irvine)	1
2000	Ferrari (F1)	1 (Michael Schumacher)	1
2001	Ferrari (F1)	1 (Michael Schumacher)	1
2002	Ferrari (F1)	1 (Michael Schumacher)	1
2003	Ferrari (F1)	1 (Michael Schumacher)	1
2004	Ferrari (F1)	1 (Michael Schumacher)	1
2005	Ferrari (F1)	2 (Michael Schumacher)	2
2006	Ferrari (F1)	2 (Michael Schumacher)	2
2007	Sabbatical	—	—
2008	Honda (F1)	14 (Rubens Barrichello)	9

Year	Team	Best Placed Driver	Constructors
2009	Brawn (F1)	1 (Jenson Button)	1
2010	Mercedes (F1)	7 (Nico Rosberg)	4
2011	Mercedes (F1)	7 (Nico Rosberg)	4
2012	Mercedes (F1)	9 (Nico Rosberg)	5
2013	Mercedes (F1)	4 (Lewis Hamilton)	2

But it is hard to learn from unalloyed success. I also knew that Ross had left Formula One in circumstances that were not of his choosing because, in the Spring of 2013, Ross had called me to get my thoughts on the increasingly difficult situation in which he found himself at Mercedes GP. My advice then was simple: 'Don't do what I did, don't leave, stick it out because you are going to win the 2014 World Championships. You have put together two excellent drivers [Hamilton and Rosberg], a new Mercedes power unit, and a technical team that you believe in. Don't walk away and let others take the credit for your work.' But he did walk away six months later, and sure enough, the team he put together has been untouchable since then, and are well on track to win their third consecutive double title in 2016. With Ross, I thought, we can learn from many victories, but also some defeats.

So, in early 2016, I met up with Ross in a quiet country hotel in Oxfordshire to put the idea to him. I suggested that we do a book on the subject of strategy together, and that we do it in the form of a dialogue. Ross agreed and in the spring we sat down for a series of sessions which we recorded at Ross and Jean's house. The main part of this book is a fairly raw transcript of those sessions. We have left them pretty much as they were recorded, to give a good sense of the discussion: the more raw, the better. We have split the discussion into two main sections: Part I is a review of Ross's career and Part II covers his thinking on strategy, and the elements that make it up such as leadership, rhythms and routines.

Based on these sessions, I have pulled together some observations of what I see as the consistent patterns in what Ross did and how he describes it. I have also boiled these down to some basic principles. These principles are set out in Part III, but I think it is useful to introduce them briefly here so that readers can have them in mind as they read the discussion – and see if they reach the same conclusions as I have.

Observation 1. Strategy is a system.
Ross defines strategy as a philosophy from which process flows. But it is a philosophy of *processes*. He describes it as 'integrating, applying processes and approaches, smoothing out'. Ross developed his approach to leadership in the 1980s and he applied it consistently at Jaguar, Benetton, Ferrari, Honda Brawn and Mercedes. This was his system and he describes its various aspects for us.

Observation 2. Avoid unnecessary conflict.
Ross exemplified the principle that strategy is about winning, not fighting. The only place that he allowed conflict was on the race track, and then only between his whole team and the others.

Observation 3. Build trust consciously.
For Ross, trust is a conscious thing. At its heart is the principle that underlies ethical teaching from Confucius to Christ:
treat people how you wanted to be treated yourself.

Observation 4. Know yourself and know the other.
On the plus side, Ross attributes his rigorous routines to
the need to control a certain natural 'laziness' through the
structure provided by rhythms and deadlines. On the downside, Ross was brought down by his failure to understand
the people he was up against and, to an extent, himself. He
would have survived if he had just been up against the external enemy, but the combination of the external enemy and
the internal division between himself and others at Mercedes
was lethal. In my questions of him, I tried to explore how
this happened – how did someone with such good human
understanding get into this situation?

Observation 5. Embrace humility.
Ross is fiercely proud of his achievements and in no doubt
that these are *his* achievements. Still, he has much less ego
than many people who might have less justification for it.
As a result, he was able to be generous with his colleagues,
encouraging others to take the podium and share the success.
This is a rare, and disarming, characteristic.

Observation 6. Invest in people and culture.
Ross did not take a group of people with him from team to
team; in fact there are only a few cases in his long career of
people who worked with him at two teams. Instead, Ross
worked with the people he had, taking time to get to know

them and not allowing himself to make rapid decisions based on early impressions. Within his teams, Ross fostered a culture of openness and order.

Observation 7. Take the measure of time.
Ross has the measure of time. Formula One is about speed – on and off the track, and the feedback loop is agonizingly compressed. But, time and again, Ross would take the focus off the short term and put it onto achieving a step change in what is (for Formula One) the distant future of the following season.

Observation 8. A complete process leads to a competitive product.
Ross talks about a 'complete car' – that means for him a competitive car. To achieve this completeness, Ross first of all sought to bring together all the key components – engine, chassis and tyres for the most part.

Observation 9. Develop and apply a set of rhythms and routines.
Having established an integrated team and structure, Ross instituted rhythms and routines that ensured the completeness of the process of designing, manufacturing and racing cars. These routines constantly reinforced alignment around a shared vision, clear accountabilities and systems for constantly checking in on progress.

Observation 10. Just adopt!!
Ross is clear that you have to respect the competition and learn and steal from them: people, ideas, methods, anything that can make you more competitive.

Observation 11. Define the line – and own it.

The point is to understand the governance of your activity, define the line clearly for everyone, and then operate up to that line. Not a millimetre beyond what is acceptable, but equally not a millimetre short either. Any gap represents lost competitiveness and wasted opportunity.

Observation 12. Strive for simplicity, manage complexity.

There must always be a bias towards simplicity but complexity cannot be avoided, so it must be managed through shared vision, clear accountability and the rhythms and routines described above. No one can manage everything.

Observation 13. People innovate naturally.

Formula One demonstrates that in the right environment and structure, people innovate naturally. It is astonishing how much they can achieve when their creativity is given the right conditions.

Observation 14. There is a place for data – and intuition.

While Ross relentlessly pursued data, he also emphasized the place for judgement, intuition and surprise.

Observation 15. Strategy can be studied and applied.

Strategy is a process by which we overcome obstacles to achieve a goal. It is not a plan, it is a *process*. Furthermore, that process is subject to principles, perhaps rules even, that can be studied and applied. Total competition requires a complete, integrated and inclusive process.

The cumulative effect of the way that Ross worked is that he was able to grow over four decades and adapt both to developments in the sport and to his own situation – working in several different teams and cultures. This is an important point. As Sam Michael, the former technical director of Williams and then sporting director of McLaren, observes, Ross has an ability to present complex engineering problems in a simple way. The more complex the technical issue, the more valuable that skill becomes. Equally, by following a steady and consistent set of rhythms and routines, Ross has been able to manage the increasingly complex and integrated set of technical and organisational challenges that Formula One has presented over time. Finally, the ability to get the best out of others, and to help them work together, has also become all the more critical. With the notable exception of Adrian Newey, other technical directors and Team Principals have not been able to keep up as well. This is especially true of those who manage by charisma and work by instinct. It is not, perhaps, an exciting message, but it is an important one: following a rigorous and engaging process is a much more adaptable and sustainable approach than relying on one's own genius. That genius can all too easily become a liability and, of course, the more success you have, the greater the risk that you over-estimate the magnitude of your genius and its applicability in all circumstances. The good news is that if achieving great success does not depend on genius, then it is open to more of us to do so.

I had the opportunity to observe much of how Ross worked as a competitor for nearly five years. I think it says a lot about the man that I can work with him now to explore how he bested us all time and again, but also how he came to be bested by others in the end. Ross and I want this book to be interesting to people who enjoy Formula One, but more importantly we want it to be useful to people trying to overcome obstacles to achieve their own goals. People in public service, business, the arts and sciences and not-for-profits who are trying to make a difference. And people trying to improve their own and others' lives.

There are things that can be done to make the chances of success greater and we hope that this book helps not only to describe those things, but also to inspire people to have a go. We both believe that the methodology of Formula One has wider application – and above all, that it teaches us that a group of motivated people can achieve astonishing things when they are given the opportunity.

PART I

Ross Brawn's Career

R One of the things I say when invited to address young people, all sorts of people, is to use the phrase, 'Luck is preparation waiting for an opportunity.' And that's been my mantra in life. The breaks will come and if you are not ready for them, you won't be able to take them. Therefore my approach was always to try and prepare myself; and to work for people who I thought would give me a good opportunity. My philosophy was always to be the ideal employee. So whoever I worked for I tried to fulfil my obligations to the best standard I could. I guess it is something my dad and my family taught me. And I was very fortunate that my first mentor was Patrick Head. So I started at the top. I started with a guy, not an easy guy, but a guy who had great standards, ambition, determination. I followed a very long way behind in his wake in those early days.

A Let's have the facts from when you started. What were you doing before you were in motor racing?

R I did a mechanical engineering apprenticeship at the Atomic Energy Research Establishment in Harwell. That was a proper training apprenticeship. It wasn't a form of cheap labour which unfortunately some apprenticeships can be. It was a properly structured apprenticeship. I did two weeks in the facility at the AERE, then one week at College in Newbury. So it was a split course.

The first year was very much the basics: you were given a rough piece of metal and told you had to file it down to a piece one-inch square. Teaching you the basic craft skills. I was an instrument maker and that is precise engineering, fine engineering, you could call it. I learnt to use lathes and mills, how to weld, how to fabricate: all the basic engineering skills. It was a four-year apprenticeship and it was only in the last one or two years that I was put out into the production workshops but still doing my training. Through that I did an Ordinary National Certificate in Engineering, and the next phase was to do a Higher National Certificate. While I was in the first year of that, in 1976, I saw an advertisement in the local *Reading Evening Post* for Frank Williams.

I went along just out of curiosity. My dad knew Frank, but I didn't use that. Maybe he made the connection with the name. I've got no idea, I never discussed it with him, but my father knew Frank very well, although it was Patrick Head who interviewed me. We just walked around the workshop and he gave me components and said, 'Can you make that?' And I remember he gave me an upright which, at the time, was a cast magnesium upright. And he said, 'Can you machine that?' I said, 'Yes, that wouldn't be a problem' and I explained how I would do it, how I would set it up and what tools I would use, and he seemed to accept it.

I would have been 22 years old then. Patrick thanked me, but I didn't hear anything for quite a long time. Six to eight weeks. And then I got a phone call asking me to come and work for them. I said, 'I would be delighted, but could you put it in writing because I would like something a little bit more substantial.' Eventually a letter arrived. And I thought, well, I'm doing an HNC but I'm a bit bored working at the Research Establishment, I'll go off and work in motor racing for a year and then go back to my education, because I had aspirations to get a degree. I thought I would do a year in motor racing and see how it goes.

So I went to join Frank and Patrick at Bennet Road in Reading. I asked Patrick why it took so long for them to make their mind up. I was, apparently, the second choice. The first guy turned up, started work, didn't like the job and disappeared. I was the backup. That was the start of my career in motor racing. That first phase didn't last very long, because Frank really was pretty strung out. The first Friday I got my pay cheque and I was going to pay it into the bank on Monday. But as soon as the cheques arrived the workshop emptied. When they all came back, I said, 'Where have you all been?' And they said, 'You're slow off the mark, if you don't get your cheque in quick, you won't get it paid.' Because Frank would just run out of money and not all of the cheques would get paid. They were hand-to-mouth days. The guys told stories of paying the electricity bill themselves so they could keep Frank going and having a whip round.

He had a sponsor called Walter Wolf and Frank was in such financial dire straits that Walter took over the company and appointed Peter Warr as the Team Principal and Frank got relegated to head of marketing, which didn't suit him, of course. So, Frank and Patrick left and in due course they set up Williams Grand Prix Engineering. I didn't like what became Walter Wolf Racing. I stayed for the beginning of the year and we won our first race (my first race), with Jody Scheckter driving, but I was getting itchy feet even though I'd only been in motor racing for a relatively short period.

At the beginning of 1977, I decided to up sticks and become a Formula 3 race mechanic, when I had an opportunity to work for Team March. They ran two teams in Formula 3, one from a factory in Bicester and one in Reading, which was convenient for me. I went on a semi-nomadic lifestyle as a Formula 3 race mechanic, because quite a lot of the races were in Europe. In a Formula 3 team we had two cars, one engineer, two mechanics, and a gopher. A short while into the season starting, the money of one of the drivers dried up, and we ended up as a one-car team. So I toured Europe and I used to rope my mates in to share the driving. The remaining driver was a Brazilian called Aryon Cornelsen-Filho, whose highlight was pole position at Snetterton. He was sponsored by Caixa Bank. I did a year of Formula 3, which was great fun. The first race I did was the Easter meeting at Thruxton. I'd never changed ratios in a car out in the field – I'd done it in the workshop practising – so I had the instruction manual in front of me while I changed them. My boss at March walked passed and said, 'That's not very professional, is it?' and I said, 'Well, it's more professional than putting the ratios in wrong.'

Max Mosley was running March but I had no contact with him that year. We were very much a satellite team, Reading was where March built their engines, they had some work- shop space and they had more customers for Formula 3, than they had space at Bicester, so they ran a couple of cars out of Reading. It was a great year, Monaco, Austria, Monza, plus the British championship. It was pretty busy. The beginning of '77 was when I met my wife Jean, so I was courting Jean the year I was a Formula 3 mechanic. My wife-to-be got a proper introduction to what racing was about, and we got married in that year. She came to some of the races. And made the sandwiches and tea. Great fun.

A At that point you'd had a technical education, but you were now on the racing side. Later in your career, you were on both sides: on the pit wall directing the race, technical director back at the base, and ultimately Team Principal as well. Back in '77 did you have an idea of which way you wanted to go?

R When you're that young, you don't have that much foresight. You are looking at what interests you and excites and motivates you. I did quite a bit of engineering of the car that year, because when we lost the other car, there was no justification for having an engineer. So the boss of March Engines, Peter Hass, used to come to the races and help, but he didn't know that much about the cars. I was applying the little bit of knowledge that I had built up over the couple of years I had been in racing. But there wasn't much we did to the car – there were roll bar or spring changes or tyre pressures – so I was learning as I went along and it was a great experience because there was lots of scope. Aryon and I used to go testing. You could run a car with one mechanic and a gopher, so we used to go off testing just the three of us. We used to get a set-up sheet from the March works team and that was where we would start and we could play around from there.

I wouldn't say that at that stage, I had mapped out what I was going to do. But I can say that while I enjoyed the racing, the main thing for me was the engineering, the deeper stuff, that was exciting. We used to do little tweaks on the car, which would annoy the people in Bicester immensely, but we just improved little bits. I had done kart racing as a kid, slot car racing, these were all competitive environments where you knew small things accumulated, especially in a controlled formula. We were playing around with bits and pieces. I wasn't obsessed with being a race mechanic; I really enjoyed the engineering more.

During the year, Frank and Patrick contacted me, said they were going to build their own car and I agreed to join as soon as the season finished. In early October, I joined Frank in Didcot where he had taken over an old carpet factory by the power station. That was the little 5,000 square foot unit. This was 1977 and I was the eleventh employee. It was the beginning of a great period but I almost left Frank in '78, because we had been sent to do a test in Austria. As I mentioned, I had got married in '77 and I was feeling quite homesick at times. You know, newly married, away from home a lot. In those days, you often did a couple of races and a test altogether so you would be away for six weeks. Frank had sent me to Austria to do a test and we arrived at the circuit and we couldn't test because Frank hadn't paid a bill that was outstanding from some point before. And I got so angry I resigned over the phone and told Frank I was going to leave. I downloaded all my problems. And he said, 'Look, I'll buy you an airline ticket to come back and see your wife. Have some R&R and let's forget about it.' Which he did and I went back, saw Jean and calmed down and then ended up staying for seven years. In a wonderful period because the team grew. We won two World Championships with Alan Jones and Keke Rosberg.

A You won four World Championships.

R Including Constructors', yes.

A *Do you like to count Drivers' or Constructors'?*

R Both.

A *How many have you won altogether?*

R Twenty something.

A *Let's go through them. So you've got Williams, which was two Drivers' and two Constructors'.*

R Yes. And I count those because I was very involved with the team. People often forget I was part of that. Then with Benetton we won two Drivers' and one Constructors': the Drivers' in 1994 and 1995. And we won the Constructors' in '95. And at Ferrari we won six Constructors' and five Drivers'. And Brawn was one of each.

A *That's 10 Drivers' and 10 Constructors'.*

R And with Jaguar we won the FIA World Sportscar Championship for constructors and drivers, which I am very proud of.

A *So, 22 then.*

R And Le Mans 1990 with Jaguar.

A *Not bad. Has anyone done better?*

R I don't know. I never added them up.

So that philosophy of being a good employee has stuck with me all the time. I had been at Williams for seven years, but I had hit a bit of a glass ceiling because Frank Dernie had come in. I liked Frank very much, he was good fun and very, very bright. But he had become head of R&D. I was head of R&D when it was a small thing. But as the company grew, Frank [Williams] and Patrick thought they needed a more academic approach and Frank is very bright, very creative. I was the brawn and he was the brains. That was a good combination. I enjoyed Frank Dernie's company very much and still do. He's a very good friend. But it was stymieing my career because I was bumping up against him all the time. So this opportunity came along at a new team. Neil Oatley, who was the chief designer at Williams, was going. I was going. We had been a bit suppressed, Neil under Patrick, me under Frank, and here was an opportunity to go off and start this new thing, the Beatrice Formula One team, owned by an American, Carl Haas. It showed lots of promise but didn't really come to anything in the end. It closed after two years because Beatrice had a leveraged buyout and the new owners didn't want to sponsor Formula One. So they paid off Carl Haas and it all came to an end after two years. It was a really important two years for me because suddenly I was responsible for designing some of the car.

There were three designers – Neil, John Baldwin and myself. I took care of all the aerodynamics and the bodywork; John took care of the chassis and structure; and Neil had the overall responsibility for the project. And interestingly, Adrian Newey came in right at the end. Adrian was working in America on Indy cars for Carl Haas and he joined us. I worked with Adrian for a couple of months before I left. And, in fact, the project then closed a short while later.

I then went to work for a company called Arrows which was being run by Jackie Oliver and Alan Rees. Jackie had tried to employ Neil Oatley, Neil decided to go to McLaren but kindly told Jackie he ought to speak to me. Jackie had never heard of me, but he rang Patrick who apparently gave me a good reference. So I went along and met Jackie and got the job as chief designer. That was the first car that I designed myself: the Arrows. I was there for three years in the late 1980s. We didn't do too badly. Our first car used a customer BMW four-cylinder. I had a couple of good designers, solid, who helped me a lot – another Bob Bell, not the Bob Bell I came to work with in later years, but another designer. And I was still designing cars myself. I had a little workshop out the back of our house and I set up a drawing board in there. My *modus operandi* was four days in the office managing everything else that was going on. Then Friday, Saturday and Sunday, I would work at home designing things. So I would turn up on Monday with an armful of drawings. I specifically designed the chassis and various other parts. It was a nice little set-up.

The difficulty was Jackie and Alan always ran out of money halfway through the year, so we would make a great start and we'd fade during the year, which got increasingly frustrating. Derek Warwick and Eddie Cheever were the drivers. We should have won at Montreal, but the engine blew while we were leading the race. We finished fifth in the Championship one year. It wasn't bad. It was a great period for me, because it was the first time I had taken on that level of responsibility.

Derek and Eddie also drove sports cars for Tom Walkinshaw, and they enticed me to join Jaguar because there was a new sports car formula which was Formula One with covered wheels, really. It was fabulous going in to a new regime with new rules, where everything was completely open. In fact the rules were very loose, because nobody had challenged the rules as much as they did in Formula One. In sports car racing, there was a more traditionalist approach so the rules had never been interpreted to the degree that was second nature in Formula One. So I went into sports car racing and we rode a horse and cart through the rules and came up with a car that was three or four seconds quicker than anyone else. And we won the Championship in 1991. This was one of my favourite cars, the Jaguar XJR14. It's the last car I can truly say I designed, because thereafter I became more of a director of the design process. But that was the last car I would say I put pencil to paper and genuinely designed, along with the team, of course. So it's one I quite like and a great looking car.

When I joined Tom Walkinshaw at Jaguar, he said, 'We are going to go into Formula One. We are going to do a couple of years' sports car racing and then you and I are going to go into Formula One.' And he tried to buy the Ligier team, which came back to haunt me later because Tom and I had a deal that when he bought the Ligier team, I would get a shareholding. My shareholding would accumulate over a certain period, until he and I would become pretty equal partners in Ligier. So I had agreed all that with Tom, and he was trying to find the money to buy Ligier and that didn't come off in the end. In the process, Bernie Ecclestone had put Tom in contact with Flavio Briatore who was having problems with his team at the time, Benetton. And we took a sort of left turn and joined Benetton at the end of 1991. In '91 we'd been very aware of this hot little German driver who we were battling with in sports car racing, because he was the only one who ever gave us any trouble. So Tom and I knew

Michael Schumacher very well. And when he started to make his move into Formula One, Tom really was the architect in getting him into the Benetton team.

A Because he was going somewhere else, wasn't he?

R He started at Jordan. Eddie Jordan didn't have the knowledge that we had and didn't do a robust enough contract with him. Eddie did a one-race deal with him. And of course he turned up at Spa and was impressive. Eddie then tried to get him on a longer deal, but we had already got our foot in the door, and it was a bit nasty at one stage. I say Tom was the architect. I know Flavio always tries to take the credit for discovering Michael, but Flavio didn't know what Michael looked like when he joined the team. Tom negotiated the contract on our side. On Michael's side there was Willi Weber, who had supported Michael all the way through Formula 3. So he was always part of Michael.

Well, it was delicate because Michael started driving with us mid-season and we had to get rid of one of the existing drivers, Roberto Moreno. Nelson Piquet, who was the other driver, I think realized he was in trouble with Michael, and he was coming to the end of his career. Nelson kicked up a fuss and said we had acted dishonourably with Roberto and he wasn't going to put up with it, so he left the team at the end of 1991. So in that first year, Michael was already rattling Nelson to the point where Nelson realized that Michael was our boy. He had come into the team and if he was doing that in the first year, he was going to be in even more trouble in the second year. Nelson cleared off and Martin Brundle joined the team for 1992.

A I don't know Nelson Piquet at all, but he had a reputation for being quite a psychological player with his co-drivers. With Williams in 1987, I think it was in Mexico where Nigel Mansell religiously never ate foreign food, being very English, and made the mistake of going out before the Grand Prix somewhere and got Montezuma's revenge pretty badly. Apparently, Piquet removed all the loo paper in the garage.

R Well, there was a famous incident where he insulted Nigel very personally just before a race. Nelson would do anything he could. Of course, he was a bit impotent with Michael because Michael was our boy. We knew Michael. We had come through and there's this brash German. He knew Michael had few weaknesses in that respect. This young fit kid from Germany, as fit as a butcher's dog.

A Let's just have a quick digression on psychological warfare between fellow drivers. How did you handle it?

R I guess one of the things I probably pride myself on is within the team avoiding creating an environment for that psychological battle. You can't avoid it completely, but the blatant and ugly stuff I think I generally managed to avoid. It can be destructive to the team, because it can seep into the mechanics, into the engineers. I always wanted a competitive spirit between all the crew, but it was a balancing act of then pulling them back together and saying we are all in this together. This is one team. So if you do something to benefit your driver at the expense of the other driver, that's unacceptable.

A But would it be fair to say you had a lead driver, or would you say you were balanced?

R Yes. I think that's fair. I think there were periods for sure, particularly with Michael Schumacher at Ferrari. If it was a criticism – and I'm not sure it is a criticism, because I would accept it as it is – but if it were a criticism my defence would be that I always resolved it in my own mind by saying, 'My support goes to the faster driver. If someone is faster than Michael, I would never favour Michael.' If a driver came along who clearly was quicker than Michael, it would be stupid then to make those 50/50 decisions in favour of Michael. Because it is the 50/50 decisions, where you have to go in the direction of the driver who is going to achieve the most for you. You can't deny that and that to me is logical. If you've got a 60/40 decision and you make it against the guy that should be getting the 60, then I think that's unfair. There were times, however, reflecting back on it, when I wish I made different decisions, for example in Austria in 2002. [This was a controversial event in which the team ordered Rubens Barrichello, who was leading the race, to let Michael Schumacher pass him on the finish line for victory. The crowd was furious but the FIA was powerless to punish the team. On the podium Schumacher took the trophy for first place from the Austrian Chancellor and handed the trophy to Barrichello, and then took the second place trophy from the Austrian Deputy Chancellor. For this the team and the two drivers were fined $1 million.]

In our defence, and it's not a strong defence, but in that early period of Ferrari we were so desperate and paranoid for success that the far-reaching consequences of those sort of decisions were not reflected on that much. We had this complete commitment to Michael winning the championship. We considered him to be our best opportunity and that proved to be the case. We wouldn't compromise at any stage. I think there's a necessity, and I learnt during that period, that if you start to alienate the other driver too much, it becomes destructive and therefore the whole thing suffers. And as I gained experience, this was what I often discussed with Michael. 'Look, I can suppress the other guy. I can give you every decision you like, but then you will have a problem because there will be a guy who is disillusioned. He'll cause problems in the team. He won't do anything constructively or willingly. He'll try and hide information from you. It will just become a destructive process. You've got to respect the other driver.' There's that fine balance between making those 50/50 decisions and not destroying the other driver. I remember in later years the case with Alonso and Massa at Ferrari in an early race of the Championship when Massa was told to back off and let Alonso through. It just destroyed Massa – what's he got to look forward to?

Rubens was probably the main competition Michael faced in my time at Ferrari. He won races and we did try and give him an opportunity. And I always said to Rubens, 'If after two or three races you are leading the championship by a decent margin and you are our best opportunity, you can get those 50/50 decisions – so do it and you will find out.' But he never did it.

A There's a story that Eddie Irvine was driving for you, where he was asked to move over and he did a rather snappy negotiation. He said, 'Okay, what's it worth?'

R He did that, but not in the car. We gave him a bonus for Michael winning the Championship. Drivers have race bonuses. Drivers have Championship bonuses. And Eddie, being pretty astute, part way through the year said, 'Look, if I'm going to help Michael in every way possible, then surely I've got to get a bonus if he wins the Championship?' And actually, when you think about it, it's logical.

A And that wasn't done from the cockpit?

R No!

A It's a pity, isn't it?

R 'Luca, Luca, come on.'

A [For the record, that last remark was not addressed to Luca di Montezemolo, but Luca, Ross's poodle, who is of course named after Luca di Montezemolo.]
   There is a theory that drivers have three things they are interested in: racing, money and sex.

R Well, that applies to Eddie, that's for sure! I'm not sure in which order ...
   I think sometimes we probably forget how much of a thrill they get from racing. Because we don't do it ourselves. We are involved. But I think because we are so involved with them we forget how much they really enjoy racing. How much they enjoy being out there in these cars and competing with each other, sometimes beating the others, and how much thrill there is in that. I have often thought, and said it on

some occasions, that Michael was extremely well rewarded because he was the best at what he did during that period, but I'm convinced he would have done it for a fraction of what he was being paid. And they all would. If you change the references for these drivers and said you are all going to get paid $500,000 a year instead of $50 million a year, would they still do it? They would. It's just the references. When they see someone else getting paid a certain amount, they have got to get a bit more.

A The driver market is quite distorted. Going back a few years there were only two teams that paid lots of money: Ferrari and McLaren. And I have never quite understood why because if you were Ferrari or, in those days, McLaren you didn't need to pay $50 million, because everyone wanted to drive for you. It seems unnecessary.

R I think a lot of it is the ego of the Team Principals. In that they get into a competition with another team and this competitive spirit applies to contractual negotiations as well. They don't take a step back and say, 'If we were all sensible, we could have these drivers for a fraction of what we are paying them.' I remember when Jos Verstappen, Max's dad, was the hot number in Formula One. He'd had some reasonable results in racing, but he had never done Formula One, and suddenly two or three teams seemed to get the hots for him, and it turned into a bidding war. It was crazy. And Benetton won the bidding war because Flavio was determined to win it. He was against Ron Dennis and someone else. None of them would back off, with the result that Jos got a long-term contract, having never driven in Formula One before. Jos was pretty good, but he wasn't Michael Schumacher. But sometimes that happens.

* * *

A Let's come back to your career. So, we have got you to Benetton.

R I joined Benetton with Tom and it was a little bit messy at the beginning, because there was an existing infrastructure and then Tom came in with me. Rory Byrne and Pat Symonds had left Benetton at an earlier stage and gone off to Reynard, but that was not working. So Pat and Rory were available and I brought them back in, because I knew them. We had a really weird situation for the first few months where there was Gordon Kimball, who was the incumbent designer, and then there was me and Rory Byrne and our group. And Flavio and Tom decided to let both groups design a car and see which one was the best. I said to Tom, 'This is lunacy. We are wasting resource and we are never going to get anywhere.' And I think Gordon Kimball realized it was stupid. So the engineers themselves got together and decided to sort it all out so we could focus on one car. So we put the design team together. We were living in the aftermath of John Barnard's period there, which had been pretty fraught.

We had a sensible budget, I never thought it was exceptional. We had a works engine from Ford, which was quite an important thing. We had a reasonable couple of first years. Michael started to win some races. We were occasionally giving some of the bigger teams a bit of aggravation. We had new regulations coming in for 1994, so, early in 1993, I took a small group of designers to support the existing 1993 programme and pointed Rory and the rest of our designers at the future 1994 car. This was our big opportunity to make a step change in where we were in Formula One.

A Did you have anything to do with the banning of active suspension? [This was a system that enabled the cars to vary their ride height and therefore aerodynamic performance. It was one of the reasons for Williams' dominance in 1993 but was banned at the end of that year.]

R No. Pat Symonds was pretty good on active suspension and we were quite keen on it. I don't believe we set out to stop it. I've got a feeling Ferrari were behind all that from memory. I think they were really struggling with active ride.

Anyway, we were working very closely with Cosworth and there was a group there that was dedicated to the 1994 engine. And Rory was focusing on the 1994 car with all the new requirements and new regulations. That was the first time that I had taken such a structured approach to the new regulations, new car etc. New cars tend to evolve during the year, but this approach was to ringfence a load of resource, use it just for the new car, have proper reviews and progress meetings. I would still chair the review meetings and go to design meetings. So I was probably the person with a foot in both camps, but Rory was the chief designer and 1994 was his priority. And in 1993 we didn't have a bad year from memory. I would need to look up where we were, but we won a race and had lots of podiums. But we were really focused on 1994. And then we went testing over the winter with the 1994 car and clearly it was very competitive.

So '94 we set to, and it was a great year, the car was fabulous. But it was the first year when I really got embroiled in the political environment of Formula One. And, of course, tragically, it was the year when Senna and Ratzenberger got killed at Imola. So we had a very quick car and the rules were being changed. It was the year when there were claims against Benetton for using traction and launch control. And the rules were changing because of the accidents with Senna and Ratzenberger. I think everyone was truly shocked by the events and there was a huge political battle going on. Tom and Flavio were on one side and Max Mosley was on the other. And they were at loggerheads. I remember a meeting at Barcelona where Tom and Flavio came out of it and said, 'Max has resigned. He's gone. He's finished. We are going to have someone new.' And I knew Max reasonably well by then and I thought, 'Well, this'll be interesting to watch.'

And, of course, they had stabbed the beast but they hadn't killed it. Then it became very unpleasant after that. We got hauled in by the FIA, after Imola, and all our electronic black boxes on our cars were confiscated. A company called LDRA (Liverpool Data Recovery Agency) got involved in investigating what was in our black boxes. The first time round they found nothing amiss, so we were given the black boxes back. And then the war started between Max and the teams, and particularly Flavio and Tom. The black boxes were confiscated again. The FIA came along and said, 'These are the numbers, can we have those black boxes again?' So, having returned the black boxes, they took them again. They said they had some new methodology where they were going to be able to find out what we had been up to. In the end, we went to Paris to the Court of Appeal, and I remember some very unpleasant days there, but we were acquitted.

When the FIA went after us a second time, I had taken a short break. In those days there was a gap in the early part of the year, so I had nipped off to Mauritius for a quick holiday. And I just spent the whole time on the phone. I remember my phone bill was something like £1,000. I got a phone call from Flavio saying, 'We are in trouble with the black boxes, don't worry I've done a deal, we are going to lose the points for Imola, but everything will be okay after that, they'll forget it.' And I said, 'We're not going to lose the points for Imola, Flavio, because we have done nothing wrong.' And Rory and I resigned. We told Flavio that we were not going to accept his deal. So Flavio backed off and we went into battle over the thing.

That whole period was a new aspect to Formula One politics, something I had not experienced before. And it was an education for me.

In the end we won the Championship after a coming together between Michael and Damon Hill at the Australian GP, the last race of the year. People can debate what happened in that incident but there was a lot going on that year and it has to be seen in that context.

I think 1997 (which also came down to the last race and ended with a collision between Schumacher and his rival for the Championship, Jacques Villeneuve) was different in a way. I've mentioned this about Michael before. Michael had a blind spot, he was so competitive he didn't see things the way you or I would. He did it in Monaco in 2006 when he stopped on the track in qualifying. And he did it two or three times in his career. I don't know if he did it with Damon in 1994. I never discussed it with him.

But if you look at '97, after that incident, Michael came into the pit screaming blue murder, 'Villeneuve had me off, Villeneuve knocked me out of the race ...' And I said,

'Calm down Michael and have a look at the TV.' And he calmed down and had a look at the TV and went very ashen-faced and realized what he had done. But in the heat of the moment, I promise you, he came into the garage convinced that Villeneuve had had him off. It was a pretty fraught race, because we'd all got into the habit of using our second cars in strategic ways. We were doing it with Eddie. We'd have races where Michael would tear off and Eddie would be told to control the pace of the others so we could build a lead ... it was like a chess game. And in that particular race, Frentzen had screwed Michael for quite a large part of the race. So Williams were giving us back some of what we'd given them. And that was fair enough. But I think Michael had got quite frustrated with that. That's not an excuse, but he had.

A If Formula One is about anything, it is about competition. If there are rules, the game is to maximize your opportunities. I think that applies to drivers as much as it does to cars and teams. And if somebody doesn't think that's fair, then that's just not Formula One. The object of a team in Formula One is to win World Championships for the drivers and for the team. I'm sure lots of people would disagree and say that's not gentlemanly – but that's just what the sport is about. It's about winning. The reason why we are sitting here is because you won 20 Formula One World Championships. And what we are interested in is how you win World Championships. If you want to have a discussion about how you don't win World Championships, then that's a different conversation with any number of people.

R You see, that manoeuvre that Michael made on Villeneuve which didn't come off. In slightly different ways, he would have been making it ten times in a race weekend. He would chop someone. He would force his way through. He would show who's boss on a corner. And that's all part of being what he was. If you were racing Michael Schumacher, you knew you've got no quarter. If he saw a gap, if you left an inch, he would take a foot. The reason for his success was to create that character, create that persona, the intimidation of the other drivers. And that is all about Formula One.

A That's fair enough. When I was with Williams, Rubens was driving for us and Michael was racing for Mercedes. I think it was at Budapest, but Michael had Rubens right up against the wall on the main straight and it went on for some time, and there was dust coming off Rubens' wheels from the wall. And Rubens just didn't lift and he took Michael at the end of the straight. And afterwards Michael was asked, 'That was too close, wasn't it?' And he said, 'No, it wasn't too close because he got through.'

R It's fascinating. Probably Rubens would have backed off with most other drivers, but he wasn't going to back off with Michael. That's the dynamic that's always going on between drivers. The dynamic that goes on between drivers builds, it builds in practice, it builds in testing. They all get an impression of the ones who aren't respectful in practice or testing. The guys who don't look in their mirrors. The ones they find intimidating. They build a picture of what they are all like: their competitors. And they use that or take advantage of it, or manipulate that when it suits them.

So 1994 was a very traumatic year, especially with the loss of two drivers. I was put through the wringer politically with all that was going on with rule changes, with Tom and Flavio going to war with Max. It was a very trying year, but I think an important year for me because it gave me that experience. Gave me the resilience that came from dealing with all those matters that then helped me in subsequent years when things got tough.

A So, in 1994 there were two critical moments. One is the approach that you took in 1993 bore its first fruit: focusing on the '94 car because of the new rules, with a dedicated team, keeping them insulated from the pressures of the current year, and the review process you applied. This became something you did again at Ferrari, Honda and Mercedes. The second thing is that 1994 was the year when the political and technical dimensions of Formula One came together for you.

R It's a very interesting point. My career was largely engineering-based, but as it progressed so did the involvement with the politics – beyond the engineering politics because there were always the technical meetings, deciding what's good for you, what's bad for you, and trying to get rules changed. We moved on to the bigger politics of Formula One. Some people come in to the sport with their mindset already engaged in that arena. And mine, I don't think, was. I always loved the engineering, always loved the technical side, always loved the racing. I accepted the politics was part of what made Formula One so fascinating: the whole thing. But I never saw myself as someone who really would go for the jugular in terms of politics. Might do in engineering – but I always tried to keep a fair approach. This is not really politics, but if I could prise an engineer out of another team whatever it took, within reason ... I would be relentless in that. Wouldn't have any qualms about it. But particularly later in my career in 2009, there were a lot of difficult situations. Because of the role I had then as a team owner I had political situations which slightly took my breath away, not at the vindictiveness but the sheer callousness of people.

It is probably the arena I am least comfortable with in Formula One. I think I can deal with it. I had to deal with it. But it's the side of Formula One that I used to find the most frustrating, because sometimes it was the most illogical. It was the most emotive area of Formula One. I've been invited to become involved in Formula One again and help perhaps shape the regulations or help shape the future of Formula One. And that invitation is to get involved in the politics of Formula One, because that is what it's all about. Almost as if someone said, do you want to come back and do a bit of engineering? I could be tempted. But to have to deal with all the politics of Formula One, that was probably the side I enjoyed least of what I did. And therefore the side that is least attractive to me.

* * *

A We will talk a little about the future of Formula One. Let's finish your career first.

R In 1994, we had the Ford engine and we won the Championship. In 1995, we moved to the Renault engine, which was considered to be a better opportunity. We had a bit of fading interest within Ford, I think, during 1993. So they did a 1994 engine, but showed a lack of conviction and, of course, when 1994 was successful they tried to turn the wick back up again. But by then we had already courted Renault and managed to get a Renault engine for 1995. Beginning of '95 was pretty troublesome – we had some issues with the engine that we didn't get to terms with quickly. But then as we got the engine sorted out in 1995, we won the Drivers' and Constructors' Championships that year.

But '95 was the year Michael announced he was leaving. That was a pretty bitter blow to me. I had been very close to Michael, but I hadn't seen that coming. He hadn't informed me. He was in dispute with Flavio over money, because Michael had a parity deal with whoever the other driver was. So his contract was that he never got less than the other driver. Michael discovered that Riccardo Patrese was getting paid extra. Michael found out, and Riccardo was more than willing to give him all the details, that effectively Riccardo was getting paid a lot more, because he was getting money paid directly to him from a team sponsor. That was part of the problem and also Michael, I think, by then had itchy feet. When I asked Michael for his reasons, Riccardo's extra payments was the reason he gave, that he felt he had been screwed. That may have just been an easy excuse to move on. He'd grown with the team. Benetton had been his first proper Formula One team, he knew the people very well and we knew him. We had all been through a lot together and he was leaving us. He was leaving us and it was a bitter blow.

But I was determined to carry on. There was no discussion of my joining Ferrari at that stage. It hadn't really occurred to me, although my contract ended at the end of 1995. So I looked at the team and decided what the team needed to do to move on to the next level. The team structure was a bit odd for historical reasons. A lot of the factory was run by a chap called Joan Villadelprat, who had been Flavio's man when we arrived at Benetton. And I was Tom's man. There was a segregation, in a way, in that I was running design and some of the racing. Joan was running manufacturing and the race team mechanics. And I felt there was some conflict that was not constructive and I wanted to have overall responsibility for the whole thing and restructure the group. Benetton agreed. Flavio agreed. My new contract was drawn up and I was going to have total responsibility for the whole thing. Except I didn't.

When 1996 arrived, they wouldn't implement those changes and became resistant to implementing those changes and I got frustrated. The situation wasn't helped by the fact that we had Jean Alesi and Gerhard Berger driving for us. Gerhard had been a late addition to the team. Jean joined in the season when Michael announced his departure. We were quite excited by Jean. He was a huge talent, he needed careful management, but we thought Jean would be a really good asset to the team. And then at the last minute Flavio announced that he was also going to take Gerhard Berger. Because I think when Berger saw Michael coming to Ferrari, the writing was on the wall for him there, there was no point in staying around. So Berger jumped in to the Benetton team as well and that was the worst thing we could have done.

Berger and Alesi had had a fractious relationship when they were both at Ferrari. So we now had two new drivers who came to us with a very difficult relationship. Alesi went bananas when he heard Berger was coming. So we had this team that was all going to be focused on Jean Alesi and shaping itself to Alesi, because we thought that Alesi was an unfulfilled talent who hadn't achieved his potential and we could unlock it. And suddenly we stuck Gerhard Berger into the mix. Without much consultation with the team, Flavio did a deal with Gerhard. And one of Gerhard's objectives was to screw Jean – and he was very good at it.

They just had a relationship that wasn't constructive to the team working well. Gerhard would want a completely different car to what Jean would want. We would go testing and Gerhard would give an opinion and Jean would give a different one and it was very, very difficult to manage. So I was getting disillusioned. We had a very good car in 1996, as good as we had had previously and we didn't win a race. The team wasn't gelling. We went from being World Champions to not winning a race. We had several races we should have won and they went wrong for various reasons. Some of it was reliability, but some of it was the drivers.

During '96 Michael struggled a bit with his relationship with John Barnard at Ferrari. He only really knew the relationship he had had with me in Formula One. Then he went to Ferrari and it was a completely different way of doing things and he wasn't that comfortable with it. Just before Monaco '96, Willi Weber contacted me and asked if I would have a chat with Jean Todt. I met Jean at Monaco and that is when we started the discussions to join Ferrari. And then in about September, I told Flavio I was leaving and that I considered they hadn't met their obligations over the contract. This new structure was very important to me. Flavio constantly avoided implementing it, because he knew it would be difficult with Joan Villadelprat. I quite liked Joan, I had nothing against him, I just felt the structure had to be different. So, of course, then they went into reverse: 'We'll do the new structure, we'll implement everything.' The Benetton family got directly involved, but my mind was committed to the other job. Eventually we resolved the contractual issues and I was released.

But then like a little Exocet missile from the side, Tom Walkinshaw came in and said, 'I've got a contract with you for you to work with me, because back in 1991 you signed an agreement, we were going to buy Ligier and you were going to have shares in Ligier.' And I said, 'Hang on, Tom, you can't do that. You lost the opportunity to buy Ligier and it ain't ever going to happen,' but Tom took us to the High Court. He said that he had a contract with me, that I was working for him at Benetton and that he was going to buy Ligier, that there was nothing which said he wouldn't buy it in the future. And therefore, if in the future he bought Ligier, I was obliged to come and work for him. Anyway, the High Court threw it out, as you can imagine, but he appealed it. So now Ferrari are gagging for me to join, because I have been released from the Benetton contract. But Tom's causing a fuss. And they paid him off in the end. I can't remember what they gave him, but they paid him.

That was actually the end of my relationship with Tom. It ended very sadly. I think it was because of his frustration that I was leaving, because we had been together quite a long time. Tom had a dream that he and I were going to have a Formula One team. Tom had become a little bit distant from the Formula One team by then, because he had his own problems going on with his own business. So we didn't see so much of him. I think the fact that I hadn't discussed all of this with him in detail rankled him. So he reminded me that he was still there. And that was a shame because Tom and I had had some success, we had some good times together and I didn't speak to Tom for quite a long time after that. It wasn't until he was very ill, before he died, that I really started to speak to him again.

* * *

So I joined Ferrari at the end of 1996. When I started there, I'd never seen the Maranello factory. I had done a three-year contract with Ferrari; there were clauses where they could pay me off for the whole three years and get rid of me – pretty strict clauses, because I figured that I might go there and things could blow up and be told to go, but at least the next day I would be written a cheque. It was a lucrative contract, not mind-blowing, but more than I was earning at Benetton. They also did a lot to help me with the costs of moving to Italy. I didn't have a bonus for winning the Championship – I've never been a massive fan of that. Later in my career, as I moved up the pay-scale, I did start to get more complicated remuneration packages which revolved around success, but at Ferrari I didn't get points money or race win money. I asked for a remuneration package which reflected the fact that we were going to win the Championship. And if we didn't win the Championship, they would sack me. It was going to go one way or the other; either we would win and I would stay, or we wouldn't and I would go.

I don't think that bonuses are true incentives. I have always had the view that money can be a stronger *disincentive* and a problem, rather than an incentive. If people are doing things just for money, then they have got the wrong motivation. The real issue is that people get upset if they think they are being treated unfairly. If someone is doing a good job and he sees the bloke next to him getting more for doing a lesser job, he gets upset. But it is not the absolute numbers, it's the comparative numbers. It's the fairness. So, I have always thought that those arrangements were potentially demotivators.

Later, when I went to Honda, and by then I had earned my spurs, I wanted a fairly substantial sum to start again after my sabbatical. They said, 'We will have to split this into performance and base remuneration.' And I can understand that, especially when you are talking big numbers – when you are earning more than the chief executive, especially in a Japanese company. So we did it on the basis that ultimately we would win World Championships: in the first year the performance element was guaranteed because there was no way we were going to win, and then the guarantee tailed off as I was supposed to be bringing the team up.

I walked into Maranello, and I didn't know what to expect, and that was the first time I realized what I was in for. I have to say that I was very pleasantly surprised. There had been a core group at Ferrari, Nigel Stepney and others, who knew what a racing team was about, and the thing was pretty well organized. Their quality control systems were a level above what I was used to, because they had had some quality issues so they had taken the head of quality control from Fiat and put him in the race team and said, 'You've got to sort this out.' He knew what he was doing, knew it was a racing environment and he couldn't do everything he had been doing in a road car environment, but he created a deep culture of quality control. There were more people of course. So I was pleasantly surprised.

In fact, as you start to walk around Ferrari you wonder why they don't win every World Championship. Testing was unlimited and they had two test tracks at Maranello and Mugello, a nice new wind tunnel that was just being finished, a great machine shop – everything that was needed was there. What I also experienced was that the attitude of the core worker was excellent. First-class craftsmen, technicians, really high quality people. That area of Italy is famous for many things, cars, guns and swords – that was the region that used to make all the suits of armour. It had a blacksmith culture, and there were people who were third-generation workers for Ferrari, their fathers and grandfathers had worked there, so lots of experience.

On the other hand, what became apparent was that because of the management culture there, middle and top management were watching their backs the whole time. Their whole philosophy was to preserve their own position. That was the biggest challenge. Great workforce, wonderful, passionate and committed people who were proud to work for Ferrari; but middle management were petrified of putting a step out of line and therefore were not functioning properly. Not long before I arrived, they had sacked a man in the machine shop, and it was like a public hanging. This guy had machined a piston incorrectly, and despite what I have said about quality control, it was the engine that blew up in the warm-up lap at Magny Cours the year before. They'd had an investigation and this guy had got hung, drawn and quartered and sacked: 'This is what will happen to anyone that doesn't keep up the standards.'

I thought that was shocking: the system had broken down, he hadn't broken down. And I wouldn't allow this to happen, which led to my only conflict with Luca di Montezemolo. When Luca was looking for someone to blame for a problem we had had, I said, 'Luca, it's me. I am responsible for it all. If you want to blame somebody, you blame me.' That happened in a debrief. And it was in the paper the next day: 'Brawn is responsible.' That was the only time I fell out with Luca, but we got over it. And after that we had a good relationship.

So arriving was actually a very pleasant experience. Rory Byrne didn't come straight away, he was off in Thailand, so it was about two months before he was able to join me and this was the end of 1996, and we were preparing for the '97 season. This had been my ambition to work at Ferrari, and I was really enjoying the country and the people. It was really awkward family-wise, because my kids were still at school in England and Jean, my wife, was splitting her time between the two countries. When we had a long-haul flight to a race outside Europe, I would fly in and out of London so I could have a day either side with the family. We had a lot of help from parents and so on, and we managed to see a reasonable amount of each other. Later, about halfway through our time with Ferrari, as the kids left home and went to university, Jean was able to move over.

A When would you say that things first clicked for you? The first time that you felt at Ferrari, 'This is my car, my team and we are going to win this year.'

R Well, we almost won the World Championship in the first year, 1997. Frustratingly, we almost won in 1997, 1998 and 1999 – we took the Championship down to the last race in each year and we did win the Constructors' in '99 but not the Drivers' because that was the year when Michael broke his leg. That was a car failure, obviously very upsetting. We had a brake nipple come loose. It happened very early on in the race. Clearly between the warm up and the race, it had come loose. Interestingly, the design of the brake nipples changed after that. They were screw nipples, just like a road car. Now they are aircraft dry breaks [hydraulic connections that self-seal when disconnected], the obvious thing to do all along and now standard in Formula One. We were pretty convinced that he would have won the Championship that year, because I think we had the best car. Eddie Irvine took it to the last race, which shows you that if we could do that with Eddie, we could have done it with Michael.

A Between joining at the end of 1996 and 1999, when you won your first Championship with Ferrari, what were the main things that you did to get to the point where you were in a position to win?

R First, we built a design office there, we moved the total technical responsibility into Maranello. We integrated the engine and chassis divisions. The new head of engines was Paolo Martinelli, who was totally receptive to an integrated approach. Paolo wasn't old school Ferrari, who believed that the chassis was something just to carry the engine round on. In the past, Ferrari had been so engine-oriented, that the chassis was just whatever they could get by with. Paolo understood, or I convinced Paolo without much effort, that we had to have a car, not an engine or a chassis, we had to do the whole thing, to do the integration. We put the engine design division next to the chassis design division. We built the design offices next to each other. They couldn't be the same, because we had some physical constraints. But there was only a 20 yard walk to go from one to the other. We only had one metallurgy group that supported the whole programme. We moved people around, we had people in the chassis group go and work in the engine group and had people go from the engine team to the chassis group for periods of time. Paolo and I would look at the workload and we would help each other out when there were challenges.

So I was able to realize my dream of having a car, not an engine and a chassis – Paolo was in charge of the engine, but I think he would say himself that he followed my lead on racing. He had the technical responsibility for the engine, but in terms of strategy and approach, timing, and what we were trying to do, Paolo was happy to support whatever I felt was the right thing to do. I always had a pretty consultative approach, but then I would take the responsibility at the end of the day. I was never autocratic in going in and telling Paolo what we were going to do. I would go in and say, 'Paolo, these are my thoughts, what do you think?' And he might have a different solution. He was quite a confident person but not that outgoing, so it gave space for me to become the reference point for people. We weren't competing. This was important because when I was appointed, Paolo and I were at the same level. But this is the key: he and I never got to the point where I said I was in charge. That would have been a difficult relationship, in a way you've failed. Paolo recognized that because I was at the race track, if something went wrong with the engine at the track, then I had to take the final decision.

A So, you reversed the traditional hierarchy of engine and chassis at Ferrari?

R I think you're right. Before me, the engine group was in charge, then they brought in John Barnard on the chassis side, who was a strong character. But he was based in the UK, so he and the head of engine didn't have so many opportunities to go out for dinner or have coffee, so therefore you had this problem. When I came in, I chatted over coffee, I went out for dinner, did all the normal things. It was easier for me, I was alone there; in the evenings I either went home and sat by myself or I would invite Paolo or someone else out for dinner. I used that opportunity to talk about work, but also have a bit of a social, which always helps. I was building relationships, we had this synergy, the completeness of the car. During that period, of course, I was also reinforcing the organization, bringing people in for aerodynamics, starting to build up the team.

A How did you address the culture of fear, people worrying about getting things wrong, in case they lost their jobs?

R That's a gradual thing, I don't think you can turn a switch, you have to set an example. They knew I was different because I wanted to be called Ross. Everyone else was called 'Mr X' or 'Presidente'. There was one instance that I never gave any consideration, but was quoted back to me. I was in the workshop, I asked a mechanic where the toilet was, and he said, 'Your toilet's upstairs,' but I said, 'No, I just need a toilet. Where's the nearest one.' He said, 'Well, that's the mechanics' toilet over there,' so that's where I went. But I have to say I was rather glad I didn't have to use it for everything, as it was the type known as a 'Franz Klammer'.

It was not intentional on my part, but it registered with people. They thought, 'He's not got airs and graces, he's one of us, he's an ex-mechanic, he did the things we did.' They knew my background, they knew when I looked at the car and spoke to them about things that I had a good idea of what I was talking about.

Throughout my career, I very rarely lost my temper. Jean would say, 'You lose your temper more with your family than with the people who work for you.' I would say, 'That's a conscious thing, isn't it?' Family is emotive, work is professional; I think if you get to the emotive stage at work, you've failed. In business life, you shouldn't lose control. There were moments on the pit wall, I confess, when it got a bit ragged. But that's the only environment. Passion is not to be ignored. I hope I displayed passion and enthusiasm, and emotion of that sort.

That was the priority in those first few years: to get people to regain their confidence, and know that management weren't going to cut their legs off if they did anything wrong. This process I had with race debriefs on the day after the race, which were inclusive, 30 or 40 people, to go though the logistics of the weekend, what didn't work and then summarizing that in a state of the nation speech to the factory. Jean Todt always attended those and gave a rallying speech, but my speech was the one that was critical, it would be more specific. Before that, debriefs had taken place only when there was a drama, then they all got together and had a tense discussion. Only when there was a crisis, they weren't consistent, which is not correct. You have to have process improvement all the time; improvement only happens when you have these systems that enable you to do it all the time.

When I was at Brawn GP, I was invited to go along and watch some Accident and Emergency training at St Mary's Hospital in Paddington. We went along to observe a mock A&E drama. The idea was that we would say what we thought they could learn from motor racing, anything that we could contribute. So, they had a mock-up theatre, this guy came in, he'd supposedly been stabbed, they quickly substituted him for a model, and they all piled in to save him, then he went into crisis. There were some interesting observations I made. The first was that nearly always the teams don't know each other. So when they come together in A&E, someone takes charge but they may not know the others. That was odd to me, that you would be in a crisis situation without knowing everyone around you. But having said that, it just means that the processes needed to be robust enough that you could deal with it. What really struck home was that after everything was finished, I said to the staff that were there, 'When do you hold your debrief to decide what worked well, what didn't, what problems you have and what you need to do?' They said they didn't have debriefs. I said, 'But surely you must get together and discuss things?' 'Only if the patient dies.' Only when someone has died do you discuss, when it's too late. And at that time it's emotionally charged, because you are all worried about the consequences. 'Why don't you have a normal session when everything's been okay and you can see all the things you'd like to improve?' They said they don't have time. That was shocking for me. I said, 'That's the biggest thing you have to do, give yourself time to improve the process. You have got to have a system where improvements can be developed. If problems recur several times, then it's got to have priority.'

So I think that the system I'd developed was quite significant, probably more than I gave it credit for. That Monday morning debrief after the race, where everyone got together, was the message. I insisted that the message I gave to the heads went to the staff. This is the message, this is the priority, this is why this happened. Also I would take the opportunity to give them an overview of the political landscape, such as the drama with double diffusers at Brawn GP. Everyone in the team cared, they were all concerned about it. They want to hear from the horse's mouth what's going on.

* * *

A By the beginning of 1999, you had got Ferrari to the shape where it had the best car on the grid. You didn't quite get both Championships in 1999 but you did that in 2000, 2001, 2002, 2003 and 2004. The first, and so far the only, time any team has won five, back-to-back double World Championships. What was that period like?

R It was the ultimate of what we had been trying to achieve. There were lots of problems, but a great attitude in the team to deal with them. The whole team was buzzing, the whole thing was working really well. We got onto the crest of a wave each year. We would get the car done, there would be a programme to develop the car, and then pretty soon Rory and his team would start on the next year's car. You start to get this strength and discipline to maintain it, and you build people's confidence.

One of the things I was really proud of in that period was the reliability of the cars, which was tremendous. We really established what could be done with a Formula One car. We had, I think, 53 consecutive podiums. Nigel Stepney was very strong on reliability and he was one of the reasons, because you still need the personal touch. You have all the systems in place, but you still need people who care, and he was very proud of the fact that we had 53 podiums. When that run ended, he was distraught.

A What did you learn from the success that you had during those years?

R That's a very good point. What you expect and what you see, is that in the first year or two of success, everyone is happy for you. 'It's great, Ferrari is winning. Formula One is in heaven again.' And then as you continue to win, people start to claim it's tedious, it's predictable, it's spoiling the sport. I had a wonderful letter from an Italian Ferrari enthusiast, saying, 'You have ruined my Sundays, because I sit in front of the TV and you win every race. I am disappointed if you lose but I know you're going to win. Years ago, if Ferrari won, I would be out on the town, celebrating with my friends. Now you've made it normal.'

A *The good news is, he is happy now.*

R Getting more serious: everyone is happy at the start, then the attitude changes and they try to bring you down. I sympathize with the problem that Bernie and Max had because Ferrari was winning everything. I think Max took a more pragmatic view that we were just doing a great job, but Bernie was pulling his hair out because of the impact on the commercial side of the sport. For five years we won every race and it was predictable. Myself, I think there was some good racing going on. It wasn't as straightforward as people remember, there were pretty decent challenges from other teams. Dealing with the politics of that, working out how to make concessions, give people a bit of scope: if you just stonewall everything, then eventually they will knock the wall down and you have nothing, so you have to find some compromise, accept rule changes. I was never that bothered by most of the rule changes, because I figured that as an organization we would deal with rules changes better than anyone else.

The one rule change that scuppered us was the introduction in 2005 of the rule that you had to do the whole race on one tyre. Over several seasons we had developed a sprint race philosophy where we did several pit stops. Bridgestone were developing soft, super-grippy, short-life tyres. We were developing cars with small fuel tanks. We were optimizing that approach and we were focused on three or even four pit stop races. We had gone down that route, and our cars and particularly our tyres had all been optimized.

Then we heard this clever argument built: 'Wasn't it terrible for the environment that all these tyres are getting wasted and thrown away. We are going to have an environment where you can only have one set of tyres for practice and one for the race.'

A Do you think that Max introduced the new rule deliberately, because he knew that your car and tyres were built around sprint racing and this was the biggest spanner he could use to shake things up?

R Well, Max and Bernie did it together. Bernie would not have had the idea. Max would have understood the implications. We were completely screwed, we didn't have the knowledge of the rubber or technology to make a one-race tyre. In fact Michelin, who were the other tyre manufacturer, had a different approach to Bridgestone and their tyres got *better* as the race went on. We had a tyre that just fell apart and we couldn't make one that was strong enough. So for the majority of 2005 we really struggled. We started to get it together at the end of that year, we eventually started to find some solutions. We had to have a second go at strengthening Bridgestone to understand why we couldn't make a tyre that would be competitive over the length of a race. We brought an engineer in that we had identified working for Bridgestone Italy in the research centre, and we gave him a high level of responsibility in the race programme. So, this deep integration was again part of solving the problem.

And things got better. In 2006 we put in a Championship challenge – we still had difficulties with the one-race tyre – but we were competitive and we won some races. And we would have, we should have – these are big words in Formula One . . .

A Irrelevant words . . .

R They are irrelevant words, yes, that's a good description. We had an engine failure in Japan, which was very unusual, and the Championship went down to the last race in Brazil. Michael was fabulously competitive, much faster than anyone else the whole weekend. Then we had a fuel pump failure in qualifying, and we started the race tenth. As Michael charged up the field, because he was so much faster than anyone else, he got clipped by Fisichella, who was Alonso's team-mate at Renault, and he punctured the tyre. As he punctured it going into turn one, he had to drive all the way around the circuit with a puncture. He was lapped by everyone, but he set off from the pits, and unlapped himself from everyone, and he finished fourth from being a lap behind everyone. He was stunning – every lap was faster and faster.

This was the last race before he retired. But the message was that by 2006 we were competitive again. We had adapted. The thing I learnt from that period of domination is, you're going to be brought down by one thing or another; either the other teams steal your people, maybe you get complacent about the reasons for your success, you take your eye off the ball, or you become bad for the sport and everyone gangs up on you and changes the rules.

A How did the process of changing the rules work and how did you fight it?

R The way the FIA's technical regulations were then, a majority decision had to be made at least 18 months before it could be implemented. A unanimous decision could be implemented on shorter notice, but that could be blocked by one team. But the tyres came under the sporting regulations, which were more vague, probably because no one had envisaged that the sporting regulations would affect the competitive position of the teams in the sport so much. So, we knew that the change in the rules on the tyres was a very serious threat, and it was on short notice, so I fought it basically on the technical front. But I'm sure we would have called the FIA to try and stop it politically also. We wouldn't have been passive about it. But the more we protested, the more they rubbed their hands.

It wasn't the only issue. Particularly during the second half of that five-year dominance, people were throwing mortars at us the whole time. You're constantly defending yourself and heading off the issues. The technical regulations were part of my responsibility. 'They want to do this to the rules, it's clearly aimed at us, let's steer it a bit off course, and get it in a form that we can deal with.' Ironically, we had been our own worst enemy; no one else would use Bridgestone as they felt that they wouldn't get fairly treated, because the relationship between Bridgestone and Ferrari was so close. In fact, McLaren were the first major team with Bridgestone, but we forced them out because we had such a good partnership. So we had created this situation in a way, we had Bridgestone almost exclusively, so everyone else thought the one-race tyre was a wonderful idea.

A To get a change through, the FIA had to initiate it, they had to have the majority of the teams on board, Bernie, then it went to the F1 Commission and the World Motor Sport Council, where Ferrari had a very strong influence. And, after all, in the Concorde Agreement, Ferrari even had a veto over changes in the regulations, so theoretically you could have stopped any change. You didn't use the veto.

R I think that subconsciously, deep down we recognized that we weren't doing the sport much good. Winning was our responsibility. It was what we were there for. But if the sport was really suffering because of what we were doing, if no one else could beat us, do you accept it, just decide, 'How many Championships do you have to win?' That was not a conscious decision. I never thought, 'They are going to screw us for a year but . . .' By then there was a doubt: 'Are we damaging the sport?'

A Did you ever sit down with Luca and Jean and say strategically, 'This is a very serious threat to us. We have a veto. We can stop this.'

R I didn't know that we had a veto then. We didn't use it and I don't think Jean would have ever used it, because we knew it was wrong.

A I think Ferrari did try and use it later in 2009 to stop the FIA introducing the rules for the 2010 Championship.

R I didn't know about the veto until later in my Ferrari career. We would have had the conversations about doing everything we could do to stop it. But I wonder if we knew subconsciously that for the good of the sport, we had to accept the new rules. After a while into that period of dominance, you start to defend yourself. That happens in a small way all the time: whenever any team has a competitive advantage, the other teams will try and change the rules to remove it. That was part of my role. If I saw that the rules had gone in a direction that was favourable to another team, I would try and move them back the other way. When I was leaving Mercedes at the end of 2013, and we knew we were going to be very competitive, I said to Toto Wolff, 'You have several challenges, and one of the biggest that you will have is politically maintaining your dominance.' I told him he had to start thinking about how to deal with that; he was going to have shells exploding over his head.

In any event, after a period of complete dominance, 2005 was a tough year. You have to hold the team together after it stops winning races. I remember in Hungary – which is quite a hard track on tyres, the worst track – I came on the radio to Michael and said, 'You have to pull over, because they are coming up to lap you,' and he said, 'No, you're joking. This is ridiculous, we can't carry on like this.' And it was pretty unusual for Michael to make those comments over the radio, but he was so frustrated, it shows the point we had reached. It was a tough year to keep the team together.

Through it all, in 2005, I never ever felt any threat towards my own position. I had always made sure that I had contractual security, but, in fact, my contracts only ever got discussed when they were renewed. I never felt Ferrari was talking to someone else. I trusted Jean implicitly. Luca I did trust in that respect, I could read him. I would have known if there was a problem of that severity.

It helped in 2005 that there was this very specific reason why our performance had dropped off. In spite of everything I have said about partnerships and unity, the problem was that Bridgestone didn't have a tyre that was suitable to that form of racing. But we never criticized Bridgestone – and that was vital. Once you start to criticize a partner like that, you may feel that you are spurring them on – but you're not. During that period, it was always 'we we we', never 'them'. And that was a weakness of Red Bull in its treatment of Renault. Red Bull might not have won those Championships without an engine partner as strong as Renault, but they never gave Renault enough credit when they were winning. And when there was pressure, after their performance dropped off, the relationship broke down immediately. In 2005, I made a conscious effort, and everyone did, to demonstrate that we were all partners in it together. I had a very good head of vehicle dynamics, someone I knew and still know socially, and he said to me in a later period, the most impressive thing for him was how we managed to keep the team together in 2005, when the media was going berserk. For him, it was a greater achievement than winning all the Championships, to hold the team together in 2005, and come out to win races in 2006 and then the Championship again in 2007. That was another Championship where I had left the team the year before – but it was my car and my team. When I went back to do an Italian driving tour in 2014, they had an exhibition in the Ferrari museum of all my cars that had won the Championship, and I had my photograph in front of those cars, and they included the 2007 car, because they said very graciously that it was mine.

A One of the ironic consequences of the new tyre rules in 2005 was the disastrous race at Indianapolis that year, which did very serious damage to the cause of Formula One in the United States. This was the race when only Ferrari and the other two Bridgestone teams raced, because the Michelin tyres were not safe on the high-speed banked section of the circuit. There had been the option of putting a chicane in there, but the FIA would not allow it. What is your view on the decision that you took to race there?

R We didn't take any decision. We were in a period when we were feeling very aggrieved because of what had gone on with the tyre rules, feeling persecuted. So our mindset was not to have much sympathy when the perpetrators of the one-race tyre had a problem. It was terrible for Formula One. I think we probably would have gone along with any solution that had been proposed. There was talk of putting in a chicane, and I don't think quite honestly that we put up a massive objection to that. It was Max who said, 'You can't put up a chicane to suit one tyre manufacturer, when the other tyre manufacturer is doing a good job and has shown that it is perfectly possible to design a tyre that will work safely at Indy.' He was also concerned about the fact the circuit hadn't been safety homologated with a chicane.

What about with the cars: if you found that a car has a problem with a feature of the track, would you change the track for the good of Formula One? For the good of the sport, we clearly should have done something else, but it escalated and it came to be a stand-off, a principles decision. I think that at Ferrari, we stood back a little that weekend and let it happen. We were passive in that I saw it as out of our hands, but we didn't encourage a solution that would have been to our disadvantage.

A Your philosophy was to win, and I haven't seen a lot of evidence that you did things that resulted in you not winning.

R I think that on the day, you are out there to win, but you take a slightly more benevolent view of what is good for F1 when you have sufficient timescale. I genuinely can put my hand on my heart and say that I was willing to look at what was for the good of the sport, as long it was for 18 months' time. If it was for tomorrow then it was difficult. It was also your ability to respond. If the one-race tyre rules had been in two years' time, then you would be less agitated, you would have had more time to develop a solution, that would have been fairer to Bridgestone. Whether that would have made a difference is another question, and until you are in the heat of the battle you don't know where you are or how to respond. Every resource got thrown at Bridgestone to get us back in shape, would we have done that if we had a longer timescale?

* * *

A You left Ferrari just as I joined Williams at the end of 2006. From 2007, we were on a standard tyre across the sport, with Bridgestone the sole tyre supplier. Presumably that was a decision that benefited you and you would have supported?

R The thought process would have been that we are battling in a tyre war, and we have Bridgestone almost exclusively. But there was a much bigger picture with what was going on, a big cost issue. The tyre development was very expensive, we were out every week testing tyres.

In terms of things that I learnt at Ferrari, one thing that I wasn't prepared for, was the media attention. There are three religions in Italy, of which football and Ferrari are two. In the early days, I was walking through the airport and a guy sweeping the floor stopped me and berated me about Ferrari's performance. Later, when we won our first Championship, and we flew back into Bologna airport, there were thousands of people there celebrating the Ferrari win. It's on a level you can't prepare for. All the coffee bars around Maranello have a journalist sat there all day long, finding out what the latest news is.

When I joined, there was a view that every senior manager should know what the papers were writing about the team. There would be a folio of all the newspaper cuttings on your desk each day. It would be an inch thick, and if it was a race weekend, two inches thick, and if it was an especially controversial weekend, three inches thick. When I started there, you wouldn't see much done in the first hour or two of the morning, because everyone would have their coffee and read the cuttings. I said this was ridiculous, it's crazy filling our people's heads with all the media, so I stopped it. It was a gesture; people could still get the information if they wanted it, but I thought we were sending the wrong message to staff. You can't ignore the media, but there is part of the team that has to deal with it, not the whole company. You need to give your people a message, and that isn't the message coming from the media.

A What was the basis of your decision to leave Ferrari. You were only 52. Why leave?

R There were several factors. I had the view that 10 years was a great time to have at Ferrari. I was in a wonderful, joyous position at Ferrari, success, great relationships with everyone. I felt that you need to leave on the up, we had nearly won in 2006 and then went on to win in 2007. At the end of 2004, I had told Luca and Jean that I was leaving at the end of 2006. It was time to move on, time to face a new challenge. In the background, my two girls had got married, we had grandchildren on the horizon. Jean was getting tugged a bit each way. I love Italy, but I was missing England. It all seemed to be right to say, 'Ten years is a nice round number,' give plenty of notice, and 'Let's develop the organization to work without me.'

I didn't regret leaving. Jean and Luca did try to convince me to change my mind – they couldn't see the logic. I had some difficulty to build a succession plan. The challenge of those last two years was great for me, it drew me in. If anything I was more committed to Ferrari to leave them in the best possible position I could, and leave with my head held high. And the sending-off parties were fabulous. What's been really nice is that when I've been back there, the welcome. When I went back in 2014, Luca put on a royal tour for all my friends. I was meeting mechanics and engineers and there were tears flowing and fabulous memories.

A On succession planning. You left Ferrari with a Championship-winning car. Did you leave the right structure and people to sustain a team capable of winning World Championships?

R I had identified what I felt was the optimal structure when I left. There were three key people: Aldo Costa, Nigel Stepney and Mario Almondo, my right-hand men in that period.

Rory was also easing down his commitment, he had a young family. We built a structure. Stefano was going to be Team Principal. Jean had gone over to the road car side so Stefano would be more clearly the Team Principal. There was a succession plan in place. The problem was that it was *my* view of what the succession plan should be. In fact when I left, it changed, the views changed, and it didn't evolve into the structure I imagined it would be. There was some internal friction between people, who when I was there had a clear leader. When I left, the leadership I thought would work, didn't, because those people had worked together for so long at the same level. With Aldo and Mario and others, there started to be some internal friction. This eventually led to Aldo leaving. Nigel Stepney was aggrieved that he didn't get a more senior position. He was difficult to manage, I managed, but then he became a loose cannon.

When I left, some of the glue that was holding it together was gone. I don't know if I could have anticipated that. Towards the end of my time, when I had the succession plan in place, I went away for two weeks, and while I was away, they had all decided to change what we had agreed. So, this started to show the signs of what would happen when I left. Once you leave, you can't implement a succession plan. Maybe my anticipation of what would become the natural order wasn't after I left. It didn't work out. Aldo, Mario, Nigel and Stefano aren't there anymore.

I think that James Allison has the potential to be a great technical director. What's clear when talking to people at Ferrari now is that he's got their respect, he's very committed and enthusiastic, he is very inclusive with people. In a way, he has a similar style to mine. Maybe not as active politically outside the team as I was, but that's time and age.

It is an interesting reflection of Ferrari. After they had brought James in they then convinced Adrian Newey to leave Red Bull and join Ferrari. That upset James a great deal and didn't send the right message to him, they broke his trust. And I think that's a bit of a reflection about where Ferrari are now. They are not as solid, contained, confident as they were when I was there. But I hope they get their confidence in James, and that's how they will succeed. The programmes are too long to start hopping around with engineers. You need consistency.

When I left for my sabbatical at the end of 2006, I wanted to travel the world with my wife. As you know, in Formula One, we travel the world and we don't see anything but airports, hotels and circuits. But I still had a lot of enthusiasm and energy for F1. I had agreed with Luca and Jean Todt that we would meet in the summer. So I met them in June or July of 2007, I said I was interested in coming back into Ferrari but the only position that would make sense would be Team Principal. I felt a bit uncomfortable as Stefano Domenicali is a good friend, and he was being lined up for that role. In the end, we mutually decided to draw a line underneath it.

Meanwhile, Nick Fry (the CEO of the Honda F1 team) kept calling me, in fact he had called me when I was at Ferrari. But that autumn time, it felt right. You look at Honda then and they had everything that was needed, but they couldn't score points. I knew the facilities they had, and Nick was pretty persuasive, and eventually I went to see him and tied it up very quickly. We took a trip to Japan for two days to meet the board.

A year later, in November 2008, the Honda decision came as a shock to us, we had no inkling. We knew the climate was grim. Nick and I had this odd invitation to go and meet the head of Honda motorsport at a hotel in Slough, and he was alone in the room and he was clearly very emotional and upset and just said, 'I'm sorry guys – we are stopping.' And we took a while to take that in. I said, 'What do we do, what do you want us to do?' 'Can you come with me?' Then we went into a room with a much longer table, there was a whole team of lawyers and others who had been assembled there to shut the team down. We then contacted the team HR guy, our legal director, financial director, they all came to Slough, and we started the discussion.

With the number of employees at the team, there was a process of consultation to follow, and you can't discriminate between people who had been at Brackley and others who had come from Honda. But we were in front of this group of specialists, and they said, 'We need you to go back, turn the lights off and send everyone home,' and our HR guy said, 'We can't do that, we have to go through this process. You must give everyone three months' notice and go through a consultation process.'

That gave us some breathing space, but still didn't mean that we would be spending money. So one of the first successes we had was to persuade Honda that we might be able to sell the team, but that we must have the ability to carry on designing the car, and that if we stopped doing that, we could guarantee that Honda would get nothing. They didn't believe it was possible to sell the team, but to their credit they gave us a couple of million pounds to see us through the winter, to carry on all the manufacturing and design process to keep the team alive.

There was a lot of publicity about the fact that we were seeking buyers, so we were inundated with chancers, and Nick and I spent a lot of our time discussing and negotiating with these people, while it became clearer and clearer that there were very few serious options. One guy, it came to a head on Christmas Eve, arrived in a big personalised helicopter; he was supposedly from a Greek shipping dynasty. He took Nick and me out to expensive restaurants to discuss what he was going to do. We asked Jackie Stewart, who knows most of the world's royalty, if he could find out who this man was. Turned out that he didn't exist, he had a false identity, and he is now in jail for fraud after taking the Irish banks for millions. We had a Russian oligarch, the guy who owned Portsmouth football club. We were meeting these sorts of people. We talk about Formula One being shark-infested waters, this was a different type of shark.

We were going through this experience of meeting all these people and finding it very frustrating, and we eventually started to develop the idea that we should buy it ourselves. We started to build a plan of the finances involved in taking it on ourselves, what would be the costs Honda would have to pay in closing it down compared to what we would have to ask Honda for us to take control and responsibility, the risks and possibilities. We developed a plan and convinced the Honda board that it was viable. Honda is a correct and ethical company; they found it awkward that they had brought me in on a three-year contract and then had to shut the whole thing down after only one year. That helped sway them and we showed Honda that if they went down one route, it would cost x, or the other way, it costs y, and the team would continue.

What was so rewarding in that period was the attitude of the people in the team. We had to explain to everyone, 'We are going to have to accept the Honda decision which is terrible, but if we don't work our socks off for the next three months then we will have nothing to sell, and we may as well shut it down now.' And the approach of the people was fantastic, it was so rewarding seeing the commitment they showed, in circumstances that were very difficult. We had committed that in three months' time, if we hadn't made it work and couldn't sell the team, everyone would get their redundancy package. That gave them a bit of comfort. But they went beyond that. It was interesting to see people step up or fall away. One or two people didn't cope with the uncertainty, others relished it. The Dunkirk sprit. People blanked off things they had no way of controlling, and they did a terrific job in that period. I should add that the group we put together to lead discussions on the way forward during this period included several team members from the shop floor.

We also had to sort out an engine to replace the Honda. We asked Mercedes and Ferrari. The Ferrari would have been the previous year's version. The Ferrari engine didn't really fit the car, Mercedes offered their current engine that fitted the car much better, and they were local. We owed Martin Whitmarsh, Ron Dennis and Norbert Haug a lot for their support. When we started to get things rolling, Mercedes supplied the drawings so we could work on the design, but when we bought the team Norbert came along and said there were concerns from the Mercedes board and they could only go ahead if we paid for the whole season up front, so we gave him a payment, which was about €8 million. 'Right, we will pay it tomorrow,' I said. And that settled everything there and then.

When we started testing for the 2009 season, we knew we had a potential Championship-winning car. The first test in 2009 we didn't make, so we were looking at the other teams' times. They didn't look very impressive, but you never really know unless you are there. We were very interested to know whether we had missed something, and whether we would get a dose of reality when we joined the other teams for the second test. But when the test came, our times were, as predicted, very good and we did it with a normal fuel load. In general, my policy was never to run light in testing to flatter the timesheet. It may have been a very odd occasion when we have done something to elevate the timing in testing, a tactical thing, to rattle someone, but it was never my policy to be unrepresentative in testing.

We had the early skirmishes which were all these chancers I mentioned. Then we had the late skirmishes: Richard Branson and then Bernie. Richard had approached us to sponsor the team because it was becoming a nice story, but then, before we had closed the deal with Honda, he tried to buy the team from under us which was a bit unfortunate, although we managed to maintain a relationship. Richard was in cahoots with Adrian Reynard, they were good friends. I have a letter somewhere that Adrian wrote to the president of Honda saying that we wouldn't be responsible owners and that Honda should bear in mind that Richard would be a far more responsible owner. The president of Honda very kindly gave me the letter and said, 'Make of this what you will.' His opinions of me and Adrian, who he knew, were different.

Richard Branson invited the Honda people to a meeting in London to discuss his proposal to buy the team. He wasn't aware I knew, but the Honda people asked me to come along to help negotiate this possible deal. Of course, I agreed. Richard's people were shocked to see me there, because they knew what was going on. But Richard was on Necker Island, so he had called in on a video link. He came on the video screen, but he couldn't see our side of the link, and he didn't know who was there. He didn't ask who was attending the meeting and then gave his pitch to the Honda people. 'Well, I'm sure we will be able to persuade Ross and the other management to run the team for us as we have a good relationship.' And I said, 'Richard, our relationship has just taken a step back.' 'Who's that?' he said. 'It's Ross, I'm here.'

That was Honda, they were very open with me, they trusted me, they gave me the letters, when Bernie approached them they contacted me. The second late skirmish we had was Bernie trying to buy the team. Honda had to consider all offers. Bernie's offer wasn't as attractive as ours – nor was Richard's. We had registered our proposal with Honda and when the closing date came, it was still the best offer on the table.

Then we got going.

The best thing about 2009 for me was that the same people who, the year before, couldn't get a podium, were now winning races. For me, part of the reward was demonstrating to them that they were as good as everyone else. We saw those dramatic contrasts of the despair in the winter, and the joy of winning races, winning two Championships. Some of the guys placed bets when they saw testing, and they made a few quid as the bookies took a while to catch up. That was a reason for some added celebration.

The idea of selling the team to Mercedes grew from mid-year. Norbert was a strong architect of that, he always had a dream for Mercedes to have their own team. The deal evolved during the year and became really a shoe-in. There was a perfect storm. Mercedes had been with McLaren for many years, but McLaren now had plans to become a road car manufacturer in their own right, which caused some difficulties at Mercedes, and Mercedes wouldn't supply engines for the McLaren road cars. With the McLaren road cars becoming a concern for Mercedes, Brawn GP winning the Championship, us not being natural team owners: we had a decent offer, it was a good deal for Mercedes, and it was a good deal for us. Everything worked well for everyone.

I agreed to do a contract to carry on for three years as one of the conditions for the purchase. We will discuss this all later in more detail, but we didn't have a good 2010 and 2011. In 2012 we won some races, and in 2013 we fought for the Championship so we had started to get it back. But it didn't have the impetus that it should have had, certainly not initially. I retired from Mercedes GP and Formula One at the end of 2013, pretty much on my 59th birthday, and after close to four decades in the sport.

PART II

Strategy in Formula One

INTRODUCTION

To frame our discussion about strategy in Formula One, Ross and I started by looking at the earliest recorded work on strategy, the *Sunzi*, or *Sun Tzu's Art of War*. This note highlights some of aspects of the *Sunzi* which we read and where we found interesting lessons and parallels. In the references section at the back of the book, we have provided a short bibliography of the main works that we have relied on – for those who are interested, these books could provide further reading. The extracts from the *Sunzi* are from the classic translation by Lionel Giles, with some minor changes for style.

The *Sunzi* is not about war, it is about strategy, and it goes to great lengths to argue that those who resort to fighting have failed. This passage in Book III states the position:

Sunzi said: In the practical art of war, the best thing of all is to take the enemy's country whole and intact; to shatter and destroy it is not so good. So, too, it is better to capture an army entire than to destroy it ... Hence to fight and conquer in all your battles is not supreme excellence; supreme excellence consists in breaking the enemy's resistance without fighting.

Thus the highest form of generalship is to frustrate the enemy's plans and the next best is to prevent the enemy's alliances ...

Therefore the skilful leader subdues the enemy's troops without any fighting; he captures their cities without laying siege to them; he overthrows their kingdom without lengthy operations in the field. With his forces intact he will dispute the mastery of the Empire, and thus, without losing a man, his triumph will be complete.

Just as in Formula One, the best strategists have won before they even get onto the field. If you are someone who loves intense racing, that can be a disappointment because winning looks too easy. But if you are interested in how you get to the position where winning looks easy, then you will find the sport more complex and subtle than any other yet invented. And at the other end of the field, when I joined a Williams that was struggling both on the track and financially, my view was that I had to do whatever was necessary to 'keep us intact to compete in the world'. A financially sound team has the hope of becoming competitive once again [as Williams did], but a bankrupt team cannot win.

The *Sunzi* was written in China between 500 and 300 BC, a period known as the Warring States. This was, as the name suggests, a period of constant – and constantly evolving – political and military competition between states vying to be the one to unify the Chinese world. The context in which the *Sunzi* was written was one in which states faced constant external, existential threats, from increasingly far afield, as political strategies and military campaigns moved from immediate neighbours to distant states. Armies grew from 30,000 men at most to 100,000 and perhaps more.

Technology changed: the crossbow appeared, the chariot became obsolete, massed infantry became the dominant force while the introduction of iron-making meant new, mass-produced weapons and armour. Campaigns extended in time and space. By 221 BC, when China was unified by the winning state, 148 states had disappeared during the course of over 250 major wars. This pattern of escalation is not limited to warfare: it is also visible in Formula One where the intense competition to win drives teams to seek ever more sophisticated technology, and ever greater spending. But these higher costs also mean greater consequences for those who do not succeed.

The success of Chinese states during this period was a function of internal and external strategy: internally, the states that undertook self-strengthening reforms were able to sustain themselves and the military capabilities they needed; externally, ruthless strategies were required to minimize risk and make best use of limited resources. The two reinforced each other: financial reforms generate more resources to finance the costs of expansion, while administrative reforms allow states to raise and manage larger armies, mobilize more national resources for war, and alleviate logistical problems in long-distance campaigns. Again, there is a parallel with Formula One: the better a team is at securing funding, and investing its resources efficiently, the more competitive it can be on the track.

A crucial aspect of strategy is, therefore, the political dimension of how you rule your own state so as to maximize its competitive position; but also minimizing the costs and risks of war itself. This approach was perfected by the state of Qin [pronounced Chin], which eventually succeeded in winning the competition to unite China. Its first emperor is the one who was buried with his terracotta army. Qin won by pursuing the most comprehensive self-strengthening reforms and the most ruthless strategies and tactics. Qin was not the first reformer but undertook extensive military and civilian reforms once it got going in about 350 BC. At the same time, Qin pursued a policy of turning state against state, fomenting civil dissent and finally fighting only when it had established sufficient superiority. Its methods were unrestrained and included lying and cheating, bribing corrupt kings and officials, and sowing dissension between kings and commanders: tactics that are recommended in the *Sunzi*.

THE THREE DIMENSIONS
OF STRATEGY

In Formula One the goal of strategy is to win. Winning demonstrates technical superiority, and it brings economic benefits in the form of prize money and sponsorship; and it also gives the winner political influence that can be used in technical and commercial negotiations about the future of the sport. Winning requires also that a team maximizes its political, economic and technical capabilities. So, these are the three dimensions of strategy.

This is equally true of strategy in Warring States China which required a country to mobilize its political, economic and technical capabilities in pursuit of objectives that were ultimately political and economic more than military. Strategy therefore requires the consideration of the political and economic capabilities of each side and of other potential participants, as well as of their military strength. Let us look then at how the Sunzi *addresses these dimensions, starting with the economic, and then turning to the political.*

The Sunzi *speaks extensively and precisely of the economic impact of warfare on a state and its citizens, whether they are in the theatre of war or supporting a distant campaign:*

The state's treasury is impoverished by having to maintain an army a long way from home. Contributing to the costs of maintaining an army at a distance causes the people to be impoverished. On the other hand, the proximity of an army causes inflation; and inflation drains away the people's wealth; their homes will be stripped bare, and 60 per cent of their income will be dissipated; while the government's expenses will amount to 80 per cent of its total revenue. (*Book II*)

We have seen already that the Warring States period was characterized by increasingly large armies composed mostly of infantry, deploying new technology and conducting campaigns deep into other territories. The funding of war therefore became a strategic imperative while the economic implications of war grew: the consequences of misjudgement were, as the Sunzi repeats, the extinction of the state. Effective logistics are, however, not simply a factor to be got right – they can be used offensively. The Sunzi advises that 'the wise commander does his best to feed his army from enemy soil. To consume one measure of the enemy's provisions is equal to twenty of our own ...'

The political dimension of the Sunzi presents three challenges. The first is internal: the political ruler and military commander (who were typically not the same person) must behave ethically towards their subjects and soldiers, to win their loyalty and ensure they fight well. The second challenge is that the same ruler and commander must behave utterly ruthlessly towards the enemy: nothing is out of bounds. The third challenge is a familiar one: the ruler and military commander must agree who is responsible for what.

On the second point, the Sunzi prioritizes attacking alliances before armies. It also contains political advice: 'Unless you know the intention of the rulers of the neighbouring states, you cannot enter into preparatory alliances with them ... the business of waging war lies in carefully studying the designs of the enemy.'

On the third point, the Sunzi *describes the ideal commander in five words: wisdom, trustworthiness, benevolence, courage, discipline. Once appointed, the commander must follow his own judgement, and not any orders given to him by the ruler, who cannot assess the situation as well as he can:*

> If fighting is sure to result in victory, then you must fight; even though the ruler forbid it; if fighting will not result in victory, then you must not fight even at the ruler's bidding. The general who advances without coveting fame and retreats without fearing disgrace, whose only thought is to protect his country and do good service for his sovereign, is the jewel of the kingdom. (*Book IX*)

Just as the commander must follow his judgement, not his orders, so the ruler must respect the authority he has given to the commander. The Sunzi *identifies three ways in which a ruler will confuse his army, lose the confidence of his soldiers and invite the aggression of his neighbours: ordering an advance or retreat when inappropriate; interfering with the administration of the army; or interfering with military assignments. 'The side on which the commander is able and the ruler does not interfere will take the victory.'*

The commander's wisdom lies in a dispassionate assessment of the facts. For both the ruler and the commander, emotion is the antithesis of strategic effectiveness and its consequences are dire:

> The enlightened ruler lays his plans well ahead; the good general cultivates his resources. Do not move unless you see an advantage; do not use your troops unless there is something to be gained; do not fight unless the position is critical. No ruler should put troops into the field merely to gratify his anger; no general should fight

a battle simply out of pique. If it is to your advantage, make a forward move; if not, stay where you are. Anger may in time change to gladness; vexation may be succeeded by content. But a kingdom that has once been destroyed can never come again into being; nor can the dead ever be brought back to life. Hence the enlightened ruler is prudent, and the good general full of caution. This is the way to keep a country at peace and an army intact. (*Book XI*)

In summary, the ruler and commander (once appointed) must both follow the way and exercise good judgement with a calm, dispassionate temperament. The commander must accept the responsibilities of leadership, regardless of the consequences, and the ruler must accept the consequences of delegation, resisting the temptation to interfere.

R Well, what I found fascinating about the chapter from your thesis was that battle is the last resort and the activities to avoid battle are the most critical – I mean espionage, spying, intelligence, all those things; also, the complete contrast that they were advocating between the internal leader and the external warrior. These points were in some ways obvious, but fascinating to see it illustrated so well, and in terms of the qualities that a good leader has, it really struck home to me. The other interesting aspect was the critical point they made on how a good commander needs to be given authority and mustn't be interfered with in terms of his activities. The emperor, or whoever is the ultimate leader, has to be prepared to give that authority and let them get on with it.

A I can see parallels, for example, on that last point, when you were the Team Principal of a team owned by a manufacturer. There has to be a clear delineation of what you are accountable for and what your authority is. If people start interfering with that, you can't do your job. It is interesting that there is such a long history of this subject, but also that, as you say, the ideas in there are immediately relevant.

R Yes, nothing has changed.

A That's why we still read it.

R Yes.

A And, of course, the reason why nothing has changed is that people are people and this is all about people.

R Yes.

A So, one of the first things we have to do is come up with a working definition of what strategy is. The idea behind these conversations is to start with a bit of a hypothesis and then use the evidence from your experience, and maybe mine, to say how do we refine that hypothesis into something pragmatic? We could start by asking, 'What is strategy? What do we think it means?' In the Formula One world, people use the word strategy in different contexts, race strategy and so on. So, do you have a definition of strategy in your mind?

R Well, for me – and the chapter you gave me to read illustrates this in many ways – there is strategy and there is philosophy. In Formula One, strategy normally refers to race strategy – but race strategy is game play really. It's a chess game. There's a little bit of bluffing, false calls and stuff like that, but it's really game play. You look at all the numbers and you're trying to predict as far as you can how a race is going to evolve. And importantly you have scenario A, scenario B, scenario C that you must have thought out in your mind and your models so that when they occur, maybe you don't have the perfect solution, but you have thought about it, and every lap is mapped out. If the safety car happens this lap, if it rains this lap, what are we going to do? And all those things can all be modelled. Undoubtedly, in races there are the unknowns. You know, maybe two drivers start to clash and you have got to make some unplanned decisions about what you are going to do. You can talk about those things with the drivers beforehand, but they are human beings and they don't react how they think they will when faced with the real situation.

Those are the unpredictable variables in a race. There are a whole number of relatively predictable variables in a race that you can put all together and keep crunching the numbers until you build a picture of how the race will go. And that's strategy in the simplest sense. But, going into it more deeply, the strategy of positioning yourself in the best place with your budget, your engineering team, with your political influence on the rules and how things are directed in the future, is just as vital to success, in fact even more so. What you are doing in a race is the final stage; what you don't want to do is screw up in a race. You have got the best car. So you develop a strategy that makes sure you can win with the best car. Sometimes, you know, you have been smart and someone's missed the point and you can win a race when you haven't got the best car and it's great fun. But most of the time, the job's done by then. Therefore the strategy prior to the strategy, if you know what I mean, is the most important thing.

A If we go back to the Chinese, the Sunzi *is quite counter-intuitive on this point. The book says that if you aspire to be greater than the greatest generals of the past, then you are actually worse than them. Because the really great generals are not the ones who manage to win terrible battles by the skin of their teeth – they are the ones for whom the battle was so easy that no one even remembers them. So, if you are trying to be better than the best, what you are really trying to do is have those scary, you know, just-make-it-through battles. That is the definition of being a bad general. Now, of course, a sport thrives on competition on the track, so there is a potential downside in making it look too easy. But from the perspective of a competitor, that's not the point. So, when you say, 'the job's done' by the time you go racing, you mean perhaps that at the peak, in Ferrari and the first half of the season at Brawn, the races were pretty much a given. But that's not because there wasn't a big battle to get there; it is just that you have done all the preparation.*

R I think that's a good comparison. You know when we won some of those Championships, and people would come up and say, 'That was easy, you know, you just cruised that.' They didn't realize the tension and emotion as well as work and preparation behind it all. Because we created a car, created a team that *should* win and there is also enormous pressure to make sure you fulfil your objectives, realize your potential. It's great fun to pull a victory from the jaws of defeat, but ...

A ... but you can't win a Championship like that. No one's ever won a Championship with the worst car in the field.

R No, no.

A Essentially, you pretty much have to have the best car. But it is interesting to look at the rules today versus the rules then. Back when you were racing with Ferrari, with Michael and Jean, there was a tyre war, complete freedom on engine development, and unlimited use of wind tunnels and computational fluid dynamics [computer-simulated modelling] for aerodynamic development. You could do whatever you wanted. Theoretically, a team could reinvent itself every season. If you had enough money, and you knew what you were doing, you could just say, 'We are starting from scratch.' Today, that's not the same because engines have been homologated, there is no tyre war, testing is limited, even aero is limited, so you could argue that the challenge today is to get into the right position structurally, get the right engine rules etc. and then there is potential that you can just sit it out. So we saw Red Bull win four consecutive World Championships with the previous engine formula, and if the engines hadn't changed, the chances are that they would still be winning. The change in engines gave Mercedes the opportunity to develop a better package. And it is now going to be very hard for others to beat. Not impossible, but difficult.

R I think this is where philosophy comes in. You are right, in the early 2000s there were lots of different opportunities for development and it was therefore crucial for the team to know where it should focus its efforts. And that was an interesting strategic aspect because ...

A You can't do everything ...

R Yes, what was apparent to us in that period was that the tyre could be massively influential. So you know, you would spend weeks and months in the wind tunnel and get half a second per lap gain. But you could put on a new tyre and find half a second just like that. We put a huge effort into developing the tyre at Bridgestone. We put ourselves in a position where we were the prime team for Bridgestone. And we, quite honestly, forced on Bridgestone, semi-willingly – I mean they were a little bit reluctant but we insisted – a technical structure that enabled us to use all the strengths in the team and in Bridgestone to get the best tyre. So, the tyre was never developed in isolation. We had engineers at Bridgestone and we had Bridgestone engineers working at Ferrari. And we really integrated the tyre designer and manufacturer into the car design process so it wasn't separate. I think that philosophy was very important to welcome Bridgestone and say, 'You are not a tyre supplier, we're a team. We're one. And the tyre is so vital that we are going to put everything we can into this relationship. Share everything you want, every piece of information that is in the company you can have. And we want the same from you.' And it became clear in that process there was some areas that could be strengthened. The structural analysis of the tyre wasn't great, for example, and we were able to help with that an awful lot. So, that period was all about recognizing where is the biggest bang for the buck.

A Let's just talk a bit more about that integrated team, because the perception from the outside was that you as the technical director and Michael Schumacher as the key driver played a fundamental role, especially Michael's testing and technical understanding. Did the drivers play a big role in that?

R I think they did. By then data acquisition and analysis was at a pretty good level so that helped a lot. But after the analysis, the discussions about where we should be going with the tyre, what's needed, Michael was very involved with. Rubens was good as well in that period. But Michael was relentless in the effort and capacity he had to work with the team. If we suddenly had a tyre test to do – say something had happened and Bridgestone had a new tyre to test. I would ring Michael up and say, 'Can you be here tomorrow?' 'Yep. What time?' Never any hesitation. One or two others I would ring up and it would be, 'Oh, well, I want to see my kids tomorrow, it's a birthday party' and all the rest of it. You never had those discussions with Michael, because he knew if you asked it was important. With others you had to justify why you needed it.

A In 2003, before I joined his team, I asked Frank Williams, 'What's the difference between Michael and everyone else?' And he said there were three things. He said first of all his intelligence and technical understanding. Secondly, his physical fitness. And thirdly, that he just loves being in the car.

R Yes, I think that's a good summary.

A So, he wanted to be in the car presumably?

R Yes, he loved it. He loved driving.

A And even if he was testing tyres. You may not have heard these comments but Patrick Head once told me an interesting story. It was at Budapest or Monaco, a difficult circuit, and the radios were encoded at the time but something went wrong and suddenly everyone could hear Michael and you on the radio. And Michael was in the lead and he was setting the fastest times, lap after lap, which shows up purple on the timing screen, every one like a qualifying lap and Patrick said it was astonishing listening to Michael because he would say, 'Ross, run through the race order with me.' Patrick said it was like the two of you were in a couple of armchairs in front of the fire just chatting. Meanwhile, he is driving at a level that most people couldn't imagine. Purple, purple, purple. Do recognize that description and what do you put that down to?

R Well, Michael is hugely talented but he also recognized the importance of physical condition. He was very ambitious in terms of his physical condition. Drivers tend to be driven by the team to stay fit unless they have got strong self-motivation. He had huge self-motivation. He realized it was something he was doing better than everyone else. He wasn't arrogant about it, but he loved the physical side of things. He had a regime going that gave him fabulous physical fitness. He was just a naturally talented athlete with a great self-generated training regime. So when he was driving a car, it didn't really physically strain him. We would be having a conversation the same way that we are now, while he was in the car. Qualifying laps, we had to be careful, and if you spoke to him at the wrong time you would get a bollocking. But that's obvious if you do that. In the race, I was always trying to be considerate about where he was on the track because that was only sensible. But other drivers could become distracted by the conversation and slow down or you would just get on the radio to them and they would be very breathless, trying to get the words out in between pants of breath. He never did that. He also never seemed to sweat that much after a race, probably due to his superb condition. It was all part of what he knew he had to do to become a great driver. And also – and this goes back to some of the things in your thesis – I think some of it was about undermining the enemy, the confidence of the opposition. You remember the days when Michael first came along and you would go on the podium and there would be two drivers there almost unable to stand up and Michael would be jumping around, and they would sort of be looking at him thinking, 'God, what on earth is this creature we're competing with?' He had this massive mobile gym that was taken to all the tests. Half of it was to put two fingers up to the other drivers. 'Not only am I testing, I am going in the gym at night and working out.'

A Yes, because everybody knew that. In 2003 or 2004, I had a conversation with Frank, for example, and I asked him why he thought Michael was so good. He said of Ralf Schumacher and Juan Pablo Montoya, who were his drivers, 'I would be lucky if Ralf and Juan Pablo spend together as much time in a gym in a week as Michael does in a day.' Now of course, people can have raw talent. But even if you have got raw talent, being fit helps. If you look at the drivers today, they are much fitter probably than they would have been 10 or 20 years ago, but very few of them actually push it to the level that Schumacher did. They will go to the gym, do their cycling, whatever, but even though they know that that is part of being a World Champion, they don't necessarily do it.

R Well, most of them, and in some ways I include myself in this, are lazy. Human beings who will often take the easiest route and do what they feel is adequate, and I am just as guilty in that respect. As a person I am often best driven by deadlines and targets. I like to give myself challenges, because I know that will be the thing that will drive me most and if I know there is not that deadline ... One of the ways I worked in the office was to schedule meetings for the week because I knew that ...

A ... otherwise you would go fishing?

R Perhaps not that extreme! But I knew the week would slip away. I had to structure my week quite strictly to make sure I used the time properly. I knew a technical review was coming up and so I had to do the work to be ready for it.

A So do you regard yourself as a fundamentally lazy person?

R Yes, I probably do, yes. I like an easy life – let's put it that way ... but I probably need to defend myself a bit more!

A Well, you are obviously not a lazy person. But the object of this exercise is not just that people might be interested in your experience of working with Michael Schumacher. The question is, what can they take away from this? And one of the points that I have got on my list of questions is this: is strategy something you can study? Can you learn? Because the people writing 2,500 years ago, they believed that this was something that you could and you should study. If you wanted to lead an army, then you needed to apply yourself to what makes people successful commanders. So if your point is that people are quite lazy and they have to put structure into their lives to get the most out of themselves, then that is an important lesson.

R I think it is.

A People look at a Michael Schumacher or you and they say, 'These are World Champions. I will never be able to do what they have done. And how they have done it is just pure talent.' But I don't think that is what you are saying. It is more than just talent, isn't it? There's structure and there's discipline.

R Yes. Structure and discipline are a very important part of my life. And it is very important in Michael's life. His, in a way, was an even more difficult challenge. He was very much his own man for 90 per cent of the time. And there was only 10 per cent of the time when he was in the environment when it was structured for him. You know, we would go to a race. There would be the pre-briefs, debriefs, all the things he had to do – so a race weekend was very structured. But the other ten days in between races, unless there was testing or other team activities, he would have to be pushing himself. He would have to get up in the morning with his training programme set out in front of him and make sure he achieved it. And he was very good at that. I think that's a good point. So if you recognize in yourself that you are lazy, then having that structure, committing to it, and making sure it happens, is vital.

When I was working for Frank in the early days – and this is not a criticism of Frank, just a wonderful insight – I remember one day I was waiting to see him and he came in and he had been around the factory and he said, 'Okay, that's the factory tour over for today. That's another job done.' And we all imagined he was walking around the factory because he liked to go round – and some of it was that. But he realized he needed to be seen in the factory and that has stuck with me for my working career. And I used to say to my PA, all my PAs, 'Make sure I spend time out in the factory. Make sure you remind me and schedule it in.' And that relationship was a vital part for me of achieving success and getting the right team.

A And it is not because you are not interested but because you are busy and stuff happens. My way of doing that, when I was at Williams, was every morning I would drive into the car park and I would park in front of the aero building and then I could either walk to my office or I could go into the new wind tunnel, then into the old wind tunnel and then through the aero office and the composites department, into the machine shop and then up to my office. And if I did that, it would mean that the first thing I would do every day was spend the first 45 minutes just talking to aero and talking to the team as you go through. Once you get to your office it is very hard, the day gets going and suddenly there is stuff going on. So you do put routines in. It is not that I wasn't interested enough to do it. It was because I was interested in it. But without that structure, it doesn't happen.

R I think you are interested but there are some days you would rather not do it because you are swamped, but you do it, because it is important to the function of the business and because of the relationships you have in the team.

A So, let's change direction a bit. To summarize what you have been talking about so far. You have talked about the fact that race strategy is where the word strategy is used most frequently in Formula One, but you have also talked about the philosophy of how you set things up before you even get to a race, so that the rules are at least neutral towards you. You have got the right budget, you have got the right team, drivers and so on. The way that military theorists have developed this concept is to say that strategy has three elements. One is political. The second is economic. And the third is technical or technological: money, people and technical capability. What about the economic side of the team? How important is money in Formula One?

R It's pretty vital. It's a crucial element. One can definitely state that – but there are many examples in Formula One where you can have a hefty budget and not achieve huge success, but very few people have achieved success without a hefty budget. The Brawn GP story is sometimes highlighted as a fairy tale, but in reality there was a couple of hundred million pounds of Honda money put into that project before Honda withdrew. The real birth of that project was under Honda, when there were substantial resources.

A So money is a necessary but not a sufficient condition for success in Formula One?

R Yes, it's not a guarantee of success but it is a necessity.

A Can we just flip that round because there are teams, perhaps the best known example was Toyota, which invested an unimaginable amount of money. Well, let's say a similar level to what Honda was putting in, hundreds of millions of dollars a year, for an extended period, but I don't think they actually won a race ...

R No, they didn't.

A So how do you explain that? Why wasn't the money enough?

R A close friend of mine who worked at Toyota, told me that he had met with the Toyota hierarchy and had said, 'What we need on the team is Ross Brawn or someone similar. We need someone who has had success in Formula One and under-stands how it works.' And they said, 'No, that is not the Toyota way. We don't import success – we breed it.' And I think that

was one of their failings. If you look at the high-level structure of the team, there was no Formula One experience. And
in a team you need some references to understand how you
can achieve success in Formula One. There may be different
ways that no one has thought of so far. Maybe there is a different philosophy that will succeed. However, history has shown
that so far there is a certain approach that you have to take to
succeed. And Toyota failed. They didn't have that experience,
not only technically but also politically. They were very weak
politically. They were outsiders all the time. You know this
and I know this. They never really had a strong presence in
any of the strategy meetings. The Formula One political meetings that took place deciding the future direction of Formula
One, the technical regulations, the financial aspects: Toyota
were never the heavyweights and fully engaged in that process. They almost seemed to be superficial to it. The people
they employed didn't have a presence in those meetings.
They had people from a background and careers who were
not used to that environment.

*A What you are saying is that at that time the most successful
company in the world, which Toyota was, could not apply what had
made it so successful in making cars to making cars in a Formula
One environment. They couldn't apply the logic of the Toyota production system or their leadership style, or the way they invest in
people. That just didn't work, so you could say, therefore, if the outside world can't apply its logic in Formula One, then why would the
reverse be true? Why can the outside world learn from Formula One?*

R I take the point. One of the interesting things when I went
to Ferrari was that it was probably the first time I had been

to a company which had a large industrial base as well. I had worked at Williams, I had worked at Benetton, which were very similar teams. Benetton made sweatshirts and jumpers. Frank and Patrick were a self-contained engineering company. But they were small compact teams with no real connection to a car manufacturer. I explored the possibilities in a small way at Benetton with Ford, because Ford supplied the engine and we tapped into Ford a little bit. But what I found at Ferrari was that some of the methodologies from the car industry were being applied in the race industry to success: quality control, for instance, which was far better at Ferrari than anything I had experienced before. My experience of quality control up until then was primarily 'measure it and check it after it is made to make sure it is to the drawing'. The quality control at Ferrari was deeper than that: it was having quality assessment at the suppliers to make sure that the materials and the processes they were applying, things that perhaps you can't ultimately measure, were being done properly. So, Ferrari taught me that there is a lot in the automotive industry and also in the aerospace industry that Formula One needs to apply and learn from. But I think that the reverse process never happened with Toyota. They always took that knowledge they had and assumed it would be adequate for Formula One and it wasn't. And when they went into Formula One, they didn't have people looking at the sport and asking, 'What is this world all about? Is it different to what we are good at? What adjustments do we need to make to succeed in this environment?' They tried to apply their philosophy and approach for their environment to a different environment. It is a car with four wheels, but that is about all there is in common!

A That leads to Honda. You worked with Honda at the time you were at Williams, when Honda had been enormously successful with the turbos in the late 1980s. Then you worked with them at Honda GP when they obviously had a very uncompetitive engine. Now, they quite surprisingly have come back in, and are having a pretty tough time. And interestingly one of the things they keep saying is we will not accept other people's experience. Do you think that they fundamentally have the same approach to what you saw in Toyota? They brought you in?

R Yes, they did bring me in and I guess that was a recognition that they had to change their approach. I think if you looked at the contrast between what would be the typical model of a successful Formula One team and what I perceive – and I am not that experienced – is a typical model of a successful Japanese company, they couldn't be further apart. Therefore, when you have a Japanese company owning a Formula One team, it's difficult – it's almost two environments at their extremes. How do you bring them together to perhaps exploit the disciplines and philosophies and strengths of a Japanese company in the somewhat chaotic environment of a Formula One team and racing? When Honda were engine suppliers to Williams and McLaren, there was enough influence from the Race Teams to succeed. The Race Teams did all the political negotiations. Honda didn't have to, when they were purely engine suppliers, engage in the machinations of Formula One. They didn't need to because the team took care of everything for them and defended their rights, as an engine supplier, where it was necessary. So when Toyota and Honda acquired their own teams, I think they struggled in that aspect.

A In the McLaren-Honda relationship of today, I am sure that both would say that they have an integrated chassis engine group. The famous 'size zero' concept that they seem to have put forward looks from the outside like McLaren is setting the direction. Is there a pattern here? Or is every situation different?

R There are not enough examples to really say, but when I went into Honda in 2007, I needed to try and understand why it wasn't working, what were the reasons. Here was a team with a great budget, which we have already said is vital, good facilities that were vital, and I knew some of the people in the team and they were very good. But it was struggling. And what I found was a very disparate organization. The engine group was in Japan developing an engine almost in isolation, the chassis group was in Brackley developing a car almost in isolation, the relationships had broken down, and there was no bridge between the two. It had deteriorated to a point where the technical teams were almost in a battle to blame each other for the lack of success. When I joined Honda I was in a good position, I knew what a successful Ferrari organization looked like. I knew how it performed, I knew what the engine did, and I knew how the team functioned and I knew why it was successful. I was able to come along and say, 'Actually we have got to all face up to it – neither the engine nor the chassis is good enough at the moment. How do we bring this back together?' And there was progress. We changed the management in the engine group in Japan, because they had become entrenched. And we changed the management of the chassis group. We got some fresh people together and started to try and get it to work as a team. We were installing engine dynos at Brackley and the idea was

that we could start to do dynamic engine and chassis mapping and all that sort of stuff at Brackley. There were lots of
things happening to bring everyone together as one team.

*A Just one thing on the way through there. You talk about changing
people. There are two different times when you can change people.
One is when you start and the other is at some point later on if
things aren't working out. Which would you say is your approach?*

R I like to try to do the latter if possible. I had the philosophy
that it took a year to understand a team, a year to fix it and
then the third year you should start succeeding. In my mind
these were the timescales I worked to. Your first impressions
of people are quite important, but sometimes they are the
wrong impressions. Someone can be very awkward, difficult –
but as you start to understand them, you discover they can
be contributing an awful lot. They just need a few edges mas-
saged off. And some people who are very friendly and nice
and cooperative, you realize they aren't contributing very
much. It takes time to understand that. So, first impressions
are not always the best. I would always prefer to have time
to absorb and understand how an organization was working. And also be able to spend the time to tell people what's
expected of them. Understand what they think they are there
for and make sure that aligns with what you think they are
there for. Often, that is not the case.

*A Some chief executives and managers of football teams, when
they go somewhere they will bring their head coach. Are there
people who have been with you along the way or have you pretty
much just taken whatever you have got?*

R When I went from Benetton to Ferrari, Rory Byrne came and that was a pretty vital part. We had a substantial challenge because there was no Ferrari design office in Maranello. They had one in the UK, that was operated by John Barnard, the incumbent technical director, but the design office wasn't something that could have been easily transferred to Maranello. I joined Ferrari in the winter of 1996, and the car we had for the 1997 season was a car that John had designed and we cooperated on that. During the year, John left the team and went his own way. He acquired the design facility as part of his severance package, and he went off and started doing work for other organizations. So that meant we had to build a design team and we wanted to build it in Maranello. And Rory was pretty vital to that and I don't think we could have succeeded in that environment without him. We had worked together for a long time at Benetton and I could just know that certain things were being taken care of without having to micro-manage them. So, in terms of people I took with me, Rory was pretty vital at Ferrari. When I went to Honda, I didn't take anyone with me that I recall, but I knew a number of people there that I liked and enjoyed working with.

A How much of Ferrari's lack of success, over the twenty-one or so seasons before you joined, do you put down to things like having a design office that wasn't in Maranello?

R Yes, it is quite a contributory factor, because having the chassis design office in the UK meant you had the separation between the engine and the chassis. For me, the team has to be integrated and include every aspect of the car. For me, a car is tyres, chassis, engine, everything. The car is one. Therefore, for the first time, having the opportunity to have a unique fully integrated engine package was so attractive to me at Ferrari. They made their own engine, they made their own chassis. What could be better than that? Not only are you responsible for the chassis but you are involved in designing the whole car, including the power train and that is something I wanted to be involved in. I had always taken an interest in engines. At Benetton with Cosworth we had some involvement in the design of the engine. Less so when Benetton were with Renault, because Renault had a long-established relationship with Williams, so we simply had to take an already designed customer engine. But what could be better than Ferrari doing the whole thing?

A When you started to rebuild the team under Mercedes, you did recruit Aldo Costa after he left Ferrari.

R Yes, Aldo was a present from heaven really. I have always rated Aldo. Very good design engineer. Came to the fore in Ferrari under Rory. Rory is very creative but by his own admission sometimes a bit ... he's a bit creative, let's put it that way. And Aldo was a perfect balance with Rory of practicality, pragmatism and getting the job done and knowing that it had to be done by a certain time. So Rory and Aldo worked very well together and when all the difficulties came at Ferrari and they eventually hoofed him out, that was a godsend for me. It just took some time to gradually turn his head towards England and think about working for a Formula One team again.

And touching again on the part of the thesis you gave

me, relationships are so important in all of this. Aldo joined Mercedes partly because I was there, so he had someone he could rely on and hopefully someone whom he had trusted over the years. So when I said to him, 'ABC, Aldo, that's going to happen. DEF, I can't promise but we know we want to do it. And the others I have got no idea.' He's a grown up adult Aldo, he knows that nothing is 100 per cent. But he knew I wouldn't exaggerate and he knew that what I told him was the truth and he trusted me. The same way I trust him. So there was an established relationship there. There is another point we can touch on: in building that engineering team, the relationship is vital and also that reputation you acquire within the *inside* of Formula One. Is he a good bloke to work for? I always tried to be a good bloke to work for. You know, if you could be a good bloke to work for in a professional sense – not just nice to have a beer with but in a professional sense – you would attract the best people. You could go and talk to good people and have a chance of persuading them to join your team. If you were flaky and hadn't created the right reputation, then it is so much more difficult to build a solid and successful engineering team.

A One of the points you made about reading that chapter is that there is an implicit difference between an internal leader and an external leader. The internal leader is someone who exhibits this Chinese virtue of treating other people the way you want to be treated. And that is the core value of good leadership internally. What about externally? Because, unlike internally where everyone is on the same team and you are trying to achieve the same goal, in Formula One – and in other walks of life – that is not the case when you look outside. I mean, at the end of the day only one person gets to win in the World Championship. One driver, one team. And to win in Formula One, you have to be quite ruthless. So how do you frame that? Did you ever think about where the line is, or how you approach this competitiveness?

R Yes, and I don't know if we can draw the analogy, but what is clear from your thesis is that if you have to go to war, then you have failed in a sense. We don't have that luxury in Formula One, because we have to race, we have to 'go to war'. Racing and beating the opposition is the key part of it and eventually leads to winning the World Championship and we cannot avoid that battle. We have to go out there and have the battle. However, I think there are some important principles for me in engaging and waging that. One was respect for my competitors. They could frustrate and annoy the hell out of me, but I always respected them. I always assumed that they could be doing some things better than I was doing – and asked myself what could I learn from them, how could I take that into consideration? And it might be wide-reaching: have they better people, better facilities, better budgets? What are they doing better than me? Who are they employing that I can employ who might improve my strength?

A So, who do you steal from them?

R Yes – who can I steal from them!
   The second principle is a bit of an odd one, but I always want to be able to have a glass of wine with someone after a race. I don't want to have that rage of battle carry on afterwards. I want to have respect from my competitor and I show respect to my competitor, and in the main be able to see them

at the airport to be able to have a glass of wine together without any massive undercurrents. What other aspects are there?

A *Well, there is a principle that you haven't put down.*

R Which is?

A *Is there, in Formula One, 'a line' or is it 'all is fair ...'?*

R No, there is a line. There is a line and it is what you are
prepared to do and you make that line yourself. I was always
comfortable that I have never intentionally cheated. I might
have cheated unintentionally so it might have happened,
but it was unintended. I quite frankly took the view that
sometimes you were lucky and sometimes you weren't. If
you discovered your car was unintentionally illegal but you
didn't get caught, you weren't going to take it to the authori-
ties and say, 'By the way I have just realized that our car was
illegal at that race.' You thank your lucky stars, find out why
it happened and make sure it doesn't happen again. I think
that was the case with all the teams.

A *So by definition, you could never have had a situation where it
was intentional and you got caught because there was never an
intention.*

R You knew yourself whether there was intention to cheat
and so had to face the consequences. Because I never intentionally cheated, if something was found to be illegal, then
that was because we had made a mistake. I mean the barge
boards, part of the bodywork, found to be illegal at a race

in 1999, was a misunderstanding by a design engineer. He intended it to be like it was, so you could argue it was intentional, but none of us knew they were on the car. None of us had noticed they were on the car, so the people that did the vetting and the inspection process and all that stuff hadn't found the error in his understanding.

A But that's a really interesting case, because that is a situation where you put your hand up and said, 'The barge boards are illegal.' But then the decision was ultimately taken out of your hands and the FIA's independent appeal court found them not to be illegal or there was insufficient ...

R Well, it wasn't taken out of my hands. It is an interesting philosophical aspect, because my nature in those situations is not to say anything. Just get your head down, don't say anything and understand what has happened. But there was tremendous pressure from within Ferrari to say something straight after the race. And it was a mistake in my view to say anything because there was no need.

A To say something: you mean in that case, to say 'fair cop'.

R Yes.

A So just to put you on the spot here. That wasn't your instinct to say, 'We screwed up.'

R No.

A Your instinct was to say, 'Let's just see what happens.'

R My instinct is, 'We are going to go away and understand what's happened, because I didn't understand completely how we had got there.' I got on the phone, and asked Rory, 'What has happened?' They went away to study the drawings and, lo and behold, there was an error, a misunderstanding, in the design. And somehow it had got through the system. When you look at it, you think, 'How on earth could that have happened?' And we all know things do happen. It is that analogy of holey Swiss cheese. You put walls of Swiss cheese up and eventually all the holes line up somewhere and the arrow shoots through them.

A Let's assume for the sake of argument that you looked at it, you found that there was an error. Once you had done the investigation and you knew for a fact that it was wrong, would your instinct still have been to say nothing? Or would your instinct have been to say, 'No, we screwed up, the car was illegal?'

R My instinct would have been initially to say nothing. To just control the situation. It doesn't mean that at a later stage you may say, 'We've now done the analysis, we've now understood and this is what happened.' Because what we were doing, by commenting straight after the race, we were reacting in a panic and I hate doing that. Therefore my objective in life is always to try and eliminate the potential for panic. And this was a situation where we were reacting in a panic and those impulsive statements, decisions etc. often come back to haunt you and I wished we had never – I had never – made that statement.

A But you did make that statement and, as it happened, it was true.

R Yep.

A Right? But ultimately the FIA did not take action.

R What then developed, as you always do in these situations, is that you study the regulations. You study the regulations intensely to understand. And in studying those regulations we realized there was an interpretation that you could present where they weren't illegal. It was never the intention of the regulation and it was never the ...

A 'the intention of the regulation ...'

R Yes, let's come back to that idea! And I think everyone knew how the regulation was applied, but it was an interesting lesson for me because ultimately when you go to an appeal court you are sat in front of a group of people who are qualified only to make an interpretation of the wording of the regulation. And the wording of the regulation, the intention of the regulation and the application of the regulation may be different things, because historically a regulation may have been assumed to be applied in a particular way. And we were able to convince the appeal court that the description of the tolerance on the flat floor not only applied to the flatness of the floor but to the vertical width of the floor. There was a tolerance and it said plus or minus 5 mm over this surface. So we said, 'Well, flatness on this surface – does that include the vertical edges of the surface?' It was a delicate point but we presented the argument that the plus or minus 5 mm could be interpreted in the vertical plain as well as in the horizontal plain. And that was an argument and the argument was accepted.

A Was it your idea?

R It came from a meeting I chaired. What then developed was that the FIA came to witness a wind tunnel test that had barge boards which were flat and barge boards which were not flat, to show that there was no performance gain in what we had done. It was, in retrospect, a bit of a sideshow, but it was to demonstrate when we went to the appeal court that we could say that we screwed up but we weren't trying to gain any performance. Peter Wright, who is an FIA advisor, came to that demonstration. I took the opportunity to ask him, 'What do you think about this principle? That this interpretation can be applied. Here is a table and it is not only the flatness of the table but the flatness of the width as well?' He is a lateral-thinking engineer, and he said, 'Yeah, I can see that. Yeah, I can see why you might be convinced by that argument. If you weren't familiar with the way it had been applied for years but you just come into a courtroom or a hearing. You're a judge, you're presented with this argument. Yeah, it could be interpreted that way.'

A So, two things. In 2003, when I was sitting in Frank's office on a visit, it was the time when Williams were fighting Ferrari for the championship and suddenly the FIA penalized Williams because the tread of the Michelin tyres was too wide at the end of a race. Frank said, 'You're a lawyer, I want your advice on this,' and he got John Healey who was the team lawyer to bring in the regulations. And the regulations in some places used the phrase 'at the start of the race it must be X', in some places, the regulations said, 'it must be X or throughout the race, the weekend or whatever.' In this case it says 'at the start of the race'. And so I said, 'Frank, look, I am not a specialist in this area, but I would have thought you had a pretty punchy case here. As long as the tyres were measured and complied at the start of the race, that's fine. There are other rules where something has to comply throughout a race, or at the end – but not here.' So I said, 'I think you should go for it' – which he didn't. And that had a significant impact on the 2003 Championship which was the last one where Williams were really in contention. I went to Suzuka for the final race, even then there was a chance for Williams to take the Championship, but it didn't happen and Ferrari won. This might have been a case where you looked at the FIA's interpretation of the rules against another team and thought, 'Well, I don't think that's correct, but I am very happy to live with the result.' Were there cases like that?

R I think there were. And again I go back to my issue about how the dice fall – sometimes you get the decision and sometimes you don't. In 1994, when the wooden plank was first introduced under the car to limit the minimum ride height, the regulation was that it was 10 mm thick and it can't wear below 9 mm or, if the plank is damaged, you don't measure it, you weigh it and as long as the weight is 90 per cent of the original weight then you are okay. In Spa we had worn the plank too much at the front, but we'd also smashed it, it was substantially damaged. Michael had been over some curbs and smashed the plank up. So we said, 'It's damaged and therefore you have to weigh it. That's what the rule says. If a plank is damaged you don't measure it anymore, you weigh it.' And the FIA said, 'No, we are doing both.' And we lost that one. For me that was black and white. The rules said it can't wear more than 9 mm but if the plank is damaged you weigh it, you don't measure it anymore. And it was interpreted differently to how it should have been. So I lost the one that I thought was really a slam dunk and an easy decision.

A So, let's go back to this question of the 'intention of the rules' or even the 'spirit of the rules' that came up during the year of Brawn GP, 2009. We were all in Paris for the 'double diffuser' case. And the interesting aspect of that case was that it revolved around what is the spirit or intention of the rules. And we had a lot of fun with that. I think Frank Dernie said at the time, 'The spirit of Formula One is that clever people beat stupid people.' That aside, the philosophical question is that people see a car but good Formula One designers don't see a car, they see a set of rules. And they look at those rules and they say, well, we can do this and this and this. If you can make a car that had 4-wheel drive and the rules permit it, then you should do it. The fact that someone thinks that there was no intention to have 4-wheel drive is irrelevant. The question is, can you do it or not within the rules. So the philosophical question is, does the intention of the rules matter?

R No, I don't think the intention matters. But can we go back a bit and just say, what were my principles? What were the principles I applied when I was involved? My principles were you never intentionally cheated. So I would never intentionally have anything on the car or advocate to any of my engineers to intentionally cheat. And that even includes things that can't be measured. There are requirements in some of the regulations that are extremely difficult to measure and you know full well the FIA don't have the capacity to check them.

A So you are saying even if you couldn't really be caught ...

R Even if you couldn't be caught, you don't do it. You take the strongest and most competitive interpretation of the regulations you can. This gets back into the political environment where you negotiate with the FIA technical delegates and convince them that your argument, your interpretation of the regulation, has got credibility. We know that process is not foolproof, because the stewards of the race meeting may disagree, but it's always good to have the technical delegates on your side. So always a very, very competitive interpretation of the regulations is vital.

If you do get caught with something which is . . . caught is the wrong word. That sounds guilty already, doesn't it? But if it does turn out that you have some aspect of the car design that is deemed to be illegal, or claimed to be illegal, then, having previously discussed the matter with the FIA technical advisors, you have some basis to defend it in the appeal courts. There were occasions when you just knew you had made a big mistake, you took your punishment and there was no point appealing it. But if you thought you had a run at it, I would have a run at it, because I consider that part of the game. In the barge board incident, I considered it was worth having a run at it. I knew that, in some cases, I had lost the argument when I shouldn't have lost. Equally, there would be ones I would win where I would think, 'Hmm, that was interesting.' I see that as part of the competition. Your ability to go into that appeal court and convince a set of judges that you have got a worthy argument is part of the process. You have to take a run at it, to balance out the good and bad appeal court decisions.

A So, just again, if we look at the wider world. One of the things that was very noticeable for me coming into Formula One is how different this idea of there being a line is to the corporate world that I came from. In a properly-run company, you know, if there is a line you don't usually even see the line because there are set standards of behaviour, there is a compliance and governance process such that you can't get to the point where you are pushing things to the limit. That is not how it works. In competition law, environmental law, safety, you know, you can't go to the limit. For example, if you look at VW who put in a software trick that reduced emissions during testing but then on the road allowed emissions to increase to get better fuel economy. In a Formula One world, you would say that is absolutely fine. If a test is X, then you comply with the test, but what happens on the track is a different question. It is not your obligation to do other people's jobs for them. But in a corporate world, how does your philosophy of life or of Formula One apply? Does it? Can it?

R I think our area is quite difficult. I think in our area of extreme competition, it is difficult to know how that relates . . .

A Well, maybe let's look at another example. Tax. There is a big issue at the moment about corporations paying tax. And what they say is 'we pay all the tax we are liable to pay.' It just so happens that that means close to zero in the UK if you're Google, Amazon, Starbucks etc. That is a case where the law is the law. They can comply with the law but there is an expectation, there is an intention, that big companies pay taxes where they create value and if they have £2 billion turnover here and it's profitable, to pay nothing is unacceptable. Where do you stand on issues like that?

R That's a better example. My view is the company is doing nothing wrong. Strictly speaking. The companies may have a PR and branding issue which is their judgement call, but if the tax rules allow them to bring expenses onshore or take profits offshore then the tax rules need modifying. There is no way of setting a moral level of tax. At what point does everyone become satisfied that they are paying sufficient tax? It shouldn't be a moral question. It may be a PR question for them. And that's for them to make a judgement. They may decide, 'Well, actually we are going to bring some of our profit onshore, because we want to pay some tax.' But I blame the regulatory process rather than the philosophy of the companies, because they have to compete with each other and therefore by avoiding the tax liabilities they can invest more money in the country and employ more people. They can employ more engineers. And in all of this, I am digressing, we shouldn't forget the money that they do bring into the country, because I don't know how many engineers Google employ but it's hundreds, if not thousands. So they have got thousands of employees. They are all paying national insurance and tax. Those wages are being spent in our economy. For me, it is the regulatory process that needs modifying, not the attitude of the companies. The companies have got a PR problem.

A I am not sure that this approach creates a level playing field. But the point you are making, which is not totally surprising, is that your philosophy is to look at the rules and do the best you can under those rules. And if somebody wants to change the rules, which happens all the time in Formula One, so be it.

R I think that's an important point. I never objected to the rules being changed, as long as they were changed over a reasonable timescale so they didn't benefit one team over another. I might well have lobbied to get something changed for performance reasons, that was in my competitive nature. So, if clearly someone had taken an interpretation that I didn't agree with and they were gaining a competitive advantage, I thought it was perfectly fair for me to lobby to have the rule changed.

A Let's use a practical example. Formula One is almost the only sport in the world – maybe the America's Cup is another – where rule changes also change the competitive position of the contenders. We could change the size of a goal in football, or the length of the pitch, or the offside rules, but everyone is in the same position. Formula One is not like that. You could argue that rule changes have as much influence on who is winning as anything else and I am sure that there are many cases where you've encouraged the rules to be changed and discouraged the rules to be changed, because you knew exactly who would gain and lose from those changes.

R Yes, to a degree, but I was more concerned about my own team's position. However, you have to be part of the process.

A Well, until recently everyone was part of that process. One of the astonishing things about the new Concorde Agreement governing the sport is that not all teams get to participate in the making of the rules, which I would have thought was very questionable.

R Yes, and it's failing, isn't it? They seem to struggle now even more so to make progress on rule changes and part of it is the confusion that is caused, because not all of the teams are involved and that has implications. I always thought that was a big mistake. I have never had a problem with rule changes, because I always saw rule changes as an opportunity.

A *But what if the changes are not in your favour? For example, when active ride suspension was banned for the 1994 season?*

R I was at Benetton and we had a good system. So it was frustrating to have it taken away.

A *Patrick says that Frank went off to a meeting and agreed to stop active ride, and Patrick was beside himself.*

R I can imagine – not linked up. This was the problem with Team Principals agreeing technical rule changes. I have been fortunate in a way that Flavio never really understood, so he would have to rely on us for advice. Even then he did make a few gaffs, because he didn't understand. Jean Todt simply wouldn't get involved in technical discussions or decisions at Team Principal meetings. He insisted I make the decisions.

A *I have always thought Flavio was pretty canny. Back in 2008–09, Flavio was always on about how refuelling was a waste of money, because of all the equipment we had to carry around. So we agreed to ban it, but then when Williams moved onto the Renault engine at the end of 2011 we realized that they actually had a very fuel-efficient engine. I am sure he knew that, but I don't think many people at the time thought, 'Ah, that's why he's pushing it so hard.' But my sense is that he was quite canny ...*

R For me the rules are part of the game. This again makes Formula One unique in that the participants have a large say in making the regulations. Undoubtedly, when you went through that process of trying to determine the regulations for the future, consciously or subconsciously you always had your own position in mind. You couldn't help it. But if you knew that the rule was in three years' time or two years' time, you could take a more balanced view on what was best for Formula One, than if the rule was coming in next year where you would think, 'Well, my car's got this, got that, whatever.' The timescale was vital and I always saw rule changes as an opportunity. I always loved it when I heard people going, 'Oh no, they're changing the rules again.' I would think, 'Great, how are we going to take advantage of this?'

A *If you are in a well-resourced team and you've got a good engineering group and, as you say, your engine and your chassis teams are integrated, then you don't have a lot to fear.*

R No, you welcome it.

A *Especially if you're not dominant at the time. It's more tricky if you're Red Bull and Renault and in the middle of a winning streak of four back-to-back Championships, and someone decides to change the engine formula. Christian Horner fought like hell against the new engine rules, because he had nothing to gain from them. And as it turns out, it was a major disaster for him.*

R And we were the opposite. We were very keen to have the new engine rules.

A *Absolutely. But if you had been Team Principal of Red Bull at that time, what would you have done?*

R I think, because of my experience at Ferrari, I would have tried to achieve more with Renault in the early stages of developing the new engine.

A *We can come back to how you would have responded once the rules were changed. But what would you have done in terms of the proposed changes? Would you have fought to stop the rules being changed?*

R Yes, probably in that case.

A *And you would have argued, 'Well, it's going to cost a lot of money.' Which it has. And you would have said that the V8s were good, they sounded great, they were quite fuel-efficient engines in their own way. We had the KERS energy recovery system. You could have argued quite successfully, 'Look, we've got a great little package here and any changes are just going to cost more money.' And, of course, people did try, but they didn't win the argument.*

R Well, if you remember, Renault were the main protagonists behind the rule changes. That's the paradox, the irony rather. Because they wanted a more relevant engine, that was the argument.

A *But turning to what happened after the rules were changed, you think their primary failing was the lack of integration between Red Bull and Renault.*

R That was pretty important. One of the things that became apparent to us at Mercedes during that period building up to when the new engines first raced in 2014, was that every time we asked the FIA for an interpretation or clarification of the engine regulations, it became clear we were the first ones to ask. This told me that we were ahead of the game compared with the other engine manufacturers. We were putting the work in early on the engine project when everyone else seemed to think there was plenty of time. They thought there was ample opportunity to get this job done. But at Mercedes we knew that we were going to run out of time. So the early work was vital. People like Thomas Fuhr, who was the manager at Mercedes High Performance Engines at the time, he was good at getting the foundations of all that work done. Making sure all the budgets were in place, making sure everything was there and pushing hard early on.

One thing we will get to later on is the philosophy of how you manage projects. While there has to be some crossover – because you could never totally isolate a new project from your current operations – I always had the belief in separate teams for projects like developing the new car for the rule changes of 2014. So with the new 2014 car, Geoff Willis was employed as project leader of the chassis, Andy Cowell was the project leader of the engine and they were dedicated to that project from a very early stage. That's because if you are going to truly integrate the engine and the chassis, you have to design the chassis as well as the engine at the same time. And you have got to be designing the complete car to the new regulations and know what the requirements are. Configuring chassis and engine and seeing what the cooling system is like and all the rest of it. And it was because of the optimum layout of the cooling system that we went for the unique design of separate turbine and compressor on the engine. It was interesting because Stefano Domenicali told me

Ferrari had considered that concept as well – but they had left it too late to integrate into their engine design.

A Time is something that comes up in my thesis – one of the core principles in the books on strategy is that time is crucial but it is also a paradox. And, nowhere more than Formula One is time more of the essence. In some seasons progress is so strong that, by the last race, the slowest car was faster than the fastest car in the first race. The difference between coming first and coming last was six months. So, on the one hand, time is crucial but on the other hand, you can't rush things, you can't react in panic, you need to take time to think and prepare. You also said, for example, in a new team, it's a year to get to know everyone, a year to sort it out, a year to start winning. Many in Formula One are not so patient. How do you understand and use time?

R You mustn't waste time. So even if you've got a structured plan, you mustn't waste time on it. I go back to the point we discussed earlier about being lazy. That's why I always needed a strong structure. There have been times when I've thought, 'Have I got it wrong?' I'll give you an example – when I took over Honda. I joined the team at the end of 2007 and I put an effort into the car for 2008 as much as I could, but it was designed by the time I arrived, the systems were in place and so on. I was able to have some influence, and in fact the car scored points and did much better than the year before, but it wasn't going to win races.

I'd said to the board, 'The first year is going to be what it is. We've got these new regulations coming in the second year and that's what we must focus on. I have to use the resources I have, and I will build the resources up as best I can, but I have to use the resources for us to be a success in the second year.' My ideal three-year timing plan I mentioned is compromised because of new regulations coming in, but they couldn't be ignored.

When Honda withdrew, I did reflect on it and wonder how a mediocre year had influenced that decision to withdraw. I couldn't have anticipated it but 2008 was a mediocre year despite the fact we had a couple of podiums, which the team had not had in 2007. But if I had put more effort into 2008 and maybe we had won a race, I don't know whether Honda's decision to withdraw from the sport would have been different. I just reflected on that. I am not sure I would have made any different decision with the knowledge I had at the time. But it was an interesting aspect of this whole time thing. How you use resources and so on.

But going back to what is predictable in normal circumstances, it is that race-winning cars are not designed the winter before they win the race. They're a product of several years of good work to develop the designs and engineering that you need to produce a successful car. If you have been part of a successful team, sometimes you can transplant that knowledge to a new team to some degree, or at least get you a step up the ladder. But it does take some time to get the infrastructure in place. If you go to a team that doesn't have a good driver simulator, for instance, that's something you have got to build. If you go there and it hasn't got a good wind tunnel or CFD [computational fluid dynamics] system, you can't turn a switch and immediately have a top-rate facility. If you go there and the chief aerodynamicist is not capable, it takes you six or 12 months to find the right guy, put him in the system and so on. There are things that just take time.

When you have got the organisation established, as I think it was at Mercedes, and you want to make a step change in competitiveness, then you've got to commit to making the resources available for the future, for the new regulations and the new engines. And you have to take the pain sometimes that that brings. For example, in 2013 up until the compulsory two-week summer break, we were fighting for the Championship, but it was a long shot. After we came back from the break, Red Bull surged ahead. They had made a huge step with their car . . .

A No, they had a very refreshing break!

R Exactly. We weren't in the same league anymore, we were half a second off them. And the reason for that was I had said to everyone in the months leading up to the summer break, 'Look, I don't think we can win this Championship. I'm not giving up but our focus has got to be longer-term.' So all the work in the summer was for the new car. It was all about the engine, the car. You are just using the resource in the way that would give you that chance. And Mercedes have now won two World Championships and are heading for a third based on those decisions to commit the resources in that way and have that vision of, 'Where do we want to be?'

If you keep piling in the resource on the problem you have today and never allowing some resource to go into the future, then you will never have that future.

A Even in a big team, that's not straightforward because of the pressure to perform. In an independent team, that can be lethal because if you don't deliver you lose sponsors. You were reminding me that you won the double World Championship in 2009, and then in 2014 and 2015, the last two seasons, your team was dominant again. There were three years between. And in those three years Mercedes was in Formula One. I don't know if it was even true to say it got steadily better, but it was not until, as you say, the first half of 2013 that it became a Championship contender.

R We had 2010, 2011 and 2012 in the wilderness. And 2010 suffered because in 2009 we didn't have the resources to do what we needed for the following year. And then in 2011 and 2012 we suffered to some degree, because we didn't have the resources for let's say political or ideological reasons. Mercedes had bought the team and were convinced that they could run the team without investing money into it. There would be enough sponsorship and the Resource Restriction Agreement between the teams was going to mean that we were perfectly sized for the new world of Formula One. However, it became clear that Ferrari and Red Bull were not paying any attention to the RRA. And we'd also committed to some fairly expensive drivers. I know when Toto Wolff did join, one of the good things he did was to give the board a dose of reality. I think he did it sometime before he joined, but they did budget comparisons between Williams and Mercedes. The bottom line was about the same, but we had expensive drivers. So, in fact, we were spending much less on the engineering and the car than Williams was spending.

My first budget proposal to Mercedes in 2010 was cut back by £29 million and it was hurting. So those years in the wilderness were caused because of the changing structure of the team, the lack of certainty of where the team wanted to be or needed to be, the level of commitment needed, and the team just losing momentum. Then at the end of 2011 and beginning of 2012, that winter, there were some harsh discussions with the board. Mercedes were thinking of pulling out, but then fortunately, went the other way and committed the funds to get what we needed. So Geoff Willis joined, Aldo Costa joined. We built a 50 per cent wind tunnel model – up from 40 per cent. There was a fresh impetus. We said, 'Right, we are going to go for it and if that doesn't work, that's it.' But in that process I think they lost some faith in me and started to cast around to see what else they needed, and I also became disillusioned. It was a two-way thing. I ended up leaving the team, but I think . . .

A *You didn't leave until . . .*

R . . . the end of '13.

A *You know you called me . . .*

R . . . I know, I know . . .

A *. . . in early 2013 to discuss what you should do. I said, 'Don't go because you are building this: you are going to win the World Championship in 2014 with the new team, the new engine, with Lewis Hamilton . . .*

R Yep.

A *. . . and others will get the credit . . .*

R Yep.

A And that is one thing that really surprises me, because you knew that was true. You must have had a pretty good idea.

R I think I was emotionally drained at that time. I had never had the situation where people had undermined me like that. It is an interesting thing to explore in the book. Everywhere I had been I had often had strong discussions but was always supported. At Benetton, at Ferrari and at Honda, all of the teams supported me, and then, of course, I had the indulgence of running my own team where I didn't have to answer to anyone.

A Do you think you got a bit arrogant as a result of that?

R Maybe. I think we can define arrogance in the sense that I had enjoyed a certain independence that I didn't want to give up. A certain status or responsibility in the team that I didn't want to share.

A This happens with a lot of people. Ultimately, there is a moment when they are emotionally drained and that is probably why I quit in the end as well. It's partly the feeling, 'I don't see why I have to put up with this anymore. There is no need to.' It is partly that, and it's partly that you just get sick of being chiselled away at all the time. And Formula One is pretty good at that stuff. But a lot of people in politics and in public service and in companies have the same experience. What would you do differently now, if anything?

R If I reflect on the time, I was going through a fresh experience. I had partially sold the company to Mercedes. It wasn't an easy post-sale period, in that it was half-owned by [Abu Dhabi investment group] Aabar and half-owned by Mercedes who, not long after, started to have their own difficulties between them. Aabar had come in and supported Mercedes during the financial crisis and I think had done very well out of it financially, but they were very demanding. So that relationship started to deteriorate and it reflected around the team.

We had one vote on the board and Aabar board members were lobbying us to go one way and Mercedes were lobbying us to go the other way and we were in the middle. But we knew that Mercedes were the future because we didn't really have a future with Aabar. Mercedes had the engine and the potential. That muddied the waters for quite a while. We got into the difficulty of any extra budget demands being spread among the shareholders. We still had 23 per cent of the shares and we had to stump up as well. A Formula One team of that sort doesn't make a profit in the conventional sense. What it provides is image and branding to the owners if successful. And image and branding had no relevance to us as partial shareholders.

I hadn't had the experience to think through how these things would play out and they became distractions in those couple of years. Norbert Haug was the head of Mercedes motorsport. Norbert had very good intentions but, of course, was between the board and the team. He told the board they could buy this team and it shouldn't cost them a penny in the future. And I was on the other side saying, 'Come on, you've got to invest far more heavily or else we are not going to go anywhere.' I was working through Norbert to respect his position and it just ...

What I should have done, looking back on it, was have a much clearer share structure at the beginning. We should have sold all our shares and not had this interim position of having some shares but not really knowing what to do with them. The final share price was influenced by the results of the team over a reasonable period, so that's fair enough. I don't have any issues with the way that was done. But I think the share sale, in retrospect, I would have done differently. I didn't have enough experience to realize how this would play out. It would have been more efficient if Mercedes had just bought the team outright, which they did ultimately. And I should have been stronger in making it very clear to the board that this is what needed to be done.

A Did you have access to the board?

R Yes. In fact, I had a board seat in Mercedes GP until we finally sold our last shares. We also had access to the main board of Daimler and some of their members were on both boards. And Dieter Zetsche, the Mercedes CEO, would often come to one of our board meetings to listen to what was going on.

A One of the things, again, that the classical strategists emphasized was forming alliances. Did you take the time to have alliances with the right people?

R No. I failed in that respect. In that environment I failed.

A My observation is that, for example, at Ferrari you did that very well.

R I did because it was easy, in the sense that Jean Todt was there, Luca di Montezemolo was across the road, and it was a small circle.

A But Jean and Luca are not necessarily the easiest people to work with, so there must have been a process of building up a relationship. Did you consciously do that or maybe others did it, maybe Jean did that? The perception from the outside is that with Jean, Rory, Michael, and maybe Luca as well, you had a bulletproof – a politically insulated – group of people. Nobody could get at you. Nobody could undermine you with each other. You presented a joint front. That is the perception.

R I think the core of that is always trust. And we trusted each other.

A Did you do that consciously? Did you have a band of brothers approach or is that just the way it evolved?

R It was the way it evolved – but trust for me has always been very important. I don't mind someone being frank with me. What I don't like is people not being frank ...

A The thing is, there won't be a person on this planet who doesn't say, 'Trust is important to me.' Everyone says that. The difference is that at Ferrari, you put together – or were part of – a group of people who were able to be very effective, even though Ferrari was a very political organization. Certainly before your time and afterwards, and people would say that one of the reasons why it wasn't as effective on the track as it might have been was the politics. But during that period, with this handful of people, you did it differently.

So the issue is not so much whether trust is important to you, but how do you create that environment in which you can be successful? You did at Ferrari but you didn't, arguably, at Mercedes. Even though Mercedes has gone on to be very successful. And nobody would question that largely you put that together. It is not your name on the tin because you aren't there – which is very galling. If one is brutal about success and failure, there is a difference between what you did at Mercedes and what you did at Ferrari. It may be that you just do what you do. And sometimes it works and sometimes it doesn't. Sometimes it's luck and timing and there is nothing wrong with that. Napoleon said, give me a lucky general before a good general. It doesn't matter – but what we are interested in is whether there is anything systematic that you did do when you got it right and that you didn't do when it didn't work out? And then one has to understand, why did you do those things at Ferrari, and why didn't you do them at Mercedes? What was the underlying cause?

R Let's go to Ferrari first of all. I think trust is something you have to be very conscious about. It's not just a passive thing. So when situations arise, you have to think about your response and your behaviour to instil trust in other people. Because if you don't think about it, then you won't build up trust.

A If you don't consciously make decisions that build trust, you will accidentally or unconsciously create an environment where there isn't trust?

R Yes. For example, you will have someone come into your office with a problem. And it may well involve other people.

They want to tell you things that they trust you to make a sensible judgement on how you will deal with them. It doesn't mean that you will respond to it or you may have to say, 'Look, if you want to take this any further I am going to have to involve the other people.' But you have to make those calls. People have got to know that what you say you are going to do is what you do. And it may mean often having tough decisions to make but which still create trust. So in all those situations, you have got to have in your mind that you are building trust for people and people have got to be able to trust you. It can be a personal topic. It can be a professional topic. They need to know they can trust you, even if they don't agree with you.

A You are the same person throughout 2010, '11, '12, '13. I don't imagine you suddenly started behaving in a way that people couldn't trust you. You had people in the team like Geoff Willis and Aldo Costa who you knew. You had a good relationship with Nick Fry. And Norbert was a straightforward guy. I am sure everyone has their strengths and weaknesses, but I wouldn't see him as a devious person. But for four years you were Ross Brawn and you were trustworthy and you built up those relationships which is always something you do and it is valuable to you. By the back end of 2012, you have got Niki Lauda there, you've got Toto Wolff coming in during 2013 and you've got different dynamics. Why hadn't your normal formula worked?

R Well, I guess if you look at the Ferrari situation, it was my conscious decision to have a relationship with those people. So I decided to go to Ferrari, I decided to build a relationship with Jean Todt and with Luca di Montezemolo. It is not reasonable to join a company and not try to have those relationships, build those trusts. So it was my decision to go there and therefore my ambition to make sure the relationships worked. And I realized, consciously or subconsciously, that my relationship with those people was vital to the success of the project. They are both very different, Jean and Luca, but I enjoyed their company. I know Jean trusts me but I also had the great compliment last year, before Luca was deposed, when he asked me to join the board of Ferrari. And I prevaricated, and then of course he got into his problems with Sergio Marchionne (the chief executive of Fiat Chrysler Automobiles and Ferrari) and it never happened. But I spoke to someone else on the board to get their advice and ask how the board was run and what was going on, and he said one of the reasons Luca wants you on there, is that he trusts you. That was a great compliment.

But what happened at Mercedes is that people were imposed on me who I couldn't trust. I never knew really what they were trying to do. I mean Niki would tell me one thing, then I would hear he was saying something else. Toto had that famous stroll along the beach with Colin Kolles, a friend of his, who, for his own reasons was recording the conversation. In the discussion, which became semi-public, he made various comments about me ...

A I have never heard that recording, but what was the essence of his criticism of you? Without going into too much detail.

R He said that I was resting on my money now. I had got all this money and I wasn't interested in the team anymore, and I wasn't motivated and I wasn't doing this, I wasn't doing

Brawn stands to the left of Frank Williams at the United States Grand Prix at Watkins Glen, in 1978. When Brawn joined Williams in 1978, he was about the eleventh employee. Brawn was evidently getting his hands dirty at this stage of his career. The team went on to win several championships, as Brawn took on increasingly senior roles until his departure in 1984.

Two men who played an important part in Brawn's career. Max Mosley (left) ran March Engineering, where Brawn worked in 1977 in the Formula 3 series. Later, Mosley would become President of the Fédération Internationale de l'Automobile (FIA), the owner and regulator of Formula One. Frank Williams (right) was Brawn's first boss in Formula One and Parr's boss forty years later. Here Mosley and Williams speak at the German Grand Prix in Hockenheim, Germany, July 1979.

The Jaguar XJR-14 was the last car that Brawn himself designed. Taking advantage of the relatively traditional approach to the rules in the World Sportscar series, Brawn applied the logic of Formula One in all aspects of the design of the XJR-14 and in the way he worked with the FIA to gain acceptance of his radical interpretations. The result was, in essence, an F1 car. The XJR-14 won the World Sportscar Championship in 1991.

Brawn and Schumacher in the colours of Benetton at the Belgian Grand Prix, Spa Francorchamps, in 1994. The two men worked together at Benetton, Ferrari and Mercedes and built an exceptional, and uniquely successful, professional and personal relationship.

At the climax of the traumatic 1994 Formula One season, Michael Schumacher led Damon Hill by a narrow margin into the final race in Adelaide. Schumacher was leading the race but, after leaving the track, clashed with Hill, ending the race for both drivers. This secured Schumacher his first World Championship title, and Brawn his first for Benetton.

After Schumacher left Benetton for Ferrari in 1996, he sought out Brawn, who joined him there one year later. Their partnership at Ferrari lasted a decade until Schumacher retired at the end of 2006 and Brawn took a sabbatical. Ferrari won six consecutive Constructors' titles between 1999 and 2004, the last five of those years also being doubles, as Schumacher took the Drivers' titles. The two men are pictured here at the start of this extraordinary period, on the grid at the Hungarian Grand Prix in Budapest, 1997.

In a controversial example of Brawn's ruthless application of the logic of total competition, Rubens Barrichello is ordered to allow Michael Schumacher to pass him. Rubens complies – on the finish line at the Austrian Grand Prix in 2002. On the podium, an embarrassed Schumacher insisted Barrichello took the top spot and the winning trophy for which the team was fined $1,000,000. Rules aimed at preventing Team Orders were introduced the following season, but later reversed.

For Brawn, the difficult logistics of the Monaco Grand Prix represent an opportunity. Here, a Monaco fireman watches Michael Schumacher qualifying there in 2006. On this occasion, the Ferrari driver 'parked' his car on track during qualifying which had the effect of (temporarily) securing him pole position at the expense of rival Fernando Alonso. Following a very damaging rule change at the end of 2004, Ferrari had endured a tough season in 2005. Brawn had managed to hold Ferrari together and in 2006 the Scuderia was back fighting for the Championship.

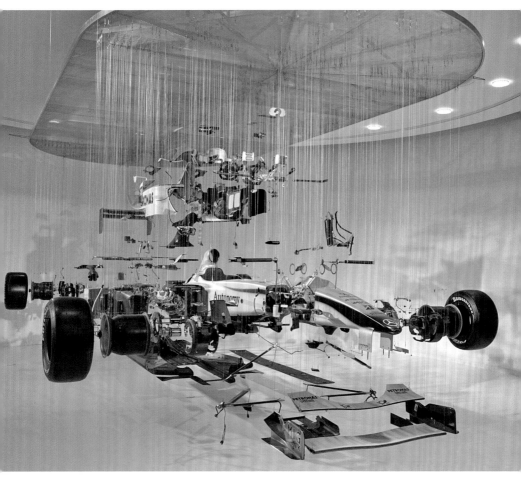

A Formula One car is an exceptionally complex piece of engineering that has to go from drawing-board to track in less than a year. It must deliver astonishing performance, total reliability and safety, in spite of having to endure extreme impacts, temperatures and forces. This image shows Michael Schumacher's 2011 Mercedes car deconstructed and displayed as a work of art.

A Formula One pitstop, with refuelling and tyre changes, involved 23 pit crew and took about 7 seconds. This is the Ferrari team at work on Michael Schumacher's car at the Malaysian Grand Prix in Sepang, 2006. Since refuelling was banned in 2010, pit stops are now completed more quickly. The Williams F1 team holds the record in 2016 with a stop of just 1.92 seconds at the European Grand Prix, Baku, June 2016.

Within the world of Formula One, 'strategy' is most commonly used to refer to the way in which the race itself is managed. The constant flow of data is used to update the race strategy, and to react to foreseeable, and unforeseen, events. Here, Brawn watches the data feed during practice for the Australian Grand Prix in Melbourne, 2013. Lap times are recorded to 1/1,000th of a second. Even though this is 1/100th of the time it takes to blink, it is sometimes not accurate enough: at the European Grand Prix in Valencia, Spain, in June 2010, the two Williams drivers both qualified with a lap time of 98.428 seconds.

Alliances in Formula One are driven by short-term objectives. The 2009 season saw Brawn GP and Williams F1 sometimes working together and at other times at odds. At the Malaysian Grand Prix, Brawn and Williams were challenged on the legality of the 'double diffuser' design both had on their cars. The two teams successfully won their case in front of the FIA's International Court of Appeal. Later in the year, at the British Grand Prix, the two teams were on opposing sides as the sport threatened to split. These issues were played out in the media through the FIA's press conferences. Above: Ross Brawn, Adam Parr, Martin Whitmarsh (McLaren) and John Howett (Toyota) in Malaysia. Below: Brawn, Parr and Whitmarsh with Christian Horner (Red Bull) at Silverstone.

Brawn, Jenson Button and members of the Brawn GP team celebrate clinching the World Championship titles following the Brazilian GP in 2009. Less than twelve months earlier, Honda had withdrawn from Formula One, and the team had faced closure. A few weeks later, Mercedes would buy the team from Brawn and, under Brawn's continued leadership, would prepare for a new period of dominance.

In 2013, Brawn's Mercedes team began its comeback in earnest, winning three races. Here, Brawn celebrates victory with Nico Rosberg at the Monaco Grand Prix in May. This was an emotional moment for both men. Rosberg was brought up in Monaco. Brawn had won the same race with Nico's father, Keke, for Williams exactly thirty years earlier, in 1983. Brawn broke his normal practice and received the Constructors' trophy himself.

What are Brawn and Bernie Ecclestone thinking about as they stand on the grid of the Belgian Grand Prix at Spa Francorchamps, in September 2012? The chief executive of Formula One's Commercial Rights Holder proved a formidable adversary in Brawn's final years in the sport.

Brawn won F1 World Championship titles with Alan Jones, Keke Rosberg, Michael Schumacher and Jenson Button. He brought Lewis Hamilton to Mercedes GP for 2013, and they won races together – but never a championship. Here, they celebrate their first win together at the Hungarian Formula One Grand Prix in Budapest, in July 2013.

that. That the team needed a fresh impetus and all that sort of stuff. Digressing slightly, he was very new to the team and he had been flattered by the board's attention. What the board had said to him, from what I understand is, 'This team is not working for some reason, you're a smart businessman, you know Williams, can you just go in there and tell us what's wrong?' So he was giving Kolles a snapshot of what he saw and he was mentally rehearsing, I guess, what he was going to say to the board about what we were or weren't doing. With Kolles, he unfortunately digressed into some personal comments about Niki and Dieter Zetsche. So I was beginning to deal with people who I didn't feel I could ultimately trust; people within the team, who had let me down already in terms of their approach.

Then early in 2013, I discovered Paddy Lowe had been contracted to join the team and it had been signed off in Stuttgart. When I challenged Toto and Niki, they both blamed each other. I met them together to have it out with them. And they both pointed to each other . . .

A It was Toto, wasn't it? Because we had been talking . . . it was just after me, I think, they were talking about Paddy coming to work at Williams and then somehow it kept going on and on and on. It was quite a serious conversation but it never quite happened, and then suddenly Toto left and Paddy went to Mercedes.

R Well, Toto always denied it to me. But if you read his recent interview in *Motor Sport*, he sets it out and he says that he was the one who got Paddy in and it was agreed before Toto even joined the team. So, anyway, clearly the trust had broken down.

A 'Failure is an orphan, success has many parents.'

R So I couldn't trust these people. And I had also failed in the point you made earlier in building relationships with people on the board which was not ... I don't know why but I just didn't have the enthusiasm to spend the time in Stuttgart.

A Which you would have done at Ferrari?

R I did, but it was almost by default it happened because we were all there, we all walked down to a restaurant on the night. I didn't make enough of a conscious effort to go to Stuttgart ...

A When you sold Brawn to Mercedes, possibly what you didn't do was say to yourself, 'How am I going to make this work?' There was always the challenge of being so remote from the new owners, and the risk of buyer's remorse – them wondering if you had out-smarted them in some way. Toto had been with Mercedes in DTM and to some extent was one of their own, plus he had not sold the business to them.

R And from my side, having sold the company to them and having been through the whole Brawn GP thing, the rescue and the success and all the rest of it. The frustration that I was now back in the semi-corporate world again, having to go to board meetings in Stuttgart and all the rest of it. Perhaps I was at a time in my life where I didn't want to accommodate it.

A So you could argue maybe it was a mistake to carry on or maybe Mercedes should have bought 100 per cent, but that wouldn't necessarily actually have solved ...

R You may be right in some aspects. I think historically, you would be better informed on this. There have been very few occasions when people have sold their companies to large corporations that a relationship carried on successfully beyond a few years.

A Well, one of your sponsors at Mercedes was a classic example. Autonomy. Bought by Hewlett Packard. Now they are suing each other.

R Yes. At least we didn't get to that!

A No. Well, they didn't pay $11 billion for you. Again, if we look at classical military theorists, they are also interested in what happens after you win. Because many people who are ultimately brought down are brought down after huge success. Napoleon is a classic example. Human beings deal very badly with success. As they deal very badly with power and money.

A So, reflecting on what we have discussed so far, if you had to hazard a definition of strategy – what would it be?

R I think it goes back to those three elements: politics, economics and technical capability. Putting all these into a place and a level that enable them to come together to achieve the objective of success, and being the interface and the overseer of all the elements to make sure that they are gelling properly together. You've got a great budget, make sure it is spent properly. Waste is a philosophy. It's not just the waste of money, it's a bad attitude. So making sure that all that resource – the human, financial, time – is all being spent on the right objectives. I consider my role was the strategy of making sure that you had the processes and approaches that enable those things to be built and that all the elements were being used properly. So if you look at the engineering team, working hard to make sure all those people were motivated, had clear objectives and had the resources they needed to achieve those objectives. And smoothing out all the ripples and sometimes waves that occur when people work together. That was my objective. Behind all of that you have the planning, the timescales, you have projects and innovation. But as the Team Principal of a Formula One team, for me it was getting all those elements to the right level, but importantly, all crossing over to really get the most out of them.

A Is strategy a process, a philosophy, a set of values?

R I think it's a philosophy because the process flows from the philosophy. Your philosophy is to have that process. Your philosophy is to have this attitude. Your philosophy is to have this level of commitment. So it is a philosophy in my view. And that's a philosophy which you are not born with. It's a philosophy that you develop over your years of experience and years of knowledge.

A A simple definition of strategy is that it is how you overcome obstacles to achieve a goal; while the definition of intelligence is the ability *to overcome obstacles and achieve goals. So, strategy is essentially the expression of human intelligence. When you say strategy is a philosophy, the philosophy is really your approach to overcoming obstacles to achieve your goals, and you worked out through your experience, for example, that building trusting relationships is absolutely fundamental to doing this. Now, a lot of people might say that – but they don't actually do it. But the question is this: is building trusting relationships fundamental only to your strategy, or is it fundamental to all possible strategies? I believe that building trusting relationships is always essential to strategy.*

R I think you are right.

A So in other words, the way we are as a species, if you want to be ultimately successful you have to build trusting relationships. One can look at what you have done and say that you have developed your own way of being successful in Formula One that is based on your knowledge and experience and the environment in which you have been working. But equally, you could say that there is an objectively correct way of overcoming obstacles and achieving goals and it so happens that you found it. And when you followed those rules, you succeeded, and when you didn't follow them, you did not. There is a right way of doing it and there is a wrong way of doing it. And you have got closer to the right way of doing it and therefore you have been more successful.

R It's difficult for me to judge, because that's the only way I know of doing it. But that's my approach. You've made me reflect on some things. Probably the lack of trust in the Mercedes situation, certainly the hierarchy, was the thing that became disconcerting for me, and the thing that I wasn't used to having to deal with. Now, the reasons we are getting into that situation were probably my own making, so I accept that. But once that situation was created, I couldn't deal with it comfortably. It wasn't what made me happy. It wasn't what made me motivated or made me get out of bed in the morning. All the other obstacles that were in the way of achieving my ambitions of winning races and championships in the past were obstacles I was happy to take on. Because that trust element was big enough with enough people that if there were some failures I could just deal with them, because they were in the minority. Here in Mercedes, I had a situation where at a high level I couldn't trust. Even with Paddy Lowe, I was never quite sure – he was quite happy to jump in and take my job. I couldn't trust those people, so I saw no future unless I was willing to go to war and remove them. I saw no future with people that I didn't feel I could trust.

A *The situation had two distinct phases. Phase one where you were in a relationship with the board etc. and it was what is was. Limited, not ideal. When it got really drastic was when other people were brought in without your agreement or consent who then became your competitors. So whether it was Niki or Toto or Paddy – there was no way that you were all going to make it. I am not saying that you are an egotistical person, but there is no way there were going to be four bosses in that organization.*

R Well, it was becoming confusing for the employees.

A *Putting that to one side, ultimately most organizations have one boss: four is three too many. So, the only thing you could have done at that point, the choice you had, was either leave or fight. You could have made the decision, 'Hang on, I've built this up, I know we are going to be successful and I've got plenty of respect for the others – but I'm the guy to run this team.' You could have had that self-belief and the will to fight. In which case, you could have made a different decision.*

R I think one complication in all of that was Toto and Niki became shareholders, which was an interesting decision by Mercedes. I never really understood it. Their view was that they wanted management who were committed and I think they also took a view that by being shareholders they would gain greater respect from the team. That they partly own the team, so by coming in and being a shareholder they were putting their money where their mouth was. That's what they hoped. So there was the added complication of them being shareholders.

If I look back on my career, there have been small skirmishes but I would say is I have never had a situation where at the senior level it was an 'us or them' situation. I have never faced that and maybe I just didn't feel passionately enough about the whole project to want to have to go through that grief.

When I went to Ferrari, it was a little bit mucky at the beginning because John Barnard was a technical director – and then I was appointed technical director as well. And I had been told originally that John wouldn't be there when I joined. Then I was told that his contract was coming to an end and he was going to leave at the end of the year. It turned out he had another year left on his contract. I was a bit disappointed with that situation, because assurances had been given that all the decks would be cleared by the time I arrived and they weren't. Jean came to me and said, 'It doesn't look as though John is going to leave at the end of the year. We need another year of handover.' I was frustrated with that because it wasn't what I understood, but it did look as though John was ultimately going to depart. And I sat down with John and had a full and frank discussion with him: 'Look, this is where we are, let's see if we can make some success at least of the year we've got together.' Which we did. He was very professional about it and so was I, and we got through it without acrimony.

A The difference there is that he had accepted that he was going at some point one year out, and you knew you only had to survive a year of it.

R Yes, there was a timescale.

A At Mercedes, this would have been an open-ended affair for the foreseeable future.

R And I guess it might have ended with me being forcibly removed from the premises, which I have never had happen to me before.

A If you had stayed and Mercedes had gone on to win in 2014 – which you knew, as I did, was likely to happen – you would then have been in a very strong position probably, because however everyone felt, people would have known that you were the architect of it. Mercedes would have been over the moon and they would have been very reluctant to risk everything. If you had sat down and analysed it rationally, you could have come to the conclusion, 'If I just stick around for twelve months, I am going to be in a much stronger position.' Is there a part of you that thinks you should have stuck around?

R Yes, definitely. There are certain aspects of racing that I miss. I did enjoy the racing. I enjoyed the camaraderie. I enjoyed the relationship with the people and that bit is missing from my life now. What I don't miss is the uncomfortable aspects. Funnily enough going for a meal with Niki and Toto was good fun. Then knowing that you couldn't trust them, you couldn't lean on them, was a problem. I am sure they do have trusting relationships with some people.

TOTAL COMPETITION

Many people object to the idea that a sport such as Formula One involves a political and financial competition as much as a technical or sporting one. But the idea that sport, business, the arts and even war are 'purely' technical endeavours is as questionable as it is appealing. History provides many demonstrations that strategic success is derived from the combination of technical, economic and political factors. Amongst these, we took one example: that of Napoleon Bonaparte (1769–1821). Napoleon was regarded by friends, enemies and historians as a brilliant strategist. It is true that he was able to manage armies, control a battlefield and inspire his troops like no other general in modern history. In addition, his achievements as head of state were remarkable – in education, law and state finance. Early in his career, Napoleon was also able to count on his political instincts to get him out of trouble. But Napoleon's preparations for the invasion of Russia in 1812 represent a case study in strategic failure and a demonstration from history that politics cannot be abstracted from strategy, however brilliant you may be technically, and regardless of the resources at your disposal.

You might expect that before going to war against such a

formidable enemy as Russia, Napoleon would have sought to assemble as many allies as possible. In this instance he had many options from among Russia's neighbours. Turkey was engaged in a brutal war with Russia, Poland was ready to rise up against her traditional foe, and Sweden was looking for an opportunity to recapture Finland from Russia. Austria and Prussia were also potential allies. In the months leading up to the invasion, however, Napoleon actually invaded part of Sweden, made a vague and minor agreement with Austria, an insulting one with Prussia, alienated the Poles and allowed Russia to make peace with Turkey. He could not have started the war on a weaker political footing.

Once the invasion began, Napoleon made no effort to win over the Russian population to his cause, as he had done elsewhere. Consequently, even though Napoleon made rapid progress, defeated the Russian army at the battle of Borodino and captured Moscow, his victory proved illusory and unsustainable. In the subsequent retreat through the Russian winter, Napoleon lost 300,000 of his best troops. The failed invasion also cost him his aura of invincibility and led inexorably to his final defeat at Waterloo.

As compelling as it may seem, the lesson from 1812 has proven the hardest one of all for politicians and military commanders to learn. Fortunately for the rest of the world, one of the people who should have heeded this lesson, but did not, was Adolf Hitler. The Nazi invasion of the USSR in 1941 and the declaration of war on the United States of America six months later, were an even greater strategic misjudgement. While this instance of strategic misjudgement benefited the world, we live today with the consequences of other examples that have not.

R I hadn't realized, because I am not a great historian, that Napoleon eventually failed because his politics failed him.

Because he failed to maintain that dimension of his war effort. And failed to convince the people he was taking over that he was a better solution for them than what they already had.

I guess if you talk about politics in Formula One, it had many dimensions. But one is the alliances that you described. I had a reputation for being close to the FIA. And I think I got the 50/50 decisions. I think when things were 50/50 they fell my way more often than they didn't. And it was because I always cooperated and I think there was an element of trust that had been built up. They knew I wouldn't outwardly lie to them. They knew I'd be cute. Like everyone in Formula One, try and take clever interpretations. I think over the years the FIA never found a blatant breach of regulations. It would be a detail that had not been noticed from our side or what have you. And that political dimension, that personal relationship I had with the people within the FIA, was always important to me, but I enjoyed it as well. I didn't want to have fractious relationships with people. That's not my style. Therefore, I always felt if it was 50/50 it would work in my favour, because people don't want to kick you out of the race and don't want to find your car illegal. They have got to have a good reason. They need a 70/30 or an 80/20 to take that action. A referee never wants to send a player off really. He has got to do something blatant. And therefore there was never any value in having a confrontational approach with the governing body of the sport.

I was less successful in that, if I am honest, with the commercial rights holder. Because I was more confrontational with them and probably, almost like yourself, looking back on it that might have been a failing. In the end, I suffered because of it. Suffered maybe because I wanted to suffer in a sense that I was tired and I had reached my end and I was getting a bit fed up with everything. And therefore didn't make the effort. But I left myself exposed to the machinations of Bernie and didn't anticipate what he did.

A Which is strange because if you had thought objectively about it, you know how he works. Divide and rule.

R Yes, and I think that's because I was at a point where I was looking for a way to jump off the roundabout.

A Let's just pause there, because there are a few interesting things. I don't want to lose track of the different things you have said there, so we will come back hopefully to them in turn. But if we start with the FIA. For anyone not in Formula One, we should note that the FIA is the regulator: the judge, the jury, the referee, the authority that you have to deal with. It makes the rules and it applies the rules. The relationship between a Formula One team, or a Team Principal, and the FIA actually has a very wide application. Your own relationship with the FIA spans back over three decades and the FIA changed over that time. So, for example, the FIA before Max Mosley took over in the early 1990s was not the same as the FIA since he stopped in 2009. But there were, for much of that period, people like Charlie Whiting, the FIA's chief technical officer, whom I guess you have known for years. Before we get to the Bernie thing, it's important to know that the relationship with Bernie is not the same nature is it?

R No.

A How did your relationship with the FIA evolve over your career? Was there a time when you, because of a new role you had, suddenly thought, right I actually need to get this right? It's not just a question of whether I get on well with Charlie or whoever, this is something I actually have to think about and get it right. Or is it just an instinct with you?

R Well, the nature of Formula One is that 90 per cent of the relationship you have with the FIA is technical, because it's a very technical sport. The other 10 per cent is about the sporting regulations and what goes on in the race itself. That's a more emotive area, funnily enough, because drivers do things you don't expect. I look back on Michael's *faux pas* in Monaco where he put it in the barrier and I defended him because he was part of my team. But it was almost an indefensible action . . .

A Was it intelligence or instinct? I was stunned that anyone has the capacity to decide that they are going to park their car during qualifying in Monaco.

R It was an instinctive reaction from him, because in effect he had the fastest car that weekend and he was worried he wasn't going to be able to use it in the race because of someone beating him to pole position. Traditionally, the driver in pole position wins the race at Monaco if they do not make mistakes, so he was paranoid that someone was going to beat him to the pole. He was in pole position and he had the fastest car. But the way the races were working out in that era, that period, you could still win at Monaco even if you were not on pole because of the available strategy during pit stops and refuelling. You could have done something. I wasn't concerned and I failed in not conveying that lack of concern to him, so he became paranoid about it. And I am convinced it was an instinctive reaction, because he never discussed it. If it was premeditated, he had never discussed it. And he made a lousy job of it, because he should have properly shunted the thing into the barrier instead of just kissing it . . .

A . . . He basically parked the car on the side of this very narrow circuit in order to stop anyone qualifying faster than him . . .

R It was a half-hearted attempt because he kind of . . . Anyway, that's the sporting element of the FIA's role. All you can do is throw yourself on the mercy of the stewards. And you will get what you get. When it comes to the technical side, there's often a long build-up to technical arguments. And there is a long preparation. You make your conceptual argument, then you make your detailed argument and then you have the debates in the meetings and then you have debates with the stewards. It's never such an impulsive thing. It's a far more structured process. You've got an idea and you work out your arguments and you sit down and role play and game play the whole thing with your engineers. And I used to act as the critic of their arguments. They would come and say, 'We fancy this, so let's sit down and talk about it.' And I would say, 'Look, I am the opposition, so this is what I reckon. This is why I don't think it will work. How will you defend it?' There would be a lot of preparation to conceptual technical arguments, and by that I mean if you cast too wide because you have made a mistake, there is not much you can do. You can claim all sorts of reasons why it might have happened . . .

A But it's either illegal or it's not.

R Principally, although as we saw with the barge boards in '99 it was illegal, then we persuaded them . . .

So, 90 per cent of the contentious issues in Formula One are technical because it is such a technical sport. Therefore, that relationship with the FIA, the relationship with Charlie Whiting, who was the chief technical officer, was important because he had an understanding of the way you thought, you had an understanding of the way he thought. You knew when to approach him with an idea. You knew when you had a following wind and when perhaps you had upset him over something so there was no point in discussing it. There was all that type of personal dynamic which was normal – normal human life.

Interestingly, during my time in sports car racing with Jaguar in 1990 and 1991, I pushed the boundaries quite hard in terms of the concept of the sports car we designed. And, again, I took the FIA through what we were doing before it got protested. Because when someone protests your car, you're in crisis mode. So I said to the FIA, 'This is why we think it's okay.' Sports car racing was changing. It was going to a new 3.5 litre engine formula to align itself with Formula One. And I designed what was really a Formula One car – a sports car which underneath the body was a Formula One car. For instance, it had a Formula One construction of chassis and to get in and out of the car there were no doors, just windows. You took them off completely and the driver slid in and out. And if the driver had to get out, it was like an aircraft. You had to jettison the door. It fell off. Whereas everyone else had cut scallops in the side of their chassis in the conventional way, weakening the chassis. So our drivers kind of got in like a NASCAR stock car. They got in through the window.

Of course when it was shown to the FIA, it was completely contrary to what they expected to see so they were very, 'Ooh, no you can't do that.' And by slowly going through why we thought we could do it, they realized there wasn't a structured argument to stop us doing it. So they were onside by the time the protests arrived. There were various other elements of that car – the rear wing, the crash structure at the front – they all pushed the boundaries in a Formula One style which really wasn't being done in sports car racing at that stage. The psyche, the mental approach, the philosophy in sports car racing was pretty traditional. I came in there and upset the apple cart. And, in fact, more Formula One people then followed me into Sports Car racing. Harvey Postlethwaite joined Mercedes and so on.

So I built a relationship again: approach these issues before they become a crisis. And I have just had an example of that in real life. I am doing some work on restoring a mill. We want a hydro scheme there. Hydro schemes are very emotive for the conservationists. Before we put the final planning application in to do the hydro scheme, I invited several conservation groups to come in and look at what we were doing. And I found their approach very constructive and refreshing, in that it wasn't, 'That's a hydro scheme, you can't do that.' It was, 'Okay, we understand these things, we can live with one that's done responsibly.' Because once the protests come in, once people are stood out the front of your house with a placard, you are in crisis mode.

A What you are saying is your approach towards the regulator in the sport was to be transparent, to prepare. Some people would not have done that, because they wouldn't trust the regulator not to spread the technology out there. Or they would think, no, it's just better to keep it to ourselves and then we will fight the case as and when it happens. But your track record shows that it is not as effective, is it?

R I don't think so, no. Just to pick up on your point. I have never had an occasion where I thought a confidentiality had been breached in the process.

A The important point for people reading this is that we all get into situations where we have to make arguments on purely logical or technical grounds. Like putting forward an investment in a business or a planning application. Fundamentally it seems like it is a technical issue: does this meet the investment criteria or the planning rules? But this purely technical argument is being addressed to people. When they see the document on the table, do they want to approve it, or do they want to knock it back? And that can be down to personality or chemistry or track record. What you are saying: you invested a lot in making sure that when it came to a decision, people were prepared and were on your side.

R Yes. It wasn't a surprise. The reason I mention the debate with the FIA being a large per cent of technical issues is because that's always been my role: technical in some form or other. So even as a Team Principal I was very technically oriented. While I kept a keen interest at Brawn GP, for instance, Nick Fry would handle the business and commercial side. A Team Principal can't handle everything. You delegate and want to be kept informed of what's going on. My delegation was always towards the business and commercial side, while I wanted to keep very close to the technical side because I felt that was always what I was better at. That's where I had my experience, my relationships and so on. In the team, I felt more comfortable dealing directly with the FIA hierarchy myself. With the caveat that you don't want to over egg the custard. If you are involved they think, 'Blimey, this is important, why is he involved?' So just make that judgement of, 'Do I really have to be involved, or can I just know what's going on and don't make a fuss over it?' Because if you make a bit of a fuss about it, they might start to think there is more to it.

My orientation was always towards the technical side. From the point of being a chief designer at Arrows to being a technical director at Benetton and the various titles that that role carried within the different teams. I was ultimately responsible for the technical side. I think there is one comment I would like to make here. Bob Bell was my technical director at Mercedes. Bob was a good bloke, very reliable and a good asset to the team. Trustworthy. It was a shame he left Mercedes, but anyway, he was interviewed recently in *Motor Sport* and I was proud to hear some of the things he said. He said that ultimately if there was any drama in the team, I would stand up and take responsibility for it. That aspect was very important to me and I just thought that was a natural thing. Even if someone else had caused the drama, caused the problem. And it might be someone or something I didn't even know about. It was important for me personally, and for the team to know, that I was prepared to take it on my shoulders when there was a drama.

There was an issue that Mercedes had in 2013 when we did a test for Pirelli. It was a time of pretty severe crisis for Pirelli. They were having tyres fail left, right and centre and they were complaining that they had no proper testing capacity with cars that were relevant. They approached us to run a test. We didn't have a previous year's car available, which, as a team, is what we were supposed to tyre test with. Our team manager asked Charlie Whiting, 'Well, if it's a Pirelli test, it's not a car test, it's not a team test, is it?' It's a pretty tenuous point, I have to say. But in the circumstances of Pirelli's crisis, we agreed to do the test. There is no doubt that any time you test a car, you get some benefit from it. You can't avoid it. I think we were pretty conscientious in trying to set the lines over which we wouldn't stray to do the test. And the test helped Pirelli. But, looking back on it, I didn't instigate the test. It wasn't my idea, but, ultimately, it was my responsibility and I agreed for it to happen. When the shit hit the fan, I had to take the responsibility for it and sort it out. And in the end because of the arguments we presented to the FIA we got our knuckles rapped. We didn't get any more than that.

A No. I seem to recall that the issue there was that nobody knew that you were doing the test.

R Well, none of the other teams knew we were doing the test, but the FIA and Pirelli knew. It was odd, in that we stayed on in Barcelona after the race. Our trucks didn't leave the paddock and we didn't break down the garage – so anyone who had been slightly observant would have wondered what was going on. The one mistake we made, the drivers wore black helmets, which was a daft thing to do because it looked subversive. It was a stupid idea. It wasn't mine. Someone else got involved and I was stupid not to just stamp on it and say, 'No.' Because it just looked silly.

STRENGTHS AND WEAKNESSES

The Sunzi *emphasizes the need for a commander to know himself and know the enemy:*

Hence the saying: If you know the enemy and know yourself, you need not fear the result of a hundred battles. If you know yourself but not the enemy, for every victory gained you will also suffer a defeat. If you know neither the enemy nor yourself, you will succumb in every battle. (*Book III*)

A This comes back to a theme we discussed last time which was that at a certain point in your career, you stop fighting the battles that you would have fought even a couple of years earlier, because you just haven't got the energy.

So the relationship with the FIA I think is clear. When we look at the relationship with the commercial rights holder – which people would identify with Bernie Ecclestone – it is more compli-cated. Formula One is relatively unusual in that in most sports the regulator doesn't matter a huge amount because they might decide how big the ball is or whether you use touchline technol-ogy, or whatever, but that doesn't really affect anyone very much or it affects everyone the same. In Formula One the rules matter enormously, and changing the rules matters as we discussed. But the other oddity about Formula One is this three-way relationship between the teams, the regulator and the commercial rights holder. You said that earlier in your career the relationship with the commercial rights holder wasn't your responsibility because you had people like Flavio Briatore or Luca di Montezemolo doing it. But later, when it was your responsibility at Brawn and then at Mercedes, you delegated it, largely.

R Yes.

A If we look at people in leadership positions, like everyone else they have things that they are good at and comfortable with and they have things that they don't particularly like doing, or don't think they should be doing, or they don't think they are so good at. And they tend not to do those things. Unfortunately, those are the things that bite them.

But it's a dilemma because it doesn't mean that you should have done it, but what you probably didn't do was to make sure that the same principles and approach that you applied with the FIA were also applied with the commercial rights holder.

R I think you are absolutely right.

A So, if you were about to go back into Formula One, what would you do differently?

R I think the point you touched on, was that I was running out of energy to have those battles, those wars and in some ways not just the wars but the time you need to put in to nurture those relationships. I had put in the miles, I had done the work and I had enjoyed my relationship with the FIA. They are genuinely enjoyable people. Charlie Whiting has been in motor racing a long time. He was a chief mechanic when I was a mechanic. We just have a background.

Bernie operated in a different sphere to the one that I was most comfortable with. It wasn't really until Brawn GP that I had to operate in that sphere. I was always asked my opinion, but I never got involved in the nitty gritty of Ferrari's latest commercial agreement. Jean always kept me advised but I was happy for him to get on with that and he was happy to leave me to my area, which is why it worked well with Ferrari. That's another point we can perhaps come back to later. So Brawn GP was the first time I really started dealing with Bernie and it was a crisis period because Brawn GP was in crisis, or Honda/ Brawn GP was in crisis, and Formula One was in crisis because we had the rebellion going on with the Formula One Teams Association (FOTA) at the beginning of 2009.

A Well, let's just get the facts and the dates. So I remember a FOTA meeting in Brown's Hotel in London on about 4 December 2008. I don't know if you came. Nick Fry was certainly there, probably both of you. And it hadn't been made public that Honda was leaving Formula One.

R It would have been December. We found out in November 2008.

A So, let's just rewind a bit. In January 2008, we all met at the FIA headquarters in the Place de la Concorde and we had that meeting where Max Mosley said, 'Right, there's going to be a serious crisis with car makers and we are going to have budget caps.' Then Max initiated the process to put in place a budget cap. Then in April 2008, the News of the World *hit him and it pretty much went quiet then until just before the Shanghai Grand Prix in the autumn of 2008 when Max announced that we were going to go to a standard Cosworth engine. By then the financial crisis was under way: Lehman Brothers collapsed in September 2008 and the Shanghai race was a month later. Then you and Nick appeared in December at that FOTA meeting and told us that Honda was withdrawing from Formula One. The race was on for you to secure the future of the team and you also needed a new engine to replace Honda's.*

R By the end of 2008, it was a pretty volatile environment. And Bernie was generally on the other side. Against the teams because the teams were starting to come together as an entity. And that didn't suit Bernie. So during that period, the FIA were in the middle and Max, by then, was starting to side with Bernie because we wouldn't make our entries and so on. So the beginning of my professional relationship with Bernie was in that era. Of course I knew Bernie: we had had lots of chats but I was not part of the group that sat down with him and discussed commercial relationships and so on. Sometimes I would support a meeting because there were technical elements. That was the beginning of it and there is a bit of a background to that. Bernie tried to buy Brawn GP. We had got the whole thing structured and set up and Bernie tried to jump in at the last minute and told Nick and I that he would give us 5 per cent each if we ran the company for him. He was going to take it over. I think it was part of Bernie's plan to get a team on side. Fortunately, Honda had

had some difficulties with Bernie in the past and weren't very comfortable with him. And the proposal he made to Honda actually wasn't as good a proposal as the one that we were making. So it didn't float. But there was that background to it.

A When you say 'buy', you don't literally pay money, you mean receive *money ...*

R Receive money, yes!

A Bernie doesn't ...

R No, exactly. It only goes one way. So, my 'professional relationship' with Bernie was starting in that environment.

A Clearly this influenced his attitude towards you and Nick and Brawn GP. Bernie likes to be the solution. He likes to create the problem and then he likes to be the solution. Was there ever an agreement between you that he was going to buy Brawn?

R No. It never got that far.

A Do you think he ever thought that? Because he also likes to do things on a bit of a nudge and wink. What do you think? Do you think he felt that you had shafted him? Or do you think he felt he just missed out on an opportunity?

R No. I think he thought we shafted him on another issue – much later. But I don't think he felt we shafted him on the Brawn GP one, because we were pretty straight up with him: 'Bernie, we don't want to work for you.'

A By the way, I don't think there are any circumstances in which he could have been allowed to buy a team as commercial rights holder, because of the conflict of interest.

R No. That was another element.

A But that wouldn't have been on his mind at that point.

R No. I don't think so. Bernie has a reputation, it might be unfair, that he doesn't like to see other people make money out of Formula One.

A Well, it has been largely true.

R Yes. Therefore while there are a lot of very rich team owners who have great quality of life, which they have worked hard for, he likes to think he has been the reason for it. And he has been to a fair degree. He certainly doesn't like other people making money out of Formula One. There was a subset of all that debate in that he owed Honda outstanding prize money. And we proved legally that that money was now owed to Brawn GP. We took over that debt. He didn't like that. It eventually got resolved, but for the first half of 2009 he wasn't paying us anything. He wouldn't give us any money. And we got to Monaco, and we actually said, 'Bernie, we are the success story of 2009 undoubtedly. You are televising our car, you are putting it out on TV, you don't have our permission. You are not paying us for it. We have got no agreement with you. We don't want you televising our car.' Of course, Bernie is very strong. 'Stuff you,' etc. But I think that got out into the CVC world [the private equity firm that owned Formula One] and they became quite concerned about it and eventually we managed to resolve all the various issues. I wouldn't say we got one over on Bernie, because no one ever does.

A *Not for long.*

R Not for long, exactly. But I think those things were in the background too. Bernie didn't have it all his own way. And whether I became a minor threat to him or perhaps I didn't play his game the way he wanted it played, which some other people are happy to do, who knows . . .

A *My analysis of Bernie is that he has to be seen to be the guy who runs Formula One. You can't do or say anything that suggests he's not. It's as simple as that. So if you had credited the survival of Brawn GP to him and you had credited your success on the track to him, and you allowed him to feel that he'd made the deal by which you bought Honda, he probably would have been fine. The way I see Bernie is that in life, stuff doesn't always go your way. There's what the military call 'friction'. Bernie is friction. If you have a weak spot, ultimately he is very good at finding it. He is very good at playing human nature. But he only has one tactic. Which is divide and rule. And I think it is worth spending a little bit of time on that. In all my experience, I have never met anyone who does the same thing so consistently, so predictably, so effectively.*

One example was the famous meeting before Silverstone in 2009 at the height of the breakaway crisis. My understanding is that you and Donald Mackenzie from CVC, Bernie and Max got together and reached an agreement that would have meant Brawn GP breaking away from the rebel teams and signing up for the FIA Championship in 2010. On the face of it, this was a great success for Bernie. But very shortly after the meeting, it unravelled.

R Nick Fry and I met Max and Bernie principally. Donald Mackenzie of CVC was in and out of the meeting. It was at Bernie's office in London. Their leverage was guaranteeing our future entries and commercial rights.

A Yes, the problem was that with the three new teams that had entered, there weren't enough places. So the question was: were you going to enter or were you going to risk not having an entry?

R The issue also was whether we were a new team or not. Eventually, Nick and I agreed that we would enter the Championship, but we said we wanted a period of grace to go to a FOTA meeting with the other teams and try and see if we could act as arbitrators in this whole process, because everyone was in dire straits at that stage. Probably a bit like Williams, we were trying to find solutions on both sides. Some were very far right, some were very far left. We were a bit in the middle.

Originally the FOTA meeting was going to be at our offices at Brackley that afternoon. We signed a conditional agreement with Bernie in the morning with confidentiality clauses. We wanted to attend the FOTA meeting and explain our situation.

That is what we agreed. We left the Bernie meeting and within ten minutes of getting down the road we had phone calls saying, 'The meeting has been moved to Renault, because Flavio knows you have signed an agreement with Bernie and no one is coming to your factory for a meeting.'

We called Max and said, 'What the hell is going on? We have left the meeting and ten minutes later Flavio knows what is going on. We were going into the meeting to try and pour oil on troubled waters and now we are in the middle of a massive fight.'

We were told that as soon as we left the meeting in London, Bernie rang Flavio and told him that Brawn had entered the 2010 Championship. So we went into that meeting with a completely different complexion on the whole situation. During the FOTA meeting, I had a call from Dieter Zetsche at Mercedes. Brawn GP hadn't done the deal with Mercedes at that stage, we were really near. But they were starting to make noises and he said, 'We need everything aligned, you need to fall back in line with FOTA.' And that's what happened. That's why we realigned to the FOTA group. There was an element of us going back on what we agreed but Caroline McGrory, our lawyer, had been very clever in writing the letter that we signed that day.

A So this is the obvious question: why did he make that call to Flavio?

R Don't know. He is impetuous, Bernie, sometimes. You wonder at his actions and you wonder if you should put them down to youthful impetuosity, but you can't!

A One possible interpretation is that it was a mistake. He didn't think about it. He just did it. You have to consider the other possibility, which is that he did it on purpose. I've often wondered if Bernie is the kind of guy who likes to throw a spanner in the works to see what happens?

R I think he does. I have seen him do it in meetings, where the meeting starts to take a direction that he doesn't like and he will suddenly chuck something in which he knows is very controversial just to blow up the meeting.

A And everyone falls for it.

R Exactly. I have seen it done so many times. I remember a meeting where, in the background, Jordan and some of the smaller teams had an outstanding dispute about how much money they were getting in proportion to the bigger teams. The meeting was discussing race formats and it was heading off in a direction that Bernie didn't like. So, he said, 'Look, before we get to that let's talk about this money issue that we've got.' And, of course, Jordan and all the other guys just lunged in there, forgetting the progress that had been made, and the meeting collapsed in chaos – this was his tactic.

A My observation of Bernie through quite a few meetings over those five years is that he never wants a meeting to reach a conclusion. If you look back at your meeting in the summer of 2009, what he was confronted with was the FIA consolidating its control over the Championship and deciding who entered and who didn't enter. And a budget cap which Bernie didn't believe in. CVC were supporting it and then you, as the current World Championship leading team, were also supporting it. So what he was looking at was a scenario where a key team plus the FIA plus his shareholders were getting together and sorting out a problem. And he didn't really have a role in that. My view is that Bernie called Flavio because he wanted to throw a hand grenade in there. Quite deliberately. I'm not saying he's not capable of being impetuous, but he wasn't being impetuous then.

R No, you're probably right.

A And it worked out for him. Because one of the consequences of his actions, in my opinion, was that over the Silverstone weekend we did all reach a compromise on the Resources Restriction Agreement that was designed to control spending in the way Max wanted and ended the breakaway. Max stood down from the FIA presidency in 2009 and there is only one person in charge of Formula One now, which is Bernie. That Silverstone meeting in 2009 was when it all unravelled. Up until that point, there had been a balance of power between the FIA and the commercial rights holder. That balance of power doesn't exist any more.

R I would agree with you on that. The other interesting aspect to this was that when I worked at Honda, Bernie several times rang the president of Honda to discuss something he wasn't happy about. And on every occasion the president referred him back to me. 'It's Ross Brawn's team, I'm sorry you are going to have to speak to him. I'm not going to get into it.' And that was perhaps typically Japanese in a way. Also Honda had had some issues with Bernie in the past. I don't recall what they were, but they were very uncomfortable in dealing with Bernie directly. They knew he was the exact opposite of their philosophy and culture and they didn't know how to deal with him. They didn't want to deal with him. So on the few occasions he tried to bypass me and go to the president of Honda about some issue he was just rebuffed, which I think frustrated him a little bit, for the reasons you have described.

In 2012 he called me around the middle of the year and said, 'Ross, I just want you to know that what is going to go on now is not personal. It's business. You and I have known each other for a long time, so please don't take any offence.' And I said, 'What is it, Bernie?' He said, 'I'm not going to tell you, but I just want you to know that it's business and not personal.' I said, 'You have got me worried now, because you have never said anything like this to me before.' And he said, 'Well, honestly we've been in Formula One together, we are all old stagers.'

Initially I didn't understand what he was talking about. Then subsequently I discovered why he said that. This was a time when we were pressing him hard on the new deal for Mercedes as part of the negotiations for a new commercial agreement for 2013 [the Concorde Agreement]. And with Mercedes' agreement we had gone to him and said we think there's a European Union element in this. Nick and I gave him a letter at Princes Gate, which he refused to accept but he did read. We ended up leaving the meeting with it still on the table, even though he had refused to accept it. It set out the legal argument for why we thought he was in breach of European Union competition rules. It had been approved by our legal office. We said to him, 'We don't want to go down this route, but you are cornering us. We've been offered a really poor deal and yet Mercedes are supplying several teams in Formula One. They have been loyal supporters of F1 for years and they feel really aggrieved that you are treating them as you are. And you have singled out these other teams for special treatment.'

And he said, 'There is no more money left in the pot. You will have to take what you get, etc. I don't care.' Then he rang Dieter Zetsche, rather like he did with you, and said that he was struggling to deal with me, and wanted someone else involved in the negotiations. Now, unfortunately,

Dieter Zetsche didn't tell me that until much later. If Dieter had come to me and said, 'Bernie has made this phone call. What shall we do?' we could have played a double act. Dead simple to get round it. Instead, Dieter got Niki Lauda involved because Bernie suggested Niki. This was Easter 2012 when I was down in my holiday home in Cornwall. We had just got the house finished and were enjoying our first stay there. Niki was in London, at Princes Gate, with Bodo Uebber, the Mercedes financial executive, and Bernie negotiating the new deal. But neither Niki nor Bodo had much of an idea what to do. So they would keep leaving the meeting and ringing me. I was sat at my desk in Cornwall just picking up the phone every fifteen minutes with the latest on what they should or shouldn't accept. Understandably, it's difficult for Niki just to walk in and understand it all. And I was having to ring Caroline McGrory and Nigel Kerr, our legal and financial directors, to get information as well. So I was pulling it all together. In reality, I was negotiating for the team *in absentia*. Now whether Bernie knew they were going out and ringing me, I've got no idea. But anyway, in the end we found an agreement.

Amusingly, the deal ended up better than any of us could have imagined. What got tacked on was a multi-million latching bonus for winning two consecutive World Championships and 24 races in two seasons. (This had been part of the deal with Red Bull – they had already fulfilled the conditions and were guaranteed the bonus through to 2020 as a way of boosting their deal.) So we negotiated to have the same terms. Bernie never imagined in a million years that Mercedes would earn it – but they achieved it in 2014 and 2015 and now get the bonus every year until 2020.

Therefore, I didn't apply the same philosophy to dealing with the commercial rights holder that I applied to dealing with the governing body. I know they are different animals, but if I look back on it now, I should have swallowed my pride a bit more with Bernie. But in some ways, I slightly resented Bernie in the approach he took and the way he tried to muscle in on Brawn GP, the aggravation he was giving us and the fact that he wouldn't pay us our TV money for six months. We were there desperately trying to get this team together. We were, if I may say, the sensation of 2009. We were putting Formula One in a positive light again. And all he was doing was busting our balls all the time on every issue.

A It's clear that you did apply a different approach. One was enormously successful for decades. The other one, when it really mattered, backfired. Do you think you could have done it differently? I mean from a personal perspective and also in terms of who you were dealing with.

R I reflect on it and ask myself, 'Did I care enough at that stage to have done it differently?' I think, during 2009, I was acting instinctively because I definitely wanted it. I wanted things to work and I wanted the team to survive and I wanted to win the World Championship, so I was doing everything in my power. I think in some ways I probably underestimated that, at the end of the day, Bernie holds the purse strings. And nobody has successfully got round that. He will go and meet his maker one day, but no one has managed to depose him; you can't go to CVC and have an argument and think they will override him. There is no higher authority.

A When you were most vulnerable was in 2009, but you were totally focused on winning a double World Championship and having your own team, etc. Plus you were financially vulnerable. So you had this situation where you were doing incredibly well on the track, but you knew it was going to get very tricky with Bernie not paying you. Your most vulnerable moment was at Brawn in 2009, but by the time he actually put the axe in, in 2012, your team was Mercedes and it was untouchable from a financial perspective. The one group of people who did not need to worry about whether they were going to get paid by Bernie, is Mercedes. It wouldn't even register whether they got the money or not. So, ironically, the one point in your career where really Bernie had nothing, no hold at all on you or on the team, was the time when he struck. What did you in was internal division, not the external threat. Bernie beat you because of internal divisions within Mercedes GP, not because he had any great leverage. He did have great leverage back in 2009 and he did his utmost to sink you or to make life very difficult for you. But it didn't work because you were united and focused. Could things have been different in 2012?

R I was vulnerable in that I had lost my mojo by that stage. So you are right. We became divided. When I look upon those two or three years at Mercedes, there weren't conflicting interests, but there were a lot of confusing elements for me in that – we touched on this last time – I had sold the team, I had a personal loyalty to Norbert, he had orchestrated the deal and was in charge of Mercedes Motorsport. Norbert made a commitment to the board that the budget cap would be the way forward and that is how Formula One was going to be, so he was desperate about proving that and therefore our budgets were constrained. And it was a mishmash really during that period. It had lost the purity that I had enjoyed, and been spoilt with, in 2009 as Brawn GP.

So even though Brawn GP was a struggle it was a purity, it was a unity. There was absolute clarity in what we were doing, who was in charge and who was doing what. And so despite the greater challenges that existed in 2009, we were able to meet them and succeed. With lesser challenges in 2010–11, something was missing. The real leadership of the team had become a little bit obscured. I didn't have a direct relationship with the board, because Norbert was controlling that. You could probably analyse it and pick out the reasons why it wasn't as successful as it should have been. I look back and I failed in that period because I should have just said, 'Look, Norbert, sorry, this is what we are going to do.' The first budget I put in for Norbert's approval was reduced by £29 million. And that was £29 million of technical development, because we were already committed to paying the drivers and the team's salaries and overheads. That's a crucial amount. The first budget we presented, thinking Mercedes were going to go for this, didn't even formally get to the board. The board had been told that Formula One wasn't going to cost them anything. And the way it was structured, on top of that, Brackley had to pay £8 or £9 million to the engine group for the engines. I should have kicked and screamed in that period and just said, 'No, that's not the way to do it.'

HUMAN NATURE

A What is it in human nature that Bernie Ecclestone is able to just tweak with powerful, wealthy, successful people, as well as all the people in Formula One? You have watched him for thirty years. How does he do it?

R There is an aura about him. There is, it's almost too simplistic I think to say, but there is an aura about Bernie in terms of his character. You're right. He snoodles up to Putin like he's his best friend and Putin seems to treat him like he is his best friend. And yet, who else would able to achieve that? It's a fascinating dynamic that he's achieved, his access to almost anyone in the world. I'd wager a bet that if he rang up President Obama and said Bernie Ecclestone wants to speak to you, he would probably pick the phone up.

A But is that because of who he is – or is it because of who the rest of us are?

R Yes, I think that is a very good point. I think it is because of who we are. I think Bernie still has this aura about him that a lot of people want to be associated with him. Still happy to take the phone call. Still happy to say that Bernie called me today.

It's human nature and I think it always existed. It existed in Victorian times when there wasn't the media. There were the dandies and the celebrities. Obviously, it is potentially intensified because of modern communications and media. In fact, we are all experiencing the phenomenon of the celebrity who doesn't do anything. The Kardashians – what do they do? Yet people are fascinated by them. So there is something in human nature that, you are quite right, the people who you wouldn't imagine, and Bernie probably taps into that. He is smart enough. I am sure he taps into it. It is part of his *modus operandi* to do that.

A I said there were two things I was really interested in, in terms of the dynamics of this relationship. So we talked about Silverstone 2009 and the sort of breakdown of that whole scenario. The other thing that fascinates me, in 2012 what you were fighting for on behalf of Mercedes was the new Concorde Agreement which started on 1 January 2013. And if you recall, in FOTA we had that agreement that no one was going to break away and make a deal before we had all tried together and the deadline we set was 31 December 2012.

But by the end of 2012, Ferrari had done a deal with Bernie. If you took the pie as being a fixed size, it was a reasonably good deal for Ferrari that obviously completely screwed everyone else. But arguably it was nothing compared with what could have been if the teams could have negotiated a larger share or could have worked with the commercial rights holder to make the pie even bigger. Now again, what's going on there? Why did Ferrari break away from FOTA and do their own deal – an okay deal but nothing exceptional? They certainly didn't change the nature of Formula One with that. They just reinforced the old stuff.

R Well, if you remember, that deal got done off the back of Red Bull signing with Bernie. Bernie was quite smart. He's very smart. Normally Ferrari was the priority signing. Get Ferrari to sign and everyone else falls in line. But Red Bull were offered a very attractive deal and jumped first. Once Red Bull had committed, Ferrari were now second in line. So Luca jumped on board, in a slightly defensive position at that stage.

A 'Defensive' because that was when Red Bull were so dominant on the track?

R Yes. And they had two teams, Red Bull and Torro Rosso. Bernie's approach was to present a scenario where he was going to build the Championship around Red Bull and Torro Rosso. He claimed he could get enough cars with customer engines and customer chassis and Red Bull was going to join him. They were all going to go off and do their own thing. He created the impression that there was enough impetus now to succeed with this approach.

It was interesting if you look at the whole dynamic again: my historical alignment was more oriented towards the FIA; Red Bull's alignment had always been with Bernie. And that came into play in this environment. So Dietrich Mateschitz did a deal with Bernie. Ferrari panicked, jumped on board and then suddenly Bernie had a deal with the two major players. The rest of us were left scrabbling for what we could get.

McLaren, under Martin Whitmarsh, were being very loyal to FOTA, in that Bernie offered McLaren a deal and Martin said, 'I can't accept that deal, because it is not right for the rest of the teams.' So, Bernie tried to get around him. He rang Ron Dennis and told him he must be mad not to accept the deal. He did the same thing he did with us but didn't succeed on that one.

A In the short term.

R In the short term, yeah. So that is how it came about. In a perverse way, you could say the current issues in Formula One, with the disparity in its financial structure, are the fault of the teams, because taking on Bernie in that way had a predictable inevitability.

A Well, only if Ferrari broke ranks.

R Yeah, but Bernie was smart enough to work out how he could make them break ranks, because they probably would have stood up while everyone else was standing up, but then he worked out that the vulnerability was Red Bull, who Ferrari were scared of in terms of performance with Red Bull winning everything. And they had two teams. He touched a raw nerve with Ferrari. So they buckled. And then that was the end of it.

A So the teams were wrong to take him on in the first place?

R I don't know if they were wrong, but they have to bear some of the consequences of where we are now. I honestly don't know what the other solution was, because he would have just stood there and would anything have ever changed? What we have now is a situation in Formula One, which is going to be amplified as time goes on, where three or four teams have the rights – the voting rights, the financial rights – and the rest are lagging even further behind.

A I think there is one extra dimension to this, which is engines. Because having money is a necessary condition, but it's not sufficient to be successful. I think the biggest challenge now is that Ferrari and Mercedes have money, both through the Concorde deal and outside. And so does Red Bull. But Red Bull doesn't have the engine.

R I think some of the dynamic has changed. The approach that Red Bull took in that period alienated them from all the other teams. Even from Ferrari, because although Ferrari jumped in as well, they knew they had been had over. So nobody had any sympathy for Red Bull and they found themselves in the fight without an engine.

A Is it worse than that, I wonder? Did Ferrari and Mercedes lead Red Bull on? They didn't just say up front, 'Christian, we are really sorry we are not giving you an engine.' Both Mercedes and Ferrari seem to have encouraged Red Bull to believe they were going to give them an engine for months.

R I don't think in Mercedes' case that was a structured approach. I think that was a result of the dynamic within the team, in that Niki Lauda wanted them to have the engine, close relationships with Mateschitz. Lauda sees himself as a statesman in Formula One. He was structuring this thing to give an Austrian team – he's Austrian – an opportunity. And he persuaded the Mercedes board that it was the right thing to do. Red Bull was a gung-ho brand. Mercedes would be seen in a really reverential light, because they had given the engine to a competitor. He convinced the board of all of this and they agreed to do it. Toto Wolff had either got a little bit wrong-footed or just taken his eye off the ball and suddenly realized there was a drama going on. The team would have been going frantic. If I had been in the team I would have said, 'No way.' I think Toto then went individually around the board with a new perspective which was, 'This is a stop-gap for Red Bull, what you are doing is giving all our technical secrets to Audi. Because Audi are in the background waiting to join. We'll give them the engine, they'll discover all our technology and then in two or three years' time you will find that Audi will jump in with a leg-up, because they will know exactly what the engine is – so you can't give it to them.' And suddenly the board panicked and said, 'No, we won't do it.' Then all this nonsense came out about how 'Mateschitz was offered the engine but he never bothered to call us back' and all this bull. So I don't think it was a structured approach. I don't think it was a case of, 'Let's lead them on until they're past the point of no return and screw them.' That was the consequence.

A Perhaps that would be giving them too much credit. But I would be very surprised if anyone running Mercedes seriously ever wanted to give your major competitor the same kit.

R They did. When I was there, when Mercedes bought Brawn GP, there were some issues with the supply of Mercedes engines to McLaren. Mercedes had a long-standing relationship with McLaren so I didn't want to do anything we shouldn't have done. But I said, 'Surely, in the long term, our focus has to be on our own team.' And several board members said, 'No, you have got to prove to us that you can beat a customer with the same engine. Because that is the sporting thing to do. That's where we should be.' Now, I don't know how much of that was tied up in past loyalty or whether that was really a truly objective view or there were other things – history or relationships – that went into that. Because my approach to Formula One was very singular, and when we supplied teams with engines at Ferrari it was last year's engine and they didn't get everything we got. Why should they? We were there for Ferrari to be successful.

A Interestingly, it is hard for people to admit that, even if it's obviously true.

Well, we talked about the two seismic events that really shape the sport today. But I think where we got to is that, short of Red Bull being able to bring Audi into the sport and forge a new future for themselves on the engine front, it's going to be very hard for them to compete.

R Yep. They are being squeezed out. Red Bull have got the worst of both worlds. They burnt their bridges before they built their new one. They forced Renault into becoming a works team.

A It's very interesting a word you used earlier on, about Niki being a 'statesman'. And on the same principle I have often thought that Martin Whitmarsh opened the door for you guys at Brawn to get a Mercedes engine.

R Yes.

A We have talked about Bernie's ability to spot people's vanity and to play to that, but this is an example, isn't it, where people have good intentions, they want to do something for the sport. But, unfortunately, that is a form of vanity. Whether it's Bernie in 2008–09, you, or the situation with Red Bull. The fact is that being a statesman is a great idea, but it's very dangerous ... there's a horrible expression, which my wife hates when I mention it, but you could say about Formula One that 'no good turn goes unpunished'.

R Right!

A You said your own approach is to develop relationships and build trust – but that only works internally. If you set yourself up to be the statesman and you don't just do what's ruthlessly in the interests of your team, you pay a price.

R I've had elements of it in the past. For example, with the famous double tunnel diffuser in 2009. [This was a design for the underside of the car that generated a high level of downforce – at a time when new rules had been brought in that were intended to reduce downforce by 50 per cent in 2009. This technology was developed by the Honda, Toyota and Williams teams and it proved pivotal to Brawn GP's success in 2009.] In 2008, there was a technical meeting which I chaired. It came at a crucial point in the development of the 2009 car where ideas were starting to come in from the aero team and it was clear that we were going to get back all the downforce that had theoretically been taken away by the new rules. We had been asked to reduce the downforce, we came up the best ideas we had – but they weren't working. So at the meeting I said, 'We have brought in rules to reduce the downforce by 50 per cent in 2009. But I know from what I am seeing, as we develop our car for 2009, that is not the case. So we are not achieving our objectives. Do we want to revisit the rules or are we all clear that we have not achieved our objectives?' And several people accused me of scaremongering, that it wasn't true – the rules *were* achieving their objectives. That was at a stage where it wouldn't have massively impacted our team if the FIA had changed the rules. We could have sorted it out. But nobody had an appetite to do it. So I said, 'Okay.' I was chairing the FOTA technical group. Do you remember? The parallel technical group.

A Yes. I am pausing because the crucial player in this was Pat Symonds. In Paris, when we had the appeal on the double diffusers, I represented Williams and I cross-examined Pat. Pat had led the working group on downforce. But he was working on a similar concept to the double diffuser and he had even put in a clarification to Charlie, I think, on whether it was legal, which had been turned down. But the point is you were saying to your technical group, 'We are rediscovering downforce which is going to negate the attempt to reduce aerodynamic affects.' And, first of all, people didn't believe you but also Pat didn't want to go down that route because he thought he was onto something similar and he didn't want a rule change that would mean he couldn't go down that path. So, in Paris, we were able to show that his objection to the double diffuser – which was giving Brawn GP such a huge advantage in 2009, but Williams and Toyota also had it on our cars – was not because it breached the spirit or intention of the rules.

R Yes.

A And that's what we nailed him on ultimately in the case. But, Ross, this is an example of one of the things you have always done well, if I may say, is that you don't glorify your own success. You are not the kind of person who gets out there in the media and talks up their own team, their performance, what they are going to achieve next season. I think it's lethal, because if you are telling the truth you are just attracting attention. And if you are not telling the truth, you let people down. Whereas you always keep it low key. This is an example of where people should have asked themselves, 'Why would Ross Brawn be telling us that he has discovered 50 per cent extra downforce, if he hasn't? What's in it for him? Is that in his nature?'

R Well, we talked about statesmanship and, as chairman of FOTA's technical working group, I thought I had some responsibility because it was early enough. I couldn't feel comfortable not to at least raise it. When it was raised everyone said, 'Up yours.' I thought, 'Thank God for that.'

A When you say something like that, people need to think, 'Why would he say that if it's not true?'

R Yep.

A Because you don't have a track record of saying, 'We've discovered three seconds a lap,' you have a track record of getting out there and quietly doing it. And then saying, 'Well, we were lucky.' By the way, at Williams, we did take what you said very seriously. And I don't know if that is one of the reasons why we also got on to the double diffuser. We certainly didn't dismiss it. Sam Michael, who was our technical director at the time, was far too intelligent to dismiss what you were saying – I remember him telling us what you had said, and understanding the implications.

R We've touched on this before. I think there's a time for when you need to be a statesman in Formula One. You need to try and do what's right for the sport. Because it is in everyone's interests to do what's right for the sport. But then there's a time when that passes and what you have got to do is get down and dirty and do what's right for your team. And there is a balance there between the two.

A Let's just be clear about something. If the people sitting around that technical working group had taken you seriously, it would have been a disaster for Brawn GP. The double diffuser gave you a huge advantage for the first half of the 2009 season.

R Probably, yeah.

A So you took a risk. It was a calculated risk. I don't know whether you thought through, 'Are they going to listen to me, or are they not going to listen to me?' You probably thought, on balance, they were just going to dismiss it as bravado. And you were right. If they had listened to you, they could have tightened up the rules, and you would have been in trouble.

R At that stage it was Honda. There was no sign of Honda withdrawing. We had three wind tunnels, or whatever it was we were churning away at. I probably had enough confidence to think, 'Well, whichever way it goes, and if the rules change now, we are probably in a better position than anyone.' So my mindset obviously wasn't Brawn GP, it was Honda. 'We have got the resources. I've got this machine working now and it's starting to move in the right direction. So even if we do decide to remove some of the loopholes, then we think we have got a big enough machine to be successful ...'

A But it would have been a risk.

R Yes. Because what happened would not have happened.

A You had taken advantage of a rule change and more or less abandoned your 2008 car and focused on 2009. You had gone a long way down the road in developing the new car and you had found a really productive area of aerodynamics. And then, remember, your lead in 2009 was very rapidly whittled away by Red Bull. You took a calculated risk, but it was a risk, and if the other teams had been smart enough to realize what you were talking about, it would have been very damaging to Brawn.

So, I am not letting you get away with the argument that there is a time to be statesman-like. I think it was a big risk and you got away with it. But I bet you can count on the fingers of one hand the number of times you have done that in your career. The numbers of time you've told the other teams that you've got a competitive advantage – which you're willing to give up. I don't think that happens very often in your world.

R No. I think at that stage, because I was chairman of the technical working group I had a slightly different perspective on things as well. Because I was trying to be statesman-like.

A All I am saying is that there is a big risk in that.

R There was. Let's go back to McLaren. Martin Whitmarsh was instrumental in getting us the engine. Ron Dennis has never forgiven him. He feels that's the reason they lost Mercedes.

A It is the reason they lost Mercedes.

R Well, it is, but only because they did a bad job.

A No, you . . .

R No, it is. If we'd been thrashed by McLaren in 2009, Mercedes wouldn't have bought us.

A Okay, but when I joined Formula One I looked strategically at the strengths and weaknesses of everyone else. And McLaren's relationship with Mercedes, the money it brought in, the quality of engineering, the status, the brand. That is the crown jewels. I am amazed and so impressed that McLaren got Honda on board. Because at least they have the potential to do that again if they get it right technically. But to give up what they had with Mercedes? Ten minutes ago you said, 'When I was at Ferrari we gave people engines, we gave them last year's engines so they didn't get all the bits.' Yet you were able to get the same kit as McLaren had on one month's notice. It got you, what, a second a lap gain compared with the Honda engine?

R Yes.

A And then twleve months later, Mercedes bought the team.

R Yep.

A So if Martin hadn't wished to be statesman-like, you would never have had that opening. All I'm saying is that Ron is right. It was a huge strategic error. Because it wasn't inevitable that they were going to lose Mercedes, but McLaren made it possible. It's a terrible thing to say, because in the world we live in today we need people and countries that are willing to be statesman-like. I suppose the sad thing about this conversation is that anyone who is thinking about it, might think twice after reading this.

I think there's a third way. You can be narrowly focused on your own interest. Or you can be statesman-like and get shafted by everyone else. But there is a middle way. There is a way that Formula One could have looked after all the teams, actually grown the sport, done the things that we talked about in FOTA. They are struggling with audience. The competition is getting narrower. It's really tough out there for teams trying to find sponsors. There's a third way where people can look at their own interests and the interests of the sport as being the same – but they have to think longer term. In the longer term, everyone's interests tend to be the same.

R Yep. Where Formula One has struggled is the short-term thinking. I was approached by someone from within the sport to give some views on where Formula One might go. I set out my thoughts and I gave my views and they said, 'Yes, but that's three years away. We need a solution now.' I said, 'There isn't a solution now. The inertia of Formula One is such that you will be sat here in three years' time and you will have the same situation you have got now and not having moved forward. Because you want a short-term answer to something that doesn't have a short-term answer. But three years will be upon you before you know it.' That was two years ago.

A *And here we are.*

R No change, and I saw him end of last year and I said, 'There you go.'

A *What was his response?*

R He didn't accept it fully. He just said that there were all sorts of problems, all sorts of difficulties.

A *Then you've got to have the clarity and the patience to look ahead, haven't you?*

R And the strength. It's no good having these ideas, then the players are strong enough to say, 'We're not interested.' You can spend your time trying to politically bring them round, but they all want to win the next couple of World Championships. They are not interested in where Formula One is in ... their perspective is different. You have to acknowledge that the perspective of a team is different to the perspective of the sport as a whole. They would rather dominate a weaker Formula One than be a mid-player in a bigger Formula One.

A *Even though the chances are some of these teams like Mercedes and Ferrari would win anyway. Max Mosley always had the ability to change the rules. If he couldn't get it in now, he would just plan it ahead and do it unilaterally. He pretty much always got what he wanted in terms of technical changes. They don't seem to do that any more.*

R Well, the FIA has become reactive rather than planning ahead, reactive to complaints. Instead of being proactive in terms of having a vision of where Formula One wants to be, it's reactive to a point where there's enough pressure that it responds. It's like the price of engines. I think it's interesting to have the engines as part of the technical challenge, given that we haven't had it for so long. But the genie was let out of the lamp with insufficient constraints, particularly financial, and it's gone berserk. Now I gather there is going to be no constraints on engine development, so goodness knows where that is all going to end up.

A And who is going to bear the cost of that?

R Yes. Yet what's intriguing is, when Mercedes, Ferrari, Renault and Honda make an engine for a high-level road car, they will be set a price target. And they will be told you have got to produce the best product you can and it has to cost $5,000 or $10,000 or whatever it is. The economics of their road cars will require the financial controllers to say, 'You've got to beat the opposition with an engine that's going to cost $10,000. If it's going to cost $20,000, we are not in the game.' So why is that challenge not part of Formula One? All those manufacturers are used to the challenge of designing a product that has to meet price targets as well as performance targets and yet that's a missing constraint in Formula One.

A It brings us right back to what we've got on this paper in front of us. The reason why Formula One is strategically interesting is because what tends to happen in conflict is that people start with limited objectives. But once they are involved, the limits go. There is no such thing as limited warfare ultimately. If it really matters. Now in Formula One, of course, Mercedes started by saying, 'We are going to balance the budget.' Then they said, 'Well, we are going to predict more money from sponsorship so we can afford a bigger budget, because we will balance it with extra revenues.' And then they said, 'Screw it, we will just spend whatever it takes to win.' The truth is, even when Honda, for example, reputedly peaked at $750 million a year across the whole programme in Formula One, that sounds like a lot of money, but at the end of the day it isn't for Honda. If they're in, they have to win and the cost of losing is much greater. The reason Formula One is so exciting is that the competition is total. *And the reason why you were so successful, if I may suggest, is that you mastered the art of total competition.*

INTELLIGENCE

The Sunzi *reflects on the vital nature of preparation and puts particular emphasis on the value of being able to predict future human behaviour based on an accurate understanding of present facts: facts that are only available from intelligence activities.*

Thus the reason the far-sighted ruler and his superior commander conquer the enemy at every move, and achieve successes far beyond the reach of the common crowd, is fore-knowledge. Such fore-knowledge cannot be had from ghosts and spirits, deduced by comparison with past events, or verified by astrological calculations. It must come from people – people who know the enemy's situation.

R Intelligence about other teams is very important. You mentioned it when I was at a meeting and I said, 'Look, the downforce is getting too high on these cars.' Sam Michael came back from the meeting to Williams and said, 'Red alert. There is something we have got to look for.' And that was an interesting bit of reverse intelligence. I had exposed my position, but I had my own reasons.

A This is something I admire in Sam: the reason he picked that up was because he listened. It wasn't about whether he thought he was better than you or not. It was listening to what you said. And he just thought, 'I don't think Ross is one for bull, so if he says he has found a frightening amount of downforce ...' The goal was to have a 50 per cent reduction in aerodynamic downforce for the 2009 season based on a new set of rules ...

R And with the double diffuser we were virtually back to 100 per cent a year before the start of the season.

I think that is absolutely right. The modesty and the ability to listen can come from all levels. You go to a meeting and there's a tendency to listen to the top teams, like Ferrari or someone. But often from someone like Minardi, or these days Haas, you can pick up little things. You've got a team like Force India out there who seem to fight above their weight, above their budget and their political position. They must be doing something quite interesting to achieve what they are doing. And they are worth listening to when they make comments.

The other way of gathering intelligence and strengthening the team is poaching staff from other teams which is an intrinsic part of Formula One. If you isolate yourself and are not prepared to seek out the best engineers, then you will be missing out. When I was looking for engineers, the first priority was always their ability. But when they join, you get their knowledge and experience.

A Did you ever have a structured programme of mapping out the key people at other teams?

R Yes, I've done that a few times. It depends on the resource. At Ferrari we did it quite a bit. I didn't have that capacity at Brawn, but then later on we had quite a good HR guy join us and as we started to strengthen the team again, and as Mercedes started to step up, one of his tasks was to lay out the key personnel from other teams.

In terms of acquiring technical information, digital photographs were always a big thing. All the teams have photographers taking the snaps of the cars and thousands were taken each race. I often wondered, for my own amusement, if we'd all said, 'Right, you can have half an hour in my garage, it would be a lot more efficient. Come round and have a good look for half an hour every couple of races.' It wouldn't half save a lot of time and money because we had people with cameras photographing everything. One of the most lucrative areas, until people finally woke up, was the engineers' clipboards. They would walk across the pit lane from the garage to the pit wall with their clipboard under their arm. Get a photo and you could see the set-up of the car. They would leave their set-up sheets exposed on their clipboards. You know how politicians now deliberately leave a sheet out if they want something to be leaked. They walk to No. 10 Downing Street with the piece of paper the wrong way round. For years in Formula One, engineers were terrible on that. My engineers had closed clipboards. They got a massive bollocking if they did anything else. The other lucrative area was data screens. Data screens on the pit wall were often displaying data. You could get your camera guy on the top of the garage to just take shots and see what was on there.

A But you would have to be able to react very quickly to that information.

R Well, one of the interesting pieces of information was fuel weight. Knowing what people were running when they were on the track. That was normally available if you looked carefully enough.

So there was a lot of intelligence gathering by all the teams. But there was this fine line again and it's morals, isn't it, about what you are prepared to accept. For me, if somebody wants to walk across the pit lane with a clipboard showing, that is stupid and I will take advantage of it. But if somebody came to me and said I've got a drawing of X team's so and so, I wouldn't accept it.

That was the line. We did have people come to us. One of the things in the early stage of any interview with a potential employee was, 'You come here with your intelligence, you come here with your experience, but you don't come here with information about other teams. And we don't want to see any information from other teams.' When I arrived at Ferrari, I discovered that someone who previously left Benetton for Ferrari had brought a lot of information from Benetton. In the end we got rid of the person involved partly because I had to assume he would do the same to Ferrari.

OPERATIONAL ART

The material for the following discussion was a set of notes on the significant development in military theory that took place a century ago under the name of 'operational art'. As has already been touched on, theorists today recognize three levels of military thought: the strategic, operational and tactical. The oldest term of the three is 'tactics' – a universal and straightforward idea that means the same today as it did in Ancient Greece – the management of a military engagement. The word 'strategy' can also be dated back to classical Athens. At the same time as the Sunzi was being recorded in China, across the world the Greek philosopher Socrates identified that a military commander needed to master a much broader range of disciplines than just tactics. Recruiting and organizing his troops, looking after their health and motivation and ensuring they were supplied with horses and equipment were all elements of the science of the military commander. As a military commander was a 'stratēgos' in Greek, the science of his position was 'stratēgia' – strategy.

The word 'strategy' remained in use in Constantinople, the Greek-speaking capital of the Roman Empire, until the Empire finally collapsed in 1453. At that point, the word strategy disappeared from usage altogether for over three hundred years. It is as if the technological changes that occurred during those centuries focused thinking on the tactical level and took attention away from a broader, strategic view of warfare.

But at the end of the eighteenth century the world began to change: the American and French Revolutions saw whole nations in arms, fighting for liberty, not the quarrels of their kings. The industrial revolution changed the materials of war, introducing not only new weapons, but new forms of transport and communication. And it was at this time that strategy re-emerged as a word and idea – war as 'the continuation of politics by other means'; and strategy as the combination of political, economic as well as military factors.

The democratic and industrial revolutions changed the nature of both war and battle. This can be illustrated by a comparison of two battles. At the battle of Waterloo (1815) Napoleon personally commanded his 72,000 troops while the Duke of Wellington commanded the allied army of 68,000 men. Late in the day, the Allies were reinforced by 45,000 Prussians. Waterloo decided the fate of Napoleon and Europe in one day over an area of about three by four kilometres. Ninety years later, in January 1905, the Imperial Russian army faced the forces of Japan at the battle of Mukden (modern Shenyang in northern China). At Mukden, 300,000 Russians faced 270,000 Japanese. The fighting lasted for six days and covered a front of 155 kilometres and a depth of 80 kilometres – an area 1,000 times larger than Waterloo. The casualties at Mukden were equivalent to the combined forces of Napoleon and Wellington at Waterloo.

One of the survivors of the battle of Mukden was a young Russian officer, Alexander Svechin. Along with other Russian officers, Svechin observed that traditional tactics were not sufficient to deal with the scale and complexity of modern battles. In addition, modern battles, in spite of their scale and violence, were not sufficient to deliver strategic victory in the way that Waterloo had done. Svechin went on to serve in the First World War (1914–1918). In that war, both sides achieved tactical break-throughs on the Western Front, but neither side ever managed to sustain its advantage to any depth. One factor was railways. Military planners before the war had assumed that railways would benefit the offensive by enabling an attacking army to concentrate troops at a single point. In fact, the railways enabled the defender to move reserves into position and stop a successful breach of the frontline being maintained in depth. At the very end of the First World War, both Germany and the Allies experimented with new, more mobile types of attack. In late 1917, the Allies launched their first attack using the tank at Cambrai. The following year, during the 'Hundred Day' campaign, the Allies used aircraft, ground troops and tanks in a combined action. Once again, neither side was able to turn tactical breakthroughs into strategic success.

After the Russian Revolution of 1917, Svechin taught at the new Red Army Academy where he conducted a study into the lessons of the First World War. As a result of his work, Svechin concluded that single engagements could no longer be decisive: what was required was a sequence of engagements that, together, transformed tactical success into strategic decision. Svechin called the design and management of these sequences, 'operational art'. For Svechin, individual engagements were steps, the operations were leaps, while strategy was the path. Finally, Svechin and his contemporaries understood that the object of strategy was to destroy the political base of the enemy, not his frontline. Strategy, therefore, committed the political, economic and military resources of the whole nation to achieve its ends.

Alexander Svechin, along with most of the senior ranks of the Red Army, was exterminated by Joseph Stalin in the purge of 1937–8. But in 1943 the operational art of Svechin and his colleagues was put into effect as the Soviet Union turned the German offensive and pushed the Wehrmacht back from Stalingrad to Berlin. Using speed and surprise, the Soviets deployed combined air and ground forces in sequenced operations that repeatedly penetrated the German army in depth, paralysing and overwhelming troops who had seemed unstoppable up to that point. The Second World War was won by the Soviets on the Eastern Front – but it took her allies more than three decades to appreciate how this had been achieved. It was not until after the Vietnam War that the US Army studied Soviet military theory and officially recognized the operational level of war. The British Army finally did the same in 1989 – the year the Berlin Wall came down.

Operational art deserves a place in our thinking alongside – or between – strategy and tactics because it recognizes that tactical and technical effectiveness are not sufficient to achieve strategic success. This truth is not limited to warfare: it applies to all situations in which the strategist is confronted with complexity, inertia or competition. And, therefore, it applies to Formula One.

R It took me a second reading to get into this material and understand what it was all about. And it was interesting. The gist of it, what I took out of it, was the development of 'depth' in warfare from perhaps two to three dimensions; and some interesting examples of quantity, quality, politics. Let us try and do a comparison of the world of military theory to the world in which I lived in. By the 1920s and 1930s, military theorists were starting to understand much more about the three-dimensional aspect of warfare and how critical the political and economic elements were becoming to a successful campaign. And the fact that so many battles were stalled at the front in World War I because defence was stronger than offence, because of developments in technology. Unlike the old days where an army would go up against another army in a field somewhere and eventually one lot would stagger out the victors, this didn't exist anymore. The battleground was 400 km wide, you couldn't get around it. Also there didn't seem to be any way of someone actually winning a battle. There are some interesting examples here of how people tried to deal with that; there were a few different approaches that went against the norm where people managed to break through, such as at the battle of Cambrai in 1918. And when I think of my own experience, what that leads you to is that my involvement became more and more comprehensive.

When I joined Frank Williams and Patrick Head, I was the eleventh employee. When I left there in the early 1980s, after we had won two World Championships, we were 200 people. Ferrari, in the end, had 1,000 people, plus an infrastructure around the team of suppliers. So what becomes clear is that, however strong an individual you are, no longer can you control all that yourself. You then need a structure of like-minded people sharing the same vision to get where you need to get to. And it may still be a hierarchical structure in Formula One, but it's a fairly shallow one now and it's getting shallower. Someone has to be the figurehead and, in fact, the FIA made it easier because you have to have a licence to be a Team Principal now. But with the spread of roles in business, financial, legal, technical as well as racing, there is a pretty strong group of people who succeed in Formula One, even if one person may nominally appear to be the figurehead.

That came across in the material on 'operational art' – that because of all the disciplines needed, no longer can a general win a war. In fact, the general becomes almost one pawn in the whole, and it was interesting reading this: how, because of military experience of previous wars and campaigns, sometimes the generals were not best placed to judge what was needed because they had a very insular, isolated view of what they were trying to do. They didn't see the big picture. In fact, they resented the so-called bureaucrats coming in and messing about with their campaigns. Because the confrontation on the front line is only *part* of the war, then it has to reflect all the other elements that need to happen to win a war.

Formula One has become like that: you will not succeed in Formula One unless you have economic strength. You can be the most talented engineers in the world, and in Formula One, but if you haven't got the economic strength to give you the resources you need to exploit those talents, you won't succeed in Formula One. If you've got a poor relationship with the FIA, a poor political position, it will cost you. A good example of the poorest political position in recent years is Toyota. They had a terrible political position there. They didn't endear themselves to anyone in Formula One. They didn't align themselves with teams, they didn't align themselves with the FIA, they didn't align themselves with the commercial rights holder. They seemed to be isolated from everyone. And that is part of the reason they paid a price. They had people running the team who had no affinity to the environment that they were operating in. Do you agree with that with Toyota? You were closer to them than I was because they were your engine supplier at Williams.

A Yes, I would say that they were very decent people to work with. I believe we got the same engine as they got. They wanted to do the right thing. They were always caught between their corporate culture and the Formula One world. They had too much money, so they created complexity where they didn't need to. Too many choices sometimes. I think their lack of political savvy only became a major problem with FOTA and the breakaway. I always thought that going to the Toyota board and saying, 'We need to form our own series. We have got to get out of Formula One, it's a disgrace, the governance is rubbish, we are being treated like idiots,' created the danger that the board would respond, 'Absolutely right. We're out.' Which is what happened after the breakaway failed. Toyota, BMW and Renault perhaps all actually had to leave Formula One, because they had made such a strong case that Formula One was an impossible place for them to be. How could they then say, well, actually we have changed our minds, and by the way we want double the budget as well?

R The thing I am probably alluding to is this need for completeness on all fronts. Who knows – how do you quantify your political astuteness? How much does it count? And when is it going to matter? But it will have an effect at some stage. At some stage there will be a call where it will go one way or the other. A 50/50 decision that doesn't go in your favour will be the thing that can make a difference. Toyota had the double diffuser. Would they have won that double diffuser case if they were fighting it by themselves?

A Not a chance.

R Why is that? Because of the position that they held in Formula One. And the people they had who would then go on to defend that argument.

A I think we ought to stick on the wider thing, but a very interesting question maybe we can come back to is, Luca put enormous pressure on the FIA to ban the double diffuser at the beginning of 2009, because he realized it was crucial for them and I think he felt that it was wrong what we had done. But also he felt that he could have influence over the process, whether through the technical department, the race stewards or the appeal court itself. The implication that the FIA would do what he asked was quite degrading to them. Because the implication was, 'Well, if we tell you that it's wrong, then you've got to implement it.' And the FIA didn't like that very much.

R No.

A But nonetheless, if it had just been Toyota versus Ferrari, history would tend to suggest . . .

R This is the interesting dynamic of all these situations playing out when we had an FIA president who would have taken umbrage at being told what they should do. There were other periods when the FIA in the past wouldn't have taken umbrage: they would have seen what they could have got out of it. And therefore the whole dynamic at that time worked in the FIA's favour as things unfolded. But I think it's the completeness and the comprehensive nature of all the disciplines you need in a Formula One team to succeed. You've got to have everyone with the same vision. Everyone with the same belief. You've got to have all your troops with the clarity of purpose, full bellies and the resources they need to succeed. That doesn't mean wasting resources – but resources they need. Napoleon trying to blitz Russia but couldn't support that many troops – that's Toyota F1 in a way.

I think also you touched on this briefly: quality of people against quantity of people. And that's vital. You need the resources, you need the headcount, to do the job but you need the quality. Therefore developing a team, growing a team, is always two steps forward and one step back. However well you think you have chosen the team, you find when you get them together some of the chemistry doesn't work and you have to take a step back. Move something out and then put another piece in. And you have to pay a lot of attention to that. You need to have a really good infrastructure of people to support that. I was never a great fan of the Human Resource (HR) department – and I still have mixed feelings – until I went to Ferrari, and Ferrari was really the first place where there was a substantial HR department that was needed and worked. If anything, that was too powerful because the HR department at Ferrari decided policy and had quite a lot of control over the way the company was run. And subsequently, at Brawn GP, we stepped back a bit but still with a good HR department, just to keep monitoring and be the barometer of what's going on. You need an HR director and some HR people who can really connect with the troops. Not just be seen as bureaucrats. I met with my HR director at Brawn GP and Mercedes every week and he had to give me a summary of what was going on and where we had issues, where we had to pay attention.

RHYTHMS AND ROUTINES

A That's a good prompt because one way to manage complexity is through rhythm and routines. How did you organize Brawn GP in terms of who reported to you, how often you got them together?

R I will talk about Brawn GP and Mercedes together. I established this approach at Ferrari. One of the secrets of Ferrari, if there was a secret, was that Rory Byrne was always back at base. He rarely came to a race, only one now and again just to see what was going on. But I knew I had him at the factory 100 per cent of the time. Because my *modus operandi* was to go to races, and going to a race means four or five days out of a two-week programme when I am not at the factory. So you need to have a good structure in the factory that doesn't rely on you but will report to you with any dramas. And you know that the work is going on.

What I instigated at Mercedes was to appoint a technical director, Bob Bell, who didn't go to races very often. Just enough to keep in touch. His job was to make sure the technical programme worked properly. I then had an operations director, Rob Thomas, who handled all manufacturing. In fact, one of the smart moves we made was to move Rob into this position from the position of head of operations at Brixworth, the engine group. We managed to persuade him to come and work in the car factory, as opposed to leaving for an outside position. He just felt he had run his course on the engine side. A very strong, good guy, very professional. So reporting to me, we had a head of operations running manufacturing, and the technical side run by Bob Bell. Then there was the head of racing who was Andrew Shovlin. And on the racing side we had Ron Meadows who was sporting manager.

On the business side, all that was delegated to Nick Fry who reported to me, but as a partnership. It was a pretty nice relationship, an easy one. Nick would take care of the commercial, financial and legal sides, where the legal side was predominantly commercial. If the legal side was technical then, obviously, I would get involved. But effectively Caroline McGrory (Legal), Nigel Kerr (Finance) and whoever was heading up sponsorship at the time, would answer to Nick.

So that was the structure of the senior management. In terms of routines, I had a fortnightly senior management meeting. The subject of that meeting was company matters: HR would give us an overview of how recruitment was going and what personnel issues we had; Bob would give the group a quick overview technically of what was coming up, where we had to focus, what problems we had; Rob would give us an overview of where he was on the manufacturing and operational sides; Nigel would give us a financial overview once a month because he had to collect his figures, so he would tell us how the budget was going; Caroline would raise any legal issues that were coming up. She was a compliance officer as well which, as you know, at large companies like Mercedes is a bit of a thing. And then we would invite other people to come and make a presentation if there was something important going on.

A Would you say this group was about formulating strategy or for information? Did it take decisions?

R Primarily information but some decision-making. It was to make sure the executive group had all the information. There would be an action list generated from the meeting. My PA used to sit in on the meeting and make the list. In terms of decisions, I would say that they were concluded by me, but with the input of the whole committee. So, in the end if I felt really strongly about something, rarely would anyone stand in my way, but I cannot remember a situation getting to that. I wanted to hear everyone's views before I made the decision. There was never a vote. We never had votes on those unless it was something like where were we going to do a Christmas party . . . it was fun to see who thought what!

A What about formation of strategy? Was your relationship with the commercial rights holder discussed in that group, or was that something you and Nick would talk about separately?

R While commercial negotiations were going on, they would be discussed in that group, because Nigel and Caroline would be there. That would definitely be a topic.

A Was there anything that wasn't discussed in that group?

R Probably not, actually, in that all of that group were considered to be confidants. If we were discussing a driver contract that would get discussed in that meeting: where the negotiations were, how much we were paying etc. It was the senior management meeting and took two to three hours. We also had budget review meetings. They wouldn't necessarily be on fortnightly, but there would be quite a lot of work put into organizing and reviewing the budgets. The way we would start with the annual budget would be to get all the departments to put in their budget presentations. Stack up the numbers and realize it was too much – but I wanted to get everything in. And then with Nigel [financial director] and Robert Yeowart [financial controller] we would start to go through the various departments with the heads to see where we could make changes and meet the overall budget. So budget reviews were a pretty crucial part of the process.

Then there were the routines on the racing side. After every race meeting and after every major test – as the tests became fewer they became more crucial – there would be a team debrief on a Monday. That would include the race engineers; the heads of departments [design, aero, composites, mechanical, manufacturing, R&D]. About thirty or forty people would come to the debrief.

That would start by running quickly through a critical fault list. I didn't expect people to tell me about every nut and bolt needed, but we did have a fault list system. Every fault raised had an identity and a fault sheet was created and it had to be fixed by design or engineering and signed off. Simon Cole, who was our operations guy on the racetrack, would collate all those and he would run through them and make everyone aware in that meeting of the major and significant faults that we had. And so the faults list would be generated. Then we would go around the table and ask one or two people to give us a summary of the weekend. So Andrew Shovlin would give us a summary from a race engineering point of view. Ron Meadows would give us a summary from an operational point of view. Then I would go round the table and ask everyone if they had any points they wanted to raise or questions they had. And then I would give an overview and tell everyone what I was expecting of them before the next race meeting: where we were, sometimes a political overview of the situation. Everyone should have left that meeting with a clear picture of what happened at the weekend and what was broadly expected of them for the next race. What were the priorities. What were the issues. The debrief could take a whole morning if it was a heavy agenda.

On Monday afternoon or early Tuesday there would be the car specification meeting. This would be to confirm the final car build spec for the next race, so the factory and race department could start to build the cars.

Then later in the week there would be what we called the performance meeting. By then all the engineers would have digested all the information from the race weekend. I would chair this meeting where I expected the engineers to present their view of the car's performance over the weekend and where we had to focus. And there would be the aerodynamicists there etc. This would be a more detailed insight into what was going on regarding the car's performance. This group consisted of the individuals that directly affected the performance, probably about thirty people again because it would have expanded out into some of the aerodynamicists and vehicle dynamicists who wouldn't have attended the general debrief. It would also include members of the engine group. This would take an afternoon. This meeting would sometimes continue into a race strategy review meeting or that would be held on another day.

Then at some point before we went to the next race, the timing depending on the scheduling, there would be a pre-race meeting where the car specification would be again reviewed for changes and we would go through an agenda for the next race to make sure that everything was under control. It was a summary of what challenges we were going to face at this next race. 'Have we thought of everything?' I would challenge people to make sure that everything had been covered. For example, if we are going to Spa, we all know Eau Rouge has certain requirements because of the nature of the corner, we know it's a high-speed track, so they would present their set-ups and how they would approach it, how they were going to run the weekend. Maybe we'd got some issues with tyres or had some problem with brakes from the last race. And I would want to know what is going to be done the following weekend. So it would be the first meeting to discuss the approach and philosophy for the next race. That would consist of race engineers and all the key performance disciplines, and Simon to follow up on issues with car spec or production.

Then after every second race I would have a whole factory debrief, with everyone. In fact in the end, because we made that a little more detailed with information slides, we had to do it in two or three tranches of two hundred people a time to get everyone into the presentation room. The team was growing and so was the amount of information we were giving. In that briefing I would give a summary of the races, how we had done. It would show where we were on points scoring. We had metrics for reliability which we would present at that meeting. Rob Thomas would do a presentation on the factory and how it was going. What the reject rates were etc. Just things to give people a flavour of how the company was doing. There would be a financial report to let them know how we were doing on budget, but it wouldn't go into massive detail. I would then give a summary to the staff and try to make it clear what our objectives were and what was expected of them. That would be spread over a day because there would be a couple of presentations in the morning and one in the afternoon. Each individual presentation would be one-and-a-half to two hours. And also we did one at night because there were quite a number of shift workers. That would happen at 8pm.

A Did you spend time with the composites team or an engineer there, or wandering through the tunnels and just sitting down with the aero teams, formally or informally?

R That was all relatively informal. Obviously, I had my formal meetings with the department heads, but I would go into the department and ask them to walk me round and show me whatever he was doing and have a chat with a few people. I would try and do each department at least once a month. Have an informal walk around.

I had a schedule of all the meetings going on and I would jump in on some I thought would be interesting for me to have an understanding and also where I might be able to contribute. There would be many more meetings going on than I could attend, but I would try to sit in the meetings or strategic reviews of the various departments. Maybe the machine shop had a strategic review of new machinery and I would try and sit in.

A If you sat in on a meeting what was your approach: to sit and listen?

R I tried to. Certainly, I would never undermine the guy who was heading the meeting. If it was something I didn't like I would try and deal with it quietly, away from the meeting. If I thought I could contribute in a balanced way, then I would. So it was just that judgement call on making sure you didn't have a confrontation with a department head in front of his team.

A How did you fill your time then?

R *[Laughs.]*

A We are talking about how you organized things during the Brawn-Mercedes transition. But was it very different in Ferrari, for example?

R No. I think that I evolved my approach early in my career, perhaps during my Benetton days. The approach developed of course, at each team, as the needs required. Going back to the formal meetings, one crucial meeting I would have was the new car review. Every couple of weeks we would have a new car review to see how that was going. This was in parallel with all the other activities, but was essential to maintain momentum on the car for the following season. We would alternate the meetings at Brixworth or Brackley as the meeting was both engine and chassis. So there would be seven or eight people round the table – three or four engine guys, three or four chassis guys – and they would give a presentation on where they were with the new project. This was particularly crucial when we were doing the new engine and chassis for the new rules for 2014.

PERSONAL ORGANIZATION

A That's meetings. How much of your time would you spend just thinking and reading – not writing emails?

R Well, you know what I did, I got a chauffeur. Which sounds a bit of an extravagant thing. But it was an hour in the car in the morning and the same in the evening when I could properly read or think. Nicole Bearne, my PA, would produce a car file for me. So when I left each evening she would give me the car file with things I had to read in the car – either that evening going home (sometimes I fell asleep to be honest, if I was pretty knackered) or the next morning – that was easier. And if I had a meeting the next morning, she would give me the agenda and the supporting notes for the meeting so when I arrived I had some insight into what we were going to be talking about. So I had a driver, which sounds a bit of an indulgence, but actually was a very efficient use of my time. And you cannot make sensible phone calls while you are driving . . . I can't concentrate. I can't think properly if I am driving. Nicole would give me a phone list of people I had to ring who I hadn't caught up with during the day and she would give me a reading list as well. I had a file every night to take home with me which was quite a nice time as I would be sat quietly in the car and I had a nice S Class in the end ...

A What about in the office because there must have been times when you couldn't finish everything?

R Yes, if we had something that was problematic, critical, I would quite literally clear the decks. Nicole would just put the barriers up and I would say, 'I need a couple of hours to think about this. I need some time with no phone calls, no interruptions, to spend and reflect on all of this.'

A Let's talk about external meetings.

R We had a board meeting every two months, one or two a year in Brackley, the rest in Germany. And for a while I was quite involved with the FIA technical working group which I eventually eased out of.

A What about preparing for those? What was your approach? Would you describe yourself as a details person? Do you like to read things carefully in detail?

R I had an engineer called Steve Clark who was working at Honda when I arrived and was an old-style engineer. Didn't quite fit in with the modern geeky approach to racing, so as a racing engineer he was slightly out of it. But he had a lot of experience and he understood Formula One. So I used him as my technical secretary. So I could delegate all of the technical working group preparation and reading of the rules and proposals and all the rest of it. He would spend the time prepping all that for me. So when I sat down and looked at it, he would outline all the things we needed to focus on etc. I didn't have to spend time myself doing all of that. Steve had a few other tasks in the factory, but eventually he ended up really as my technical secretary. I would give him all sorts of projects. There are always things you'd like to do and you never quite have the time. So I would give them to Steve and say, 'Go off and look at that for me. Go off and gather this information from the relevant engineers and come back to me with a summary of it all.' It might be something like, 'What's the consideration for a new piece of machinery? What implications does it have? Are the rules going to change where we need a CNC machine [for making metallic components] with a bigger bed because the front wing is going to get bigger?' You have to look at all of that stuff. When we went to a 50 per cent model we couldn't use a lot of our CNC machinery in the aero department. We couldn't build big enough bits on it.

A Why did you have to do that? You had the whole infrastructure of the manufacturing department.

R I guess because I was technically orientated and involved in both sides. Let's take the conversion of our wind tunnel, from using a 40 per cent scale model of the car to a 50 per cent model, as an example. We had to do a complete analysis of what we needed. We had to present a proposal to Stuttgart as it was a £2 million project. That £2 million was building a new model and buying the machinery and equipment we needed to build it. The departments would put together the information, but where Steve was helpful, he would know what was happening on the regulations, he would know what was coming in the future, he would know what discussions had happened at a working group. He used to come to the FOTA working groups and act as secretary of the group. He would just be another set of eyes on what was happening.

A So really, what you were doing with him was addressing the reality that people do their daily job and however good they are, they think in terms of what they are doing now. So part of this was to make sure that you saw what was coming and that you were anticipating things.

R Yes, he had the time to go off and think about things in a little bit more depth.

A He was good at that sort of abstract thinking, was he?

R A bit too good sometimes! He would come back with some quite obscure perspectives on things. But that was alright. That was better than not spotting the opportunities. It worked quite well. His character didn't offend people too easily, so he could go off and have a chat with people and they wouldn't get upset.

R Can we highlight anything here?

A One of the things that operational art is about is that to be effective in a complex environment, you've got to get multiple things right. Now one of the issues there is timing. Do you do things in parallel or do you do things in series? A classic example: hybrid

technology when it came in. You might take that as being an exam-
ple where you've got a major change in the rules. New technology,
it's got to be integrated to the car. You've got to procure it. It's got
to be reliable. That is almost a situation where it's not tactical and
it's not strategic. This is where operational art would say, 'How do
we identify the right technology, get it right, get it integrated into
the car for 2009?' The decision to have hybrid technology could
be regarded as strategic for the sport, but as a team implementing
it you are in an intermediate world between strategy and tactics.

Another example is the new engine regulations. It's going to
take two years to get it right. You've got to integrate what Brackley
and Brixworth are doing. You've got new rules which need to be
interpreted. It has strategic implications because, obviously, part
of Mercedes' strategy of being in Formula One was to have the best
engine. But sewing it all together and getting it right through to
winning World Championships with that new engine, I would say
that is classic operational art.

R I think this is where I enjoyed an advantage – or at least
was at the forefront. If you look at the spread of teams in
Formula One, firstly you have those teams that don't have the
resources to forward think because they are just surviving. So
a team like Sauber or Force India wouldn't have the resources
to put a project team together two years ahead of when it was
needed and support them for long enough. And then you had
teams who just didn't seem to have the inclination to want
to do it. They didn't seem to want to have the distraction,
and I count Red Bull in that. Red Bull always seemed to be for
the now, tomorrow and very short term. I'm not saying they
don't do future projects, as I honestly don't know. But when
the new turbocharged engine came on the scene, that was

a classic example where Red Bull appeared to put little early effort into Renault to help them design a new engine. And the engine is clearly an intrinsic part of the car. In 2013, up until the summer, we were pushing them a bit, but after the summer break they just accelerated away from us, seemingly putting a massive effort into the second half of the season. We didn't, because we wanted to use that resource for the future car and I think that's paid off now, Mercedes winning the 2014 and 2015 Championships and dominating.

I have always been very conscious of trying to plan for the future and trying to make sure that we devote resource to the future. I keep it pretty simple. I allocate three or four people to a future project, or however many I feel is appropriate, and I tell them they are sacrosanct. Unless we have an earthquake and we are in a massive crisis, then they stay out of the daily mainstream tasks. It pains me if these people aren't left alone to get on with their future project. We would hold regular reviews with them, because I wanted to know where they had got to. I wouldn't be the person to hold the meeting. Bob Bell would hold that review. But I would join that review quite often, because I wanted to see how it was going.

Let's look at the introduction of the 2014 regulations, especially the new engine project. Geoff Willis joined the team in 2011 and he was given the project in the conceptual stage to start laying out the car and start seeing what implications the new regulations had on the chassis and engine. This gradually, over twelve to eighteen months, got handed over to Aldo Costa, as chief designer, who then started to turn it into reality.

That early stage is where the split turbo and other aspects were conceived that made it such an effective and complete car. And so I have always been very committed to providing that resource for future projects. Our first World Championship with Benetton was in 1994. In 1993 we had active suspension, but in 1994 it was classic suspension and there were various other changes. In early 1993 I said to Rory, 'You are on the '94 car now, I am going to handle the '93 car for the rest of this year. We are going to organize how the resources are split, but as soon as the '93 car starts running, Rory, you are on the '94 car.' You sometimes have to accept a bit of pain, because in making that commitment your current programme can suffer, but it is the only way to make a step change in performance.

We have already touched on Honda's decision to withdraw at the end of 2008. We'd had an average year in 2008, because I was putting everything into 2009. I reflected on whether Honda's decision might have changed if we would have had a more successful 2008. I don't know if it would or not. I guess the worst thing would have been that we still withdrew, but we had no 2009 car to fall back on and that would have been the worst of both worlds. But it does create heat. You have to be prepared to stand up. And classically at Ferrari, there was always the pressure, you know, 'We have got to win now, we've got to succeed now.' It was very difficult at times to do things properly to put in the structure and organization: maybe the wind tunnel is not working right so you have to shut the wind tunnel down for a couple of months and get it all sorted out. That's a big thing, but you know that in a year's time you are going to be so much better off. Those are sometimes tough decisions.

As I matured in Formula One, I became more confident in making those decisions and just sticking to my guns. It was interesting that in your paper on operational art, they were talking about technology. That you commit, not knowing what the results are going to be. It's the same in Formula One: you commit, not knowing what the results are going to be. But you know that if you've got the right people with the right resources and you give them the opportunity, then they will come up with the goods. You know as well as I do, you don't know in twelve months' time where you are going to be with your aerodynamic performance. But you know if you have given them all the facilities they need and you have got bright people and they have the time, and you back them and motivate them, they will be so many percentage points better in twelve months' time than they were. It's creative intellectual work that you can't really quantify. But in time you will have a car that's 20 points better than where you are now. It's a machine. It's the same with all innovation. You have got to create the right environment, right people, right resources, give them the vision. Manage it as it goes along, do regular reviews. But it's a process.

A This is terrifically important. I really noticed this with Mike Coughlan, chief designer, who's really good at not saying, 'Go away and design me a gearbox,' but at least once a week going through how it's going so people don't get off track. And when you are a good mechanical designer, a good aerodynamicist, you have a feel. There's a reason why you are head of aerodynamics or chief designer. You don't have to be there all the time, but you do have to make sure. And it gives people a chance to test the logic of what they are doing. But in those reviews, you can't just say I've got a project team, they are off doing their thing . . .

R No. Plus it shows an interest from your side. They get an incentive from knowing that you are interested in what they are doing.

A *Did you ever lose interest at any stage in what you were doing?*

R No. The only thing I would criticize myself for is just finding the time to do lots of these things. I love the engineering side and sometimes I would let that slip, because I would get absorbed in the other aspects of running a business and running a team. And it used to give me a real refresh to walk around the workshops and see the people and go to some of the review meetings. A lot of these review meetings would happen with or without me, but I would attend as many as possible. That was a useful process. People ask how do you create innovation? Well, it's the right people with the right message and the right resources. And it comes out. People are creative.

A *Another example of that is the pit stops when we stopped refuelling. Refuelling had been the longest exercise in a pit stop: seven seconds roughly. We knew it was going to be around four seconds with just wheel changes. I think it started at 3.9 and by the end of the next season, I think McLaren were the best, I think they got to 2.1 seconds.*

R We could do them under two seconds in the workshop, we just eased back a bit in the race. Astonishing, isn't it?

A *That is a process where you think everyone would know everything there is to know about a pit stop, and it's not a very long process to start with, but Formula One halved it in two seasons.*

R When we introduced pit stops without refuelling, I recall being in a meeting and said, 'We should have standard pit equipment. Before we have all gone and made everything we should all have standard stuff – guns and jacks. I know it sounds trivial but, I promise you, we will all spend a fortune on this equipment now because that is the nature of Formula One.' No one would agree and we spent hundreds of thousand pounds every year on developing pit equipment. Because when two cars come in the pit and one leaves a tenth of a second earlier, we have the race won. So in terms of absolute time in a race it may not be critical, but in strategic time it's absolutely critical. Therefore the wheel guns got upgraded every year and the best teams will do it better, widening the gap to the smaller teams.

I'm amused at the moment about the qualifying change that's being done. I have asked why is it being done? Because Bernie wants to shake the field up a bit. He won't shake the field up one bit, because the competent teams will, within one or two races, have everything working at optimum and therefore it will just ... and in fact it may even hurt the less competent teams more, because it will be more difficult for them to get themselves out of it.

PEOPLE

A Let us talk about people: hiring, giving instructions and taking advice.

R A good example of an external hire for me, and my approach, was Mike Elliot. I recruited Mike as head of aerodynamics at Mercedes. He had been second in command at Lotus. I often think it's a worthwhile process, when you're looking for someone as a head of department, to look for someone who's hitting the glass ceiling of another team. They want an opportunity to prove themselves, they still have experience to gain, but you can help them with that and Mike was a good example. Lotus were doing a good job on the car, we had a number of people who knew Mike and said he had a good attitude and approach. Lotus were very strong and were punching above their weight. You bring in some experience and knowledge with a recruit from another good team, but at the core you must have a good person. If you bring someone in just to gain that knowledge, it is very short term. But, of course, you are always influenced by how well their current team is going.

Quite a tough acquisition, as he was very loyal to Lotus. They were financially in trouble, and he didn't want to be seen as the one who was jumping ship. It took a while to persuade him to join Mercedes. At that level, I always got personally involved. Sometimes I would have HR make the first approach, but other times I would do it. I would talk about my philosophy, the company's philosophy, why it would be fun to join and what would the opportunities be, and so on. And I would negotiate a remuneration package myself. It's impersonal if you delegate that. It gives you the chance to see reactions and you hear little things that you can follow up on. You can pick up on things and think, 'How can I help him with that, what can I do?' When Aldo joined Mercedes, I wanted him working flat out on the car as soon as he arrived. Because he was moving from Italy to the UK, we hired someone to take care all of that for him. It cost us several thousand pounds, but it was great value to the company. You want a highly paid technical guy working on the car, not trying to figure out how to get his furniture from Italy. So Mike Elliot was a good example, I nurtured him over a period to join. You want people who are difficult to get out of a team, you respect their loyalty and dedication. If someone jumps at the first opportunity, you wonder.

A Do you like to tell people what to do? Or do you like to give people what you are trying to achieve and let them work it out basically? How prescriptive are you?

R I prefer the second. Obviously, everyone always says that. It depends on the timing. Sometimes you give an order because you are in a critical situation. If you took the extreme example: on the pit wall. There's a crash, something has happened unexpectedly, etc. You know you have got to step in. 'Right, do this. Do it.' And bear the consequences because you know if you prevaricate and debate and discuss, you will lose the moment.

With car development, that was more of a mix, because the process involved sitting down at some stage in the year and identifying where you felt you were weak compared to your competitors. What were your strengths? What did you have to focus on? What did you have to put the resource into the project? So you shape the teams based on where you thought you were. And you could set targets. It's a difficult process because you say, right, we have to be a second faster, but that is a hollow command unless you support with discussion and debate.

We had metrics and my process would be to meet fairly frequently with the people to ask how they were getting on. Because they knew what the process was but they wanted to come to me to tell me that they had made some progress. That is human nature. Aerodynamics I did every week. Every Wednesday morning, I did a review with the aerodynamics group, a quick meeting, twenty minutes, the first meeting of the morning. A quick process meeting and where they were, what they had found, what were their issues. And there would be a much bigger meeting later but Mike Elliott, who was in charge of the department, would say, right, we have made this progress this week. We have found some interesting things and so on. It wouldn't be very complicated. Just so I kept them on their toes a little bit and showed my interest. They knew they had to come and see me on a Wednesday and nobody wants to go along and say, 'We haven't made any progress.' So just that process of sitting down with everyone on a regular basis helped to drive things along.

A Let's move on to taking advice and choosing advisors.

R I think I learnt to know my own strengths and weaknesses. Therefore, I was never hypersensitive about taking advice or delegating certain things, whether I was running a team or, in fact, I owned the team. There were certain functions in which I wanted to know what was going on but was happy to delegate. The obvious one was legal. I had no legal experience, but I have experience of how Formula One would be interpreted and how the processes worked. Caroline McGrory was a very good legal director who knew the letter of the law, and I had a good partnership with Nick. I think that's very important.

Throughout my career I have always been able to enjoy good partnerships with people – because I have always been happy to share the success. I hope that hasn't come out wrong. It goes back to Flavio going on the podium the whole time. For me, one of the greatest gifts I could give someone was to ask them to represent the team on the podium. It meant more to me than being up there myself. The only one I ever wanted to definitely do for myself in latter years was Monaco in my last year, 2013. We won Monaco with Nico. And I thought, 'Sod it, I'm going to go up there myself. I really want to do this one myself.' In my mind, I knew I was leaving by then. It was a special race with Nico. I'd been there when his dad had won it with Williams in 1983. It was just so many things. I took that one for myself. But it actually nearly always gave me more pleasure to put someone else on the podium. And in some ways that applied to lots of other things. To enjoy success with people. To enjoy it as a team meant much more to me than individual success. Interestingly, Michael Schumacher was very much the same. Michael wanted to be out there in the car doing battle and beating people. But then he wanted to enjoy that victory as a group. He loved being part of the team. It even extended to him organizing football matches on a Thursday night, a five-a-side game with all the team. He is very much a team player. He really enjoys the team environment.

A If you had to choose one race ...?

R Brazil 2009 would be a very special race in my career. I struggle to say the best, because I've enjoyed several. But there's some interesting aspects to that race. If you look at the season, we started with a very dominant car and Jenson Button won six races. And then, maybe the team did or maybe he did, but it all got a bit wobbly. We had this Championship almost within our grasp, but then we under-performed in the middle of the year. I think some of it, by his own admission, was Jenson feeling the pressure because Rubens Barrichello went on to win another couple of races. Rubens won Monza and Valencia and he won those races when you would have expected Jenson to continue. Jenson got a bit wobbly and we were still in the balance when we got to Brazil.

Red Bull were faster than we were at that stage. They had caught up and were chasing us hard, and then at Monza we had a great race. We got the car perfect and had a one-two finish. Valencia was Rubens. What was nice about Valencia, when Rubens won it, it was his first race win for a long time and everyone in the pit lane applauded him as he came through after the race finished. But apart from Monza, Red Bull were charging hard. And then we went to Brazil and the weather was terrible. Luckily, Sebastian Vettel made a cock-up in Q1 and dropped out. And he was our main challenger. So we thought we were in good shape. And then Jenson dropped out in Q2. We'd made a mistake with the tyres. It was drying, we stayed on with a set of full wets. Between us we thought we could still get a time good enough to go into Q3 and we couldn't. So Jenson started 14th. Vettel was 16th. But on Sunday morning Jenson came to me and said, 'It's going to be okay. I'm going to do the business today. I'm up for it and I'm going to sort it out.' And he drove a fantastic race. I know he came from behind but he overtook people, he was decisive, he was really impressive. Which was great because we won the Championship. But then I thought back, 'Why can't you do that every race? What was it that switched him on that race? And why couldn't he have had that frame of mind in every race?' Because, in a perverse way, it's a weakness because you should be doing that every time.

A Did you ask him?

R No, I didn't. In fact, he left us not long after. Yes, he announced not long after that he was going to McLaren. Which was unpleasant. But the fact that he was able to come to me and say, 'Right, I am going to do it today. I'm on top of it. Don't worry, I'm really up for it today,' it's interesting, that mentality. What was it he came to terms with? And why couldn't he have done that every race? Because he definitely had races during the year where his indecisiveness cost him. I think in Spa he had an accident which, when you look at it, he should have just taken control of the situation. There were just times when we all felt he was getting a bit wobbly. The pressure was telling. Maybe it's just the nature of sportsmen.

A Why do you think he was the one that won the Championship and not Rubens?

R I think Rubens was coming to the end of his career. But after he left us, he drove for you pretty well, didn't he? I don't know the answer, to be honest. But Jenson had the edge on him at the beginning and then in the middle of the season, when Jenson wobbled a bit, Rubens came through and won two races. I was delighted for Rubens, but for the Drivers' Championship he was the wrong driver to be winning races.

SIMPLICITY

A Before we discuss your approach to race weekends, I want to discuss a principle that cuts across all aspects of life: simplicity. Many aspects of your philosophy seem simple, but life is often complex. Formula One cars are on one level a complex piece of equipment, and yet people sometimes talk about them in terms of complexity and simplicity. Are good cars simple or are they complicated?

R Sometimes people try too hard, to make too big a jump. I think what's evolved, and a good example is in aerodynamics, is the understanding and the culture that there was absolutely no use in having downforce that you couldn't use, i.e. downforce that is generated only in a straight line. I made it clear to the aerodynamicists that it was useless if the objective was just to be able to come and show me graphs every week that had a performance improvement, which was not relevant to what was happening on the track. That, unfortunately, was some of the Honda problem when I was there. With the engine, the engineers were coming along with all these power increases which were not useable on the track. The drivability of the engine was so bad that they were chasing the wrong things.

So the relevance of knowing what performance improvement to pursue is part of having a very good complete engineering process. Certainly in the later years, as it became more understood, my aerodynamicist would come along and say, 'We've improved the car in this environment. Not straight ahead.' Straight ahead was never really that interesting to the track, apart from pure drag. It was the yaw sensitivity, the pitch sensitivity, the dynamics; and our model in the wind tunnel would be put through a whole series of pitches and rolls and dynamics to build a map of it. We were never interested in the aerodynamic map straight ahead, we were interested in the map when the car was cornering. And therefore I would make sure the aerodynamicist, the guy who was developing the aerodynamics, would go to the circuit, have access to the drivers to talk about things. He would understand what was needed. He would work with the engineers on the processes at the factory. The design engineers, the race engineers and the aerodynamic engineers would have an environment where they were all talking and understanding, just to make sure that he wasn't chasing a gold star for something that was irrelevant.

There is no doubt that the more complex the solution, the more unintended consequences you can have. Because the simpler solution you can find to a problem or to an objective, you've got less chance of some unintended consequences. If you use an exotic new material or exotic new process, you then discover there was some unintended consequence that then defeats the objective. I would always advocate simple solutions. These things have got to be made, and they have got to be serviced and they have got to be used in the field. And reliable. Complex solutions are nearly always heavier, more expensive to make, use more resource. And that balance of performance against complexity is one that should always err slightly on the side of simplicity. I wouldn't necessarily decline a very complex solution that gave good strong performance. You could never say, 'Right, we are not going to do it. It is just too complicated.' You would weigh everything up and you would look at the resource involved and so on. That process of looking at everything that was required to achieve that objective would be done. The amount of time and cost to make something. We had a ratio of cost:performance slope and if you didn't meet the cost:performance slope that thing didn't happen. Admittedly, that cost:performance slope got a bit shallower as the budgets improved. This was controlled by Aldo, who was my chief designer; I seem to remember at one time it was something like £100,000 per tenth of a second per lap. Proposals had to meet that ratio. And that cost was tooling, manufacturing, everything, the whole works. Now that doesn't mean that if you spend £1 million you go a second faster. What it means is that when you do find an improvement of a tenth of a second, it will go on the car if it costs £100,000 or less to implement. Now you can get into grey areas where the engineers present a case that this is the first step of something that is going to become much more important and then you have to make a judgement call. 'This is where we are today, but if we don't go ahead with it we are not going to be where we think we can be in six months' time.'

A If you are looking at the Jaguar back in 1990, or at the best Ferrari you did in the early 2000s, did you see those cars as kind of being elegantly simple? Or cleverly complicated?

R No, elegantly simple, I think. It depends on the phase of the regulations. When regulations have been in for a long time and there's not been any change, then sometimes things do start to get complicated due to chasing smaller degrees of performance. When you are in the early stages, then you are talking about concept and you are talking about the whole idea of the car. So with Jaguar, we put a massive rear wing on the car, across the whole width, because the diffuser height was controlled by the regulations. We put a big wing on which wasn't a diffuser any more but it was coupled to the diffuser, because it was in a position that was really an extension of the diffuser but it looked like a wing. Well, it was a wing. But that wing ramping up at the end obviously elevated the under pressures to the floors, loaded the under pressures on the floors. And that was a conceptually simple thing to do. It wasn't complicated.

A Essentially you asked yourself, 'How do we make a bigger diffuser?'

R Yeah, and there might have been some very complex way of doing it. This was a simple way.

A But you were the only people. You were the first. You interpreted the rules differently. So you could have a grand, simple idea with a very big effect on performance. Later on, in the rules, when every-one is onto the same ideas, it gets subtler.

R Yes, exactly. As the rules mature and the interpretations get refined and everyone starts to do the same thing, sometimes you get into more complex solutions to find the last fractions of a second.

RACING

When the Sunzi *speaks of battle, what is actually required is a* coup de grâce, *not a fair and symmetrical contest:*

> What the ancients called a clever fighter is one who not only wins, but excels in winning with ease. Hence his victories bring him neither reputation for wisdom nor credit for courage. He wins his battles by making no mistakes. Making no mistakes is what establishes the certainty of victory, for it means conquering an enemy that is already defeated. Hence the skilful fighter puts himself into a position which makes defeat impossible, and does not miss the moment for defeating the enemy. Thus it is that in war the victorious strategist only seeks battle after the victory has been won, whereas he who is destined to defeat first fights and afterwards looks for victory. (*Book IV*)

R We all know that in terms of the car itself, the preparation has been happening months or years before in design and development of the car. But in terms of detailed preparation, there's a need to have some meetings a few weeks before the race. Some races present specific challenges: Monaco, for instance, is different to Spa. So we would have a specification meeting immediately following the previous race. And this is on the basis of the races being on a two-week cycle. You have to modify that for back-to-back races. So almost two weeks before the race, there would be the specification meeting, and in that meeting you would have all the relevant parties – manufacturing, design, and management. And there was an agenda where you would go through every aspect of the car. 'What brakes are we going to fit for that weekend? What's the aerodynamic spec for that weekend? What's the chassis spec for that weekend? What's the engine spec for that weekend?' And so on. You would produce a working document which was called the 'car spec'. So the cars were built to that specification for that race and it would be up to the race engineer and a systems or support engineer to make sure the cars got built to that spec.

Then there would be a pre-race performance meeting where you discuss how you are going to run the car for the weekend. How the set-up of the car was going to start, why you wanted to have that set-up, whether the two drivers would start in the same place or you would have some divergence for a comparison. Whether there were any new parts to evaluate for the weekend. That was putting your programme and your performance together for the weekend. So it was: how are you going to build the cars and how you are going to run them? Those are the two primary meetings preparing for the weekend.

There would be a race strategy review in between races. You would look at how the race strategy ran for the previous race and what lessons were learnt and what was good and what was bad. The race strategist would give you his first opinion on how he thought the race was going to run. I always had one race strategist. Some teams have two, because they feel each car requires individual treatment. I was fixed on one, because I wanted each car to reflect the other car as well and look at the whole situation. We used to have someone back at the factory on each car doing the numbers, but they were presented to the same guy, our chief strategist James Vowles, who would sit next to me on the pit wall. And he would be looking at the overall view of the race and balancing what each driver needed. So we would do a strategy review and James would tell us how he thought the race might run and therefore how much fuel we had to run, what tyres, when did we want to run the tyres etc. In that way, we would start to build the plan of how we were going to approach the weekend.

The plan would be conveyed to the drivers and the race engineers for the race weekend. And then the first thing we did on the Thursday when, effectively, the race meeting started would be to sit down and set that all out to the drivers and the programme for the weekend would be discussed. So, if at that stage, the drivers wanted to give their input they could do so and there was still time to change the programme. And we would also have up-to-date weather forecasts by then so we could start to take the weather into account. Then the run plan would be defined for both practice sessions on the Friday because there wasn't a lot of time in between them. In between the two practices there would be only time to sit down, go through a quick checklist of anything wrong with the car. Because it is surprising how often the drivers forget the mirror was broken until they get in to go out for the next session. 'Oh yes, I forgot the mirror was broken.' So we had a checklist: brakes, mirrors, seat, belts etc. just to make sure everything was okay with the car and there was nothing they had forgotten.

The main job between the two sessions was for the drivers to sit down with the race engineers and talk about the car and how it was handling, what they needed to focus on and where they needed to find improvements. Then, if nothing changed, it was assumed the run plan would be as previously discussed for Practice 2. If there was a change in run plan, there was still an opportunity to sit down and discuss it so everyone knew what was happening. I was very keen that each driver knew what the other one was doing before it happened, so there was never any arguments after practice, like, 'I didn't know he was doing that. Why did he do that? I should have been doing that.' You know, all the normal children's playground stuff. We would eliminate that by agreeing everything beforehand.

Friday night we would then have a debrief immediately after practice while everything was fresh in the driver's mind. Then there would be a period for the engineers to go through all the data, spend time looking at things. There would be another meeting, a couple of hours later, after they had looked at everything, to do a summary of the day. What conclusions we were drawing and therefore what we were thinking of doing the next day. And the drivers would be required to stay for that. That was tricky sometimes, because drivers would have to go off and do marketing work for sponsors. So we had to balance that carefully. My teams were always very focused on the engineering. The marketing people knew that the engineering came first, without a doubt. But we would always be sympathetic to them borrowing the drivers. We would try to get all those commercial activities within the track if we could, because then the timings were easier.

Then Saturday morning would pretty much be a repeat. There would be a briefing, just to remind everyone what we were doing. Free practice. There would be a debrief after first practice to make sure nothing had gone wrong. One thing we did on Saturday morning was the strategy meeting because by Saturday, in normal circumstances, you've got all the information to give a review of strategy. And given that Saturday morning is a short practice, classically, it is just about getting ready for qualifying. It's rare that you get any more information about how you might run the race from a Saturday morning. You've normally got all the information from the Friday. Tyres, fuel, what the others are doing. On a Saturday morning our strategist would give us an overview. So the drivers would start to get a feel for where they were going with strategy for the race. Then qualifying.

A *Because the race strategy determines, in part, the qualifying strategy.*

R A little bit, yes. Tyres in particular. It used to be much more because of the fuel. When you refuelled then it determined how much fuel you started the race with as you couldn't refuel after qualifying.

A *Do you think it was a mistake to get rid of refuelling?*

R Well, funnily enough, Bernie talks about shaking up the races and refuelling was definitely a factor that did that. We were earlier discussing some of the races and one of the races I wanted to look at was Brazil 2009, when Jenson clinched the Championship, but I couldn't quite remember what Rubens had done. I recall now that Rubens was actually on pole, because we put him out on a fairly light fuel load in qualifying, as we wanted to see if Rubens on the front row could control the pace if we had to. So Rubens actually went lightly fuelled in order to make sure he had pole, in case we had to control the race for Jenson.

A *Also, nice to have a Brazilian on pole there.*

R That always helps. So he was on light fuel load. Webber was second and he had a heavy fuel load so, of course, as the race developed he had the advantage but strategically we could have done something with it. So refuelling was another variable.

So we have done our race strategy, then we focus on qualifying. We get to qualifying, hopefully it goes fairly well. There's a debrief after qualifying. You can't change the cars after qualifying so there's not an awful lot to do in terms of set-up. But there is a little bit – tyre pressures, differential maps, all that sort of stuff. So the drivers and engineers would have a discussion on Saturday night about what might be done but it was quite limited. On Sunday morning, we'd have a meeting to define the final race strategy. Then we would have a pre-race brief based on any changes that were available to the drivers. And then we would have what we call a race management meeting where we would go through any aspects of the sporting code that needed emphasizing. The team manager would come in and sit with the two race engineers, the two drivers and go through any directives we had had from Charlie Whiting at the FIA for the weekend. The FIA saying, 'You mustn't cross this white line,' for example. So that would be a final reminder to the drivers what they had to focus on. We'd fill them in on the weather. So it was an important race management meeting.

Then the race would take place, and an hour or so afterwards we'd have a pretty comprehensive debrief of the whole race with the drivers and engineers, including a little state of the nation speech by me on how I thought things had gone, what we were going to major on before the next race and thank everyone for what they had done. Every race, before the crew went home, I would also address the whole race team with an overview of the weekend.

A Do you know how many races you went to?

R God knows. Well, it was between sixteen and twenty a year. And I went to almost every race for thirty-plus years. I could work it out, it must be around five hundred. One thing I mentioned and I always did was call the crew together a few hours after the race and just thank them for what they had done. Everyone had to come together, talk about the race, we've done well, we've done badly. This is what we are now going to do to improve, all the normal stuff. Just to give them an opinion on how I thought the weekend had gone and to help bond the team. The drivers would attend as well. We might have had a few cock-ups and we wouldn't hide from them, but we wouldn't isolate people.

One race we had a pit stop and at the time we had the lollipop system of releasing the car from the pit stop; and our chief mechanic lifted the lollipop too early, let the car go too soon. He was destroyed. In that meeting I said, 'Look, you all know Matt, we've all relied on him for years. He's made one mistake. Support him while he gets over it. We can't change the way it is. But we trust him. And he will actually be stronger from this. It will either destroy him or it will make him stronger. And we all believe it will make him stronger. So let's get over it.' You can't hide away from those things. Ultimately, if the guy does it a couple of times you've got a hitch. And everyone knows that. If someone who has done the job really well makes one error, you get over it. So that was the race weekend.

A Somebody reading this is going to say, 'How organized?' So let's talk about what goes wrong.

R The most normal or predictable problem was that one of the cars would drop out while you were in your technical programme. On a Friday you'd normally try and have the cars doing different programmes to gather the most information. Maybe one car would run a soft tyre, one car would run the hard tyre. And one might run high fuel, one might run medium fuel. You were trying to build a matrix of information that enabled you at the end of the day to make the best decision. And you lose a car. Then you have to decide if you want to change the programme. While we would never have Plan B in practice – because we would never know exactly when that might happen – we would always be mindful that if one car dropped out what would we focus on. Which is the most important programme? Do we need to change the programme to get the information we require? So the most predictable issue was that one of the cars would have a crash or a reliability problem, or we'd have to start again with the programme. And that is one that would probably happen three or four times during the year.

The same almost goes for the weather. The leveller with the weather is that everyone is dealing with it. If it was wet on a

Friday, everyone had a wet Friday to deal with. My philosophy was always to instill in the troops that if you could deal with that sort of adversity better than another team, then you would come out on top. So, never think of a wet Friday as a drama. Think of it as an opportunity. We then had Saturday to get our act together. We are going to be better at getting our act together on a Saturday than anyone else – because it is a positive rather than a negative. I used to take the same approach with circuits. With Monaco – we have touched on this before – to me it was an opportunity because so many people hated it, for the crowds and the logistics and the inconvenience. With Ron Meadows, who was our team manager, his task was to make life as easy as he could for the team. So if there was anything we could do to make the thing run more smoothly, it was done. I would say to everyone, 'This is Monaco. Enjoy it. Embrace it, because other people hate it and we will have an advantage because we are enjoying ourselves. Don't get into a negative mode, because you've got some fan staring or you can't get to the hotel very easily because the roads are blocked. That's Monaco. That's Formula One.'

When I first started it was just a pit lane, no garages. And when it rained everyone got wet. It was the best place ever to go and look at other people's cars, because they were in the pit lane. They couldn't hide.

Getting back to the race, unplanned things also happened, for example with safety cars. People would sometimes say to me, 'You made a great call. You made a great strategic decision.' In the main, they were all pre-planned, because my approach would be to pick the race strategy and then challenge the race strategist, who in the end was James. 'Every lap, what would happen if it rained? Every lap, what would happen if it was a safety car? If by lap 4 we had a safety car, what are we going to do? If it rains, what are we going to do? If on lap 7 it rains, what are we going to do?' So he had a default map of, 'If the safety car comes out lap 7, we will bring both cars in and change the tyres.' And he would also know the last place on the track where we knew we could make the latest call to get the cars to pit. So we would know the point on the track where once we had passed that we couldn't do anything. There was no point in panicking and screaming and shouting. It wouldn't make any difference. The race strategists would plot the point at which the last call could be made and they would plot all of the laps, maybe do it in twos or threes if it was not very sensitive, as to what would happen if it rains, what would happen if there was a safety car, for example.

This was done with simulation models. They weren't terribly complicated but there were tyre curves, fuel effect and maybe a little bit of track evolution built in there, depending on how clever we were getting. Undoubtedly, when we started it was a straight tyre curve, straight car slope, straight fuel slope. And in the early days, when I was responsible for race strategy, I got someone to write a simple program where you would just put the numbers in and I could keep iterating, until I thought we had the right solution.

But race strategy is not just about running the numerically fastest race. Certainly, in the refuelling days, it was often about the competition with the people you were racing against. Again, I may have touched upon it, but there is the example of the 1998 Hungarian Grand Prix in Ferrari days, where we did three pit stops. That wasn't quite the fastest strategy, but it gave us free track time. We did three pit stops which had never been intentionally done before. When we looked at it, two pit stops was the norm, because although there was high tyre degradation it was the fastest strategy. The problem we had is that we had quite a quick car, but we hadn't qualified very well. So we knew that if we did the same as McLaren did, they could cover us. McLaren had two cars first and second after qualifying. Michael qualified third. Our other car qualified fifth. So Luca Baldisserri, the strategist, said, 'Why don't we do three stops? Because it puts us out of phase with them. Because we are out of phase, we can run our own race, run at our own pace.' So it wasn't just about looking at the numbers and saying two stops are quicker than three, so therefore we should do two. Three was more of a strategic decision because with three, while we would have to overtake back markers and so on, we wouldn't actually be held up by someone fast or be controlled by McLaren.

When we did three, it threw McLaren completely, they didn't know what was going on. They had mapped out two for us and then when we came very short at the first stop, they couldn't work out what we were doing and it threw them into a panic. If you look at that race, McLaren compromised both their cars, trying to work out what we were doing. In fact, I think if Hakkinen or Coulthard had stuck at what they were doing, we probably would have struggled to beat them. But as soon as we went into three mode, they tried to react and compromised their strategy even more and we beat them. That's the different aspect of strategy that goes beyond the numbers. It's intuition mixed with calculation.

It has been after my time, but the extra set of tyres now at races, the three types they have to play with, the free choice each driver has to choose his compounds, probably gives a little bit more scope for strategy.

Red flags or race stoppages can be great equalisers. I watched a race at the weekend where a mid-race red flag effectively created a new race. That creates another interesting aspect of the strategy, that we would have red flags and, say, 'If the race starts again, is it now a one-stop race, or is it a two-stop race? This is a 70-lap race, but model a 50-lap race because we might get a red flag.' And red flags in the early days were more common before we had the safety cars.

Then you've got the unpredictable things in the race like a crash. Crashes can be terminal, or they can be just damaging. If your car is affected, you have to come in, assess the damage and decide whether to repair the car and get back out there. Then you are into experience and intuition about whether you carry on. You have to make a critical safety decision, and in the team there was a process for doing that. Simon Cole, our operations engineer, would have the task of looking at the car to see what damage was done, to make a call if it was safe to continue and whether we could repair the damage. What we did in latter years was to take digital photographs as soon as the car came into the pit lane. So if a car was coming in damaged, we would try and position our photographer to catch the damaged area, so when the car had left we could look at the photographs to try and see whether there was anything we hadn't spotted. We can make much better observations from the photographs of the car, because digital photography changed things. It's instant. Even as the car was going back out, the team would be looking at the photographs in detail.

The *modus operandi* in a pit stop was the car wouldn't leave the pits until Simon had given the thumbs-up to the lollipop man. So the guys would go about repairing the car, he would be looking and then he would be at the back of the car and as soon as he gave the sign the car could leave. There was a system. Most of the time, if it was safe to carry on, you would, because, even if you had lost time, you never knew what was going to happen. You don't know whether there is going to be a red flag. You don't know if there is going to be a safety car. And if you can try and get out without losing a lap, then you've got a fair old chance of getting out there and scoring some points. But whatever happened, safety was paramount. Any doubt and you stopped.

A One of the more unpredictable things was the crash of Nelson Piquet Jnr in Singapore in 2008. You were there with Honda. That was a very surreal moment in Formula One history.

R Everyone wondered about it, and the reason they wondered was because Alonso made a pit stop which seemed illogical. Alonso came into the pits at a time no one would consider making a pit stop. It didn't make any sense. Then Piquet crashed and then suddenly Alonso was leading the race because he had made a pit stop before the safety car ...

A Because in those days you couldn't pit under the safety car? So you were stuffed. Unless you happen to have just pitted. In which case you were in the money.

R Yes. But nobody wanted to think that was possible. Not to anyone's knowledge had it ever happened before. And no one ever conceived that could happen. I have never spoken to Pat Symonds directly about it. He claims that he succumbed under pressure, because Renault were talking about withdrawing and he was worrying about the future. He was presented with this scenario and he succumbed. I know Pat wouldn't have done that just for the sake of winning a race. It's not worth it. So there must have been other circumstances.

We would have done very well in that race. We came in and made a great pit stop at the right time. And as we went out of the pits, we had what's known as an airbox fire at Honda. Sometimes the fuel got in the wrong place and the air box surrounding the engine induction system caught fire. And we had to retire Rubens' car. But we were in a similarly good position to Williams. Something else happened later in the race, otherwise it would have been our best result of the year. Probably a podium as you achieved with Nico Rosberg driving your car.

LEADERSHIP

A I want to talk briefly about some of the types of people that you've worked with. Let's start with Flavio Briatore.

R I like Flavio. He always brings a different perspective on things, which I think is helpful. It's always fairly extreme. So you have to moderate it. Oh yes, and he is very bright and very humorous. He has had a colourful life, that's for sure.

A What was he like to work for?

R Well, he left us alone. That was the great thing that I can say. He left us alone, and in leaving us alone he never wanted to be the reference point within the team. Externally, it was different. People at Benetton would comment that he would pass them in the corridor and not even acknowledge that they were there. It was always a bit of a running joke whether Flavio would actually say good morning to you. So he had this distance, which actually was helpful in a way because it meant that I became the point of reference for the people at Benetton. He never interfered with the engineering, he got the money, I never asked how, he always seemed to do the deals. We had the tobacco deal with Mild Seven and he always kept the Benetton family happy.

There was always a fairly healthy debate about the budgets. Because on the back of the budget discussion was Flavio's view that Formula One was ridiculously expensive and we should all be running standard cars and all the rest of it. You always had those debates and I would say, 'Flavio, when the rules say that we can use a standard car, then the budget will be that, but while we are all staying with the current rules the budget has to be this.' I quite enjoyed my time with him actually. I can honestly say he never let me down. He never double-crossed me.

One lesson I learnt from Flavio came after Michael and I won our first race together at the Belgian Grand Prix in 1992. He called me into his office and said, 'Ross, you have done a really good job. I'm really pleased we won it. I want to give you a little bonus.' I said, 'That's okay, it's not in my contract . . .' He gave me a Swatch. And I said, 'That *is* a little bonus.' He said, 'Well someone gave it to me, and it wasn't for me and I thought you would enjoy it.' In a way, that was a really valuable lesson to me. The emotions I felt about that. It would have been far better to have done nothing, first of all. Secondly, you can do things that don't cost a lot of money that people really value. And he did the worst thing of all.

He had come up from a pretty poor background. But he came up in a different way. I came up in a world where I had been a mechanic, been a machinist and I worked with people. I enjoyed their company. I enjoyed working with them. I enjoyed the camaraderie. And the old adage of treat people how you wanted to be treated yourself is still a very strong principle of mine. He didn't have that background. He'd got to where he got to, I think, fighting tooth and nail in whatever way he could and hadn't been in a team culture. He was very much an individual. So his approach, his ego, everything was very individualistic with him.

A You can't imagine two more different people than Flavio and Jean Todt. You worked for Jean for several years. What's it like working for Jean? What's he like as a type of leader?

R Jean, again, didn't interfere with the engineering. He was very good in that he delegated well. He would want to know what was going on. I had to pass his office most nights when I left and he was nearly always there at that time. If the door was open, I would pop in or he would call me in, and most evenings I would give him a summary of the day. He would want to know absolutely everything that was going on, but he didn't interfere with the engineering. He was very good with the drivers. He was very close to Michael. He would spend quite a lot of time talking to me about what the drivers had said and so on. He was a very good interface in that respect, because sometimes I would have my head buried in the engineering, in the team, in the technical side. He was very good with the money, the budgets. He fought really hard to get all the funding, particularly in the early years. In the later years, he started to become concerned about the size of Formula One budgets, their sustainability and so on, especially as his role in Ferrari changed, when he became head of Ferrari.

He's an incredibly loyal person: if you were loyal to Jean he would do anything for you. He was one of those people who, if you rang him at two in the morning because you had a crisis, you knew he would be there. You could rely on him. He could be very dogmatic with other people. An example would be my relationship with Tom Walkinshaw – Tom and I had a serious fallout, but we made up in the end. Jean Todt would never have spoken to Tom for the rest of his life. I saw that with one or two people who upset Jean. And that was it. They were marked and they could forget about it then. Very bright, very intelligent guy. Interestingly, numerically brilliant. On the pit wall, I wouldn't use a calculator, I would just ask Jean what XYZ × B was, and he would give me an answer almost instantaneously. He had this amazing numeracy.

Jean was very consultative in terms of decision-making. So he would always draw me in, sometimes with Rory Byrne, sometimes Paolo Martinelli, the engine guy, or Stefano Domenicali. He would always draw us into some of the conversations before he made his decision. Certainly, he would never reserve to himself a racing decision; even if it was a political decision with the FIA he would consult . . . Where he did work without consultation with me, was the commercial dealings with Bernie, he took care of that. Stefano would get involved but I didn't, although if I asked him he would tell me. He was never secretive about it, but it was never something he chose to divulge unless I asked. If I was interested, he would tell me. So he would very much deal with the commercial side himself. He would be dealing with the sponsors, with the commercial rights holder, with the drivers – the drivers' contracts were always negotiated by him.

A Who else did you work for who had a distinctive approach to leadership?

R I guess it started with Patrick Head on the engineering side. He was my first mentor. I would characterize Patrick's leadership style as one of respect. He wasn't, let's say, an active leader. He never came out and put his arm round you. You wanted to do well because you respected him, because he had such great standards. It was never one of inclusiveness. I always tried to have an inclusive management style in the teams I was involved in, where I included people. Patrick less so. Maybe during my time at Williams I wasn't as close to the process as I became with other teams in later years. I never saw the way he operated with Neil Oatley or Frank Dernie for instance. My management style was to be consultative, but then making a decision and expecting everyone to stick by it. I was very happy and wanted to get advice from people and hear their opinions and put everything on the table. Encourage challenge, if there was disagreement about things. Sometimes I would send people away and then come back and have a debate again. But in the end I would say, 'Right, this is the way we're going.' So people always left the meeting knowing what we were doing. Unless the meeting was one where, 'You have got to go and do some more work and we are going to come back in two or three days' time, sit down and decide what we are going to do,' my first principle was to make sure you leave a meeting with everyone knowing what they are going to be doing.

A Well, my observation would be this. All of the people we've discussed, including Frank, Patrick, Jean, Bernie, Flavio, have quite a lot of charisma. They are what people imagine of a Formula One Team Principal type. I am not detracting from their intelligence, their knowledge or their achievements. But they are not methodical, structured, detailed, process thinkers. And that's where you're different. I think what's very difficult is to be both an inspiring person to work for and yet very thorough and methodical, organized, not impulsive. The people you have talked about are not really on the detail day in, day out, which is difficult to do. You've got to be patient and interested in it. And my guess is that a number of those people you've described just aren't. In fact, they would take pride in not being involved in the detail. But the devil is in the detail. You've got to run a methodical process, you've got to be on top of the detail to understand the implications. I'm not comparing myself with them, but if I compare you with them, you combine a rigorous management approach and the ability to be a good leader as well. All those people we've talked about don't really have both.

R That's kind of you. Interesting to explain a little bit more about Jean. Jean was very successful at Ferrari, because he was determined to get the best people. He got Michael for a start. He got me, he got Rory and he got other key members of the team. But he knew he couldn't do what we could do and he had no problem with that. 'I've got people to do that' was his mantra. 'What I'm going to do is get the absolute best people and then I am going to make sure that I stay close enough that if there's any little rough edges I can smooth them out.' He was very good at that. He would come to me and say, 'You know, Michael's a little bit upset about this and he thinks you are not paying enough attention to this.' But he would do it in a nice way, in a constructive rather than destructive way. And I would think at first, 'Why didn't Michael tell me?' But then you realize that sometimes people find it difficult. And it was always positive, he was very good at massaging the whole thing. He was intelligent, but he wouldn't necessarily understand the depth of the problem or the issues. But he was very good at delegating. He didn't interfere. That was the great thing.

A Well, that system works if you've got great people. But if you don't have great people, it's a disaster.

THE FUTURE

A This brings us onto our final topic: the future of Formula One. At the end of the last session, you said, 'Well, it depends what you want Formula One to be' and we put that question to one side. So what is Formula One? Is it sport, entertainment, business? Is it about technology, creating new technologies for road cars, something that Max Mosley has always been very keen on? Is it about men racing or, indeed, women? Or is it about making amazing pieces of equipment? What is Formula One for you?

R I think because of the very nature of Formula One, it's never the vision of one person. It's always the vision of a number of people. And therefore the nature of Formula One depends on the people whose vision you're accumulating, who can convince each other that they should go in a certain direction. Formula One is going through a transition at the moment where it's got a whole new management group in terms of the team individuals. So if you look at the people who are head of the teams today, almost without exception they are different to who they were five years ago. You've now got different key people who are trying to establish what they want Formula One to be, because they are the people ultimately who make the decisions.

A *Except that the FIA and FOM [Formula One Management] are not in different hands.*

R No, but what I felt was that in our day, there was a different cocktail of people who were trying to move Formula One in a direction. And people in the main with long relationships who knew the characters involved and therefore when you listened, when you didn't listen, when you gave them credence and when you didn't and so on. So there was a certain dynamic which took Formula One in a certain direction. That dynamic has changed now and there's a group of people setting the direction of the sport who don't have a lot of experience, quite honestly, of Formula One. They have not been through the mill. We've just experienced the first qualifying in Australia 2016 which was a disaster. Which everyone said would be a disaster. You wonder and worry about the process which allowed that to happen.

A *How did that happen?*

R Well, only as an informed observer, I understand that Bernie came along to a meeting and said, 'I want to reverse the grid.' And everyone said, 'No, Bernie, you can't do that. That's against the principles of Formula One.' And he said, 'I've got to shake Formula One up. Mercedes are going to be out the front. We have the fastest cars qualifying out the front, so what else do you expect? I've got to have a better show.' And as a sop to Bernie, they came up with this alternative system. Instead of saying, 'Just leave it alone, it works quite well, it's entertaining. It doesn't give you the mixed show for the race, but if we start interfering with things we are going to make it worse,' now you and I stood up to Bernie when we didn't agree with him and in some ways we paid the price. I wonder if Bernie sometimes reflects on the fact that his habit of removing people who object to his approach is actually not helpful in the end, because you need challenges. I always welcomed challenges in my day.

A I think that he does have people who object to his views. The difference between them and us, is that they have the ability to stop him. The truth is, he can't do anything now that Mercedes and Ferrari don't agree with. So he may go in and say, 'I want an independent engine' and they say, 'We will do X and Y and come back with some new rules. Don't worry, Bernie, we'll look at this.' And then he says, 'I want to mix up qualifying and it's a boring show.' They say, 'We'll come up with a proposal.' So, he's got a bigger problem now than he ever had with people like you and me, because he's got serious opposition who can block everything. The last thing Mercedes and Ferrari want to do right now is change anything.

R I agree with you. I wonder sometimes if Formula One is like evolution. If it takes a wrong direction, it takes so long to bring it back again. I think Formula One has evolved into a direction and you can look at the decision-making process that got it there. Gilles Simon, from the FIA, chaired the group that developed the rules for the new engine. That process that drove it in a certain direction. There was no strong mandate to keep the price down. We welcomed it as an opportunity. As Mercedes, we've got the strength, we've got the resources, we've got the commitment of a parent group. This feels like manna from heaven. I didn't envisage the engine situation would end up where it's ended up, but as a team we think we've got a very strong engine group, and we are up against Red Bull with no direct engine manufacturer support. Where do you want to be? So you look at the decisions that were made and see how it ended up. With that experience, if you were doing it again, you would make sure that process was more robust. You would start with the objectives of that new engine, including cost and supply – it has to be viable for an independent engine-maker (like Cosworth) to be a supplier – and make sure the process was robust enough to achieve those objectives.

A So what are the objectives of Formula One?

R For Formula One to succeed, people have got to watch it. If people don't watch it, Formula One is in a vacuum and it will just disappear. So why do people watch it? They watch it because they want to see drivers race each other. They want to see all the entertainment of drivers battling it out. The great thing about the Australian Grand Prix this year was there were battles all the way down the field, weren't there? A very good race. Shows what the product can be like. At the end of the day, someone is going to turn on the TV, their computer, go to the race and watch it. They love to watch it because there's the individuals involved, the drivers, the gladiators. And I think they do align themselves with teams. They do align themselves with cars. And with the fact that some drivers can get themselves in the right position to do better than they should, because they are in a better car. If everyone had the same car, you and I know who would be at the front the whole time. There would be Hamilton, Alonso, Vettel perhaps. You could write the order now if everyone had the same car. But you have the slightly unedifying example of Alonso struggling at the moment, because he is in the wrong car with the wrong engine.

A Which has happened before in his career. Is there another sport where someone is World Champion one year, then 19th, then World Champion again, then 19th?

R But that's the fascination of Formula One. We should never lose that. I think that the technological aspect excites a lot of fans. I know from going around talking to people. I was at Goodwood yesterday – 'What's wrong with Honda, why aren't they winning? Why aren't McLaren winning?' It's all part of the fascination of Formula One. I don't watch sailing, but I watched a little bit of the America's Cup which has interest for me because there is the technology as well. So Formula One has to retain those elements, I think, for it to be exceptional. And that is why Formula One stands out in motor sport. But you are quite right, there are any number of motor sports which give the simple formula of the same car. I know we have the best drivers in Formula One, but I don't think it would be the same. You have got to have that technical element. And you are right that you have got the dynamics of the politics and all the rest of it coming in. The commentators talking about all the various elements, all the subterfuge in the teams – it's just a great cocktail.

What I think Formula One always has to achieve is to be accessible to the largest number of teams as possible. That's what I feel is a big challenge and where Formula One fails. Wouldn't it be great if we had thirteen strong teams, with the franchise of a Formula One team being extremely valuable, and a queue of people who want to come into the sport, because they can be profitable and successful? You've got half the teams – Mercedes, Ferrari, Red Bull – who don't have to justify their budgets. It's branding. And then you've got half the teams that are almost living off being a vanity project for the owners, and they are struggling like hell. If you could fix that – if people could cut their cloth to suit their budget but still put on a really good show – you would then have a really robust formula that people would be gagging to get into and it would be more interesting. That process would create strength in numbers, and we would get the underdogs doing well occasionally.

The problem is the disparity in commercial payments for the teams and the cost of the technology is so extreme. The ratio of cost:performance is still too steep. If you have a very shallow cost to performance return, then if you've only got £100 million you won't be two seconds behind the team that's got £200 million. You might be half a second. So you find the demon driver. Pull the rabbit out of the hat with the driver and then you are there. That's the challenge, that's the trick.

What frustrates me is the short-term thinking that we touched on before. I mentioned the discussion two years ago with someone from the technical side of the sport when I proposed that we plan three years ahead – and he rejected that. But since I've left, I've also been involved socially with someone who is very high up on Formula One's commercial side. He asked me recently, 'What's the solution?' and I said,

'Well, you need to set out a plan for the next three to five years.' And he said, 'No, no, we need a solution now. We need something now to fix the problem. We might not be around in three years.' And I said, 'Well, there is no solution now. What you are going to do now is going to be worse. Consolidate what you have and have a vision of where you want to be in three years' time, because there are contracts coming up, you can position yourself, you can get engine projects started if you feel that's what's needed. But you've got to get a vision of where you want to be in three years' time.' And he wasn't convinced that you should do that. It will never change unless you do that. Unless you think that far ahead, Formula One in three to five years' time will still be the same as it is now; where there will be desperate teams at the back, with not enough money. Teams at the front will control the environment for their own purposes. So it's frustrating that even pretty senior individuals in Formula One will not have a long-term vision and plan . . . and Bernie's one of the worst. Someone's got to fix it by implementing a proper strategic plan, or it is going to suffer even more.

I can't remember a time when Bernie initiated a fundamental strategic change in Formula One. And my experience of him in meetings is that he always comes up with something which is so diverse, so divisive, that it never takes off. Also, you have to remember that Ken Tyrrell, Ron Dennis, Frank Williams all came up with Bernie. They had a long-standing relationship with Bernie. And they had a synergy with Bernie one way or another. He was one of the reasons they became so successful. They had some massive run-ins. I remember the one where Ron, Frank and Ken believed they were due a chunk of Formula One when Bernie sold it the first time. He didn't give them anything. And they took him to court but they lost the case because their contract was with the wrong party. So, anyway, they had their long-standing relationship with Bernie. The guys around now don't have any relationship with Bernie apart from what they have experienced in the last year or two. There is a different dynamic to the whole thing. Whether that's good or bad is a matter of opinion, but I think it is bad. Bernie doesn't respect them.

If I was treating Formula One like an engineering project, I would say, 'We've got to improve the product over the next three years.' You would do your analysis, make your plan and implement it. You would do the whole thing. Start to plan it, start to progress it. You would have review meetings to make sure it was going in the right direction. Getting any form of agreement in Formula One to carry out a proper process is almost impossible. I think the players don't want it and clearly Bernie doesn't. So, fixing the regulatory and rule-changing process and achieving a fair and economic supply position would be my priority.

A Getting Ferrari on board is always key and the truth is, they are not winning so they should be open to change.

R But Ferrari is in a very interesting situation at the moment, isn't it, with the company? Sergio Marchionne's in charge. He's quite a complex character and very different to Luca di Montezemolo.

A But he's a commercially astute guy. They floated Ferrari on the stock exchange. Ferrari's marketing is Formula One. They don't do any other marketing. And they need to win. They also could be earning a fortune under Formula One. They get chump change at the moment.

R Well, I know Norbert Haug's favourite reference was that the Bundesliga pulls in more money than Formula One. By quite a large margin.

A Man versus machine: which is more important?

R I think, again, that's the great thing about Formula One. It has to be both. That's why you get average drivers winning World Championships and great drivers not winning World Championships, because machines are involved. The extreme example we have touched on is Alonso and McLaren Honda at the moment. Probably the greatest driver, after Michael stopped, of the era, and yet Alonso is languishing at the back because the machine is not good enough. I can think of one or two World Champions who you would never classify in the ultimate vanguard of Formula One. But they had a great piece of kit and they did a great job with it. That's the magic of Formula One.

I think Alonso got himself into a very complex dynamic with the team at Ferrari. I think he was growing more and more frustrated with the team. And his demands were getting more and more extreme. I think he was receiving bad advice, or he was just using poor judgement of his own. I was told that at the end he felt that he needed to be able to influence what personnel the team were employing, which was, in my view, way beyond what a driver should be getting involved in. But it had become that fractious. The team knew that they were losing a huge asset. Alonso had dragged them close to winning a World Championship several times. But they just decided that the whole process had become so negative that they were better off without him. When they brought in James Allison and some other new personnel, they wanted to create a fresh opportunity. I think, on reflection, they did the right thing in getting Sebastian Vettel in, who was a fresh mind, a fresh dynamic. I will confess I thought it was a wrong move at the time, because Vettel had had a poor last year at Red Bull. Alonso was seen as the gold standard. They're getting rid of the gold standard and bringing in someone who just got spanked by Daniel Ricciardo.

A Although Vettel had won four World Championships . . .

R And no one gave him a lot of credit for them, did they? I think he has now re-established himself as a reference point and he looks as though he is in a good place. Alonso is now in the wilderness. So I think that is what is fascinating about the man and machine equation.

A Part of the sport is that the men choose their machines. They have put themselves in a position to win, which requires judgement.

R Yeah. I mean why the drivers make the decisions they do is a different matter, but the fact is that you can end up in the wrong team at the wrong time because of poor judgement. And it's only because machines are involved. That fascinating situation where Alonso has gone from potentially winning a Championship to now not even having a look in, is because machines are involved. I think if you remove that, the team variables are down to what pit crew you have and can they set the car up properly.

The idea of entirely separate Drivers' and Constructors' Championships, where the drivers rotate among the teams and drive different cars each race, doesn't sit well with me. It would be one of those things that you would have to try and see if there were any unintended consequences. I have this love and passion of a driver and a team being an entity, pitted against another driver and a team being an entity. The idea of that driver swapping a team each weekend, I think you lose the identity of the team and driver.

In terms of innovation and technology being applicable to modern road cars, I think a good crossover is methodology. I think culture is the thing that definitely crosses over. I think you can probably pick out bits and pieces that have come across: disc brakes were first invented in motorsport and I think the use of carbon fibre in Formula One was the lead for automotive applications. It certainly got the publicity for it. But where I think Formula One is very strong is in the culture. If you wanted to develop a concept and to drive things forward at maximum pace, utilize it in Formula One.

I know, for instance, with composite technology, the composite companies love Formula One because we are willing to try things. If they've got a new resin system or a new type of fibre, they give it to the Formula One teams to explore for them, to look at the applications and come back with the feedback. If they put it in the aerospace industry, five years later they would have an answer. Put it into Formula One and five months later they have got an answer. So the culture and 'can do' philosophy in Formula One is really strong. When I have worked with manufacturers, with Ford, Honda or Bridgestone, certain companies took advantage of Formula One by placing their engineers into this environment. It was part of the training of their engineers. And I remember particularly at Ford in the 1990s, they loved it because they said they had engineers coming back who had a 'can do' attitude. 'I've been in Formula One. You've got to be on the start line at 2pm on a Sunday afternoon. There is no way round that. And you are going to get it done.' Engineers who came back from Formula One would go to test a piece of equipment and someone says, 'The rig's not available.' 'Well, let's go and make a rig. I'll make a rig.' They came back with a different approach, different culture, different philosophies. So I think that is where Formula One can be helpful to a manufacturer. If they take advantage of it. Not all of them do.

A In Cosworth, where I am a director, we feel that is one of the things we bring. Because of that motor sport discipline, we'll do things a lot quicker than anyone expects is possible. Discipline is a really strong characteristic of Formula One, isn't it?

R I think one of the interesting things about discipline for me was the discipline that we touched on when we talked about the 1994 car. The discipline of saying in 1993, 'We are going to focus on '94 and not be distracted from it.' The discipline of keeping your programme structured, and even when there is a disaster going on somewhere, having the discipline to make sure all your other functions carry on in a proper way is vital.

I watched my grandson play football the other day and they are all running across the field like a swarm of bees around the ball. And I thought, 'Isn't that like life sometimes? Everyone runs to the problem.' In fact you don't want that. You want to decide who is going to deal with the problem, get them to work on it, give them all the support they need. And then make sure the rest of the people – maybe they are kept informed about what is going on because there can be concern – but make sure they carry on doing what they should be doing. Sometimes create the opportunity for them to have an input, but in a very structured way. 'So, okay, we've got this problem. Going to have a review meeting. What has everyone got to say about it? Okay, that's your opinion. Maybe you've got an interesting perspective on it that's vital. Now, this is the team we've identified and they are going to deal with the problem, so get back to your day jobs.'

A What about the question of learning as a person and as a team? Do teams learn? Do they get better, get momentum?

R Teams definitely get momentum and the momentum comes from confidence. It comes from some success. When I joined Honda, it was a group of people who had never really enjoyed much success. And they thought the people who were winning were better than they were. I had to convince them, and I think what was helpful to the process is that I had enjoyed success. So when I said to them, 'You are as good as anyone I have worked with. Your abilities are as good as anyone I have worked with. We can make this whole thing work,' that takes the team forward. When you have not been successful and you have never won a World Championship, you think there is something special about the people that do. They are doing something a little bit different to you. The way I tried to get it across to everyone in the team was, 'You're laminating this wing. You're a carbon fibre laminator. There's a bloke at Red Bull doing the same job. Are you going to do a better job than he's doing? Because if you do, and everyone in this company does, we will win the World Championship. You don't have to do a better job than the guy designing the car at Red Bull because that's nothing to do with you. But if you can laminate that wing a little bit tidier, a little bit more reliably, a little bit more efficiently than the guy at Red Bull, that's great. Just do it a little bit better. And you can do it, I promise you.'

Guess what? They did.

PART III

Observations

Observation 1

Strategy is a system

Ross defines strategy as a philosophy from which process flows. But it is a philosophy of *processes*. He describes it as 'integrating, applying processes and approaches, smoothing out'.

For him, 'Luck is preparation waiting for an opportunity.' This echoes a maxim from ancient Rome: 'He who wishes a successful outcome, let him fight with strategy, not at random.'

Ross developed his approach to leadership in the 1980s and he applied it consistently at Jaguar, Benetton, Ferrari, Honda Brawn and Mercedes. This was his system and he describes its various elements for us:

- investing in trusting long-term relationships with his colleagues;
- an inclusive and consultative but decisive management style;
- disciplined, structured and formal rhythms and routines;
- being generous in success;
- taking responsibility for setbacks;

- looking for systemic root causes using rigorous analysis rather than scapegoats;
- being passionate but not emotional;
- being on top of the technical detail;
- working alongside technical staff and mentoring them in a structured and consistent way;
- looking ahead to prospective regulatory changes, establishing a small, dedicated project team to pursue such opportunities; and,
- seeking out wholeness, integration, completeness in both the product and the process of designing, manufacturing and racing it.

At a tactical level, whether preparing for races or for an engagement with the FIA over a potentially controversial interpretation of the rules, Ross also insisted on his team playing out and planning for likely scenarios.

Observation 2

Avoid unnecessary conflict

Ross exemplified the principle that strategy is about winning, not fighting. He was struck by the insistence in the *Sunzi* that, 'the best generals do not fight. The job is done by then.' The only place that he allowed conflict was on the race track, and then only between his whole team and the others. More than any other technical director or Team Principal, Ross established a lead driver, with the second driver explicitly playing a role supporting the lead driver and the team as a whole. He reinforced this with a single team race strategist, rather than one for each side of the garage.

This approach encouraged openness in testing and practice and reduced the risk of a clash on track, conflict within the team and the dilution of results with points being spread across two drivers.

This was controversial at times, as it was seen by some as unfair and unsporting, but it was highly effective. And Ross defends his approach by saying that he backed the driver with the best chance of winning, regardless of who that was.

Ross also believed that it was correct to supply an engine customer with an inferior engine to the one being raced by the works team. Personally, I do not agree with this, but I have to acknowledge that if the goal is to win and the rules allow it, then it is illogical for a works team (like Ferrari, Renault or Mercedes) to provide competitive engines to a customer. Quite simply, the rules should not allow it, and the FIA should not have looked the other way when this happened – contrary to the rules – in 2015; nor should the FIA have amended the rules to allow it in 2016, presumably under pressure from the main engine manufacturers. The interests of a team are not the same as the interests of the sport, and it is the role of a regulator to provide a level playing-field.

But that is an aside: conflict uses up energy and resources; it creates external risk as people seek to outwit and undermine you; and it creates risk of internal division – the ultimate danger for any organization.

Observation 3

Build trust consciously

For Ross, trust is a conscious thing. At its heart is the principle that underlies ethical teaching from Confucius to Christ: treat people how you wanted to be treated yourself.

In his relations with people inside and outside his team, Ross avoided conflict, not by being a pushover, but by actively seeking people out, being approachable and by socializing with them. I saw this myself. I recall many occasions when Ross would sit down with me and chat in an airport or on a plane or (on one occasion) a helicopter flight from Nice airport to Monte Carlo. Ross just made the effort to be friendly and good company.

The result of this was that people always wanted to give him the benefit of the doubt. Look at how significant this has been in his career: the FIA's decision in 1999 over the barge boards helped secure Ferrari's first Constructors' title for fifteen years; Honda's desire to do the right thing by him when they decided to withdraw from Formula One in 2008 helped him see off Richard Branson and secure the team; and Martin Whitmarsh and Norbert Haug's advocacy secured Brawn GP a Mercedes engine a few weeks later – leading to the 2009 titles and the acquisition of the team by Mercedes at the end of 2009.

Not everyone is susceptible to such an approach – their own ambitions are (in their own mind) simply not compatible with sharing. There are two or perhaps three figures who appear in Ross's downfall who saw him as competition. Now perhaps they see each other as competition.

Observation 4

Know yourself and know the other

On the plus side, Ross attributes his rigorous routines to the need to control a certain natural 'laziness' through the structure provided by rhythms and deadlines.

On the downside, Ross was brought down by his failure to understand the people he was up against and, to an extent, himself. He would have survived if he had just been up against the external enemy, but the combination of the external enemy and the internal division between himself and others at Mercedes was lethal.

In my questions of him, I tried to explore how this happened – how did someone with such good human understanding get into this situation? The answer is that, through necessity rather than choice, Ross made an enemy of Bernie Ecclestone in 2009 and, as Ross inferred from the remarkable phone call he received from Bernie in 2012, that was not forgotten. Ross was never that interested in the commercial aspects of Formula One, so he simply did not pay sufficient attention to rebuilding his relationship with Bernie after 2009. And within Mercedes, Ross found himself, for the first time, at a disadvantage to his colleagues. They had close relations with the board of Mercedes and he did not make the effort to build relations himself.

After a period of this internal and external conflict, Ross lost the will to carry on. Probably he no longer enjoyed going to work and he saw a long fight ahead to resolve the situation, a fight different to any he had fought up to that point and one for which he had no stomach. It could be said that this was not a lack of self-awareness, but would Ross have found himself in this position had he been more aware? Perhaps if he had realized his position earlier and acted promptly and more ruthlessly, he could have secured his future. His internal adversaries were vulnerable after the release of the compromising recording made by Colin Kolles, but Ross did not exploit an opportunity that, one suspects, his adversaries would not have hesitated to grasp.

The evidence of Mercedes' performance does not support an argument that Ross had lost his appetite or ability to win on the track, but perhaps the root cause was that after Brawn GP had won the 2009 World Championships and been acquired by Mercedes, Ross did not have the will to win off the track any longer. For a man with a single-minded dedication to winning, this was a rare but fateful lapse in that clarity and simplicity of purpose.

Observation 5

Embrace humility

Ross is fiercely proud of his achievements and in no doubt that these are *his* achievements. When Ross said that he had never added up the number of Championships he had won, it was true. But he did not want to leave any out once we started counting. Still, he has much less ego than many people who might have less justification for it. As a result, he was able to be generous with his colleagues, encouraging others to take the podium and share the success. This is a rare, and disarming, character trait.

The story of Flavio Briatore giving Ross an unwanted Swatch as his bonus for their first race win together clearly made an impression. Flavio is a very amusing and flamboyant guy, who Ross praises in other respects, but perhaps the real bonus for Ross was this lesson.

Ross genuinely projects humility, rather as Frank Williams does. It is a very significant part of how both men inspire loyalty and the desire to do well in others. In business, I have seen this most strongly in Sir Robert Wilson and Dr Andrew Mackenzie, respectively the heads of Rio Tinto and BHP Billiton when I worked for them. They just have the knack of making you want to do your best for them.

To some extent, the inability of Toyota to succeed in Formula One was a failure of humility. This was a justly proud company that wanted to win in Formula One to boost its brand in Europe in particular. But Toyota also could not accept that its leadership did not have the character, disposition or ability to thrive in the world of Formula One. Looking at the three dimensions of strategy, Toyota F1 certainly addressed the economic and technical aspects, but they did not consider the political aspects. This was a lack of humility in that they thought they could apply the Toyota production system to Formula One; but it was also because they did not want to engage with the governance of the sport which they rightly regarded as not at the levels to which they were used. The problem is that if you are going to win in this sport, you have to engage in it.

Observation 6

Invest in people and culture

Ross did not take a group of people with him from team to team; in fact there are only a few cases in his long career of people who worked with him at two teams – Rory Byrne and Aldo Costa being notable examples.

Instead, Ross worked with the people he had, taking time to get to know them and not allowing himself to make rapid decisions based on early impressions. This is one of many examples of his measured approach – and of his relentless pursuit of facts. In addition, this approach reinforced the message to the team that they were as capable of winning as the competition.

Once Ross had evaluated his people and other resources, he would then seek to supplement them with external hires. As he says, he undertook this himself, treating this as an opportunity to get to know the candidates personally, even regarding negotiations of their package as a way of understanding them better. No leader is better than their immediate team, so this is a critical part of his methodology.

Within his teams, Ross fostered a culture of openness and order. His routines were designed to ensure a steady flow of information, the ability to control messaging, to encourage the kind of culture he wanted. Not all Formula One teams and not all leaders operate like this. In particular, Ross ensured that the routines were sustained through thick and thin, and were not just reactive crisis management. I am sure that is one reason why Ferrari responded so well to the performance crisis of 2005: the rhythms just kept going. You have to build systems that are robust in good times and bad, especially when you operate in cyclical or highly competitive environments where you cannot always be winning.

The *Sunzi* observes that there is a need for both compassion and discipline in leadership:

Regard your soldiers as your children, and they will follow you into the deepest valleys; look upon them as your own beloved sons, and they will stand by you even unto death. If, however, you are indulgent, but unable to make your authority felt; kind-hearted, but unable to enforce your commands; and incapable, moreover, of quelling disorder: then your soldiers must be likened to spoilt children; they are useless for any practical purpose. (*Book IX*)

In relation to the sport as a whole, Ross observed that, 'Formula One is never the vision of one person.' How does one create a cohesive culture around that fact?

Observation 7

Take the measure of time

Ross has the measure of time. Formula One is about speed – on and off the track – and the feedback loop is agonizingly compressed. But time and again, Ross would take the focus off the short term and put it onto achieving a step-change in what is (for Formula One) the distant future of the following season. This was not only when he started at Ferrari and Honda, it was during the run of victories at the Scuderia (a rhythm he describes as being like on the crest of a wave) and then again with the new engine formula at Mercedes.

To have the measure of time – using it as a resource – is essential to strategy. When things are tough, you have to do it in order to buy yourself time and space to make that step change. When things are good, you have to reinvest the time and space won by virtue of your leadership to sustain your momentum.

Time is also an important resource in resolving conflict. When people are locked in immediate competition they are reluctant to give anything up; but precisely because they are focused on the here and now, they may be amenable to arrangements that take place in what appears the distant future. But three years pass all too quickly and those who plan ahead can take advantage of this. In addition, once a future change has been agreed and locked in, human nature is often seeking to bring it forward, since we tend not to like uncertainty, and we often over-estimate our own abilities.

I was struck also by Ross's use of the expression 'strategic time' to refer to the time that could be gained or lost in a pit stop. Pit stops give cars the opportunity to gain track position and often you will see a car emerging from the pit lane neck-and-neck with a car that has stayed out on the track. These are dramatic moments for the teams and a tenth of a second in the pit stop can make a vast difference. This illustrates the fact that time does not have equal value at different stages of a competition. But time and timing are always an essential consideration in strategy.

Observation 8

A complete process leads to a competitive product

Ross talks about a 'complete car' – that means for him a competitive car. To achieve this completeness, Ross first of all sought to bring together all the key components – engine, chassis and tyres for the most part. When he joined Ferrari, the Scuderia was designing its chassis in England while the dominant engine group was at Maranello. Ross brought them together and became the reference point for the combined programme. He also worked on the relationship with Bridgestone to such an extent that no other leading team felt able to work with the Japanese tyre-maker because they were seen to be so much a part of the Ferrari programme. Even when the troubles hit in 2005, Ross worked hard to protect Bridgestone from criticism.

To integrate the engine and chassis groups, Ross physically and metaphorically knocked down walls, collocating engine and chassis designers and swapping personnel between the two, at Ferrari, Honda and Mercedes.

From a complete process comes a complete product, and the ability to sustain exceptional performance. Ross focused on the process, knowing that the competitiveness would follow. The process was honed through rigorous and swift root cause analysis of any setbacks.

It is not surprising that completeness is essential to success in Formula One, but it is hard to achieve given the levels of performance and reliability that must be attained in such short periods.

Observation 9

Develop and apply a set of rhythms and routines

Having established an integrated team and structure, Ross instituted rhythms and routines that ensured the completeness of the process of designing, manufacturing and racing cars. These routines constantly reinforced alignment around a shared vision, clear accountabilities and systems for constantly checking in on progress. Ross *never* delegated responsibility for the process or the product, and attended to all aspects of it, without ever disempowering either the heads of department or the staff working for them. He did this by using formal and informal processes and ensuring that his involvement was positive and constructive. That requires a frequent and regular process so that things never get far out of hand and can be gently reined back without a fuss.

This also meant that Ross's teams did not have to react in

a panic to setbacks – their systems were robust enough to handle whatever was thrown at them. Ross called this 'regulating to a vision, not reacting to pressure.' System robustness is based on people and processes honed through rhythm and routine. This applied equally to preparing a submission to the FIA on a novel interpretation of the rules as to designing parts. Ross used role playing and a structured process to prepare technical arguments.

One tactical trick to avoid unnecessary errors is the use of checklists, which Ross illustrated in relation to drivers forgetting to mention broken wing mirrors or other minor details.

Most people in leadership positions evolve a set of routines over time. Ross was perhaps different in that his developed early in his career and because they worked for him, he applied them time and again as he progressed. Notice that these routines survived the test of time: working in large teams and small, and in difficult as well as good times.

My learning from Ross, is that leaders need to focus more on *process* and less on diving into *content*.

Observation 10

Just adopt!!

'Adopt' is really a euphemism. Ross is clear that you have to respect the competition, learn and even steal from them: people, ideas, methods, anything that can make you more competitive.

Formula One racing technology is generally not protected by patent (takes too long, can't be enforced and just shows everyone what you are doing), so there are differences between Formula One and other areas of life where intellectual property can be better protected and adopting may really be theft.

But people never seem to want to take ideas, systems or processes from others, even from within their own companies. They want to develop their own things. People in Formula One are no different, but leadership requires that you constantly challenge this. You have to foster a culture not only of innovation but of looking outside for ideas. Also, when you take someone's ideas, you need to do it swiftly. The whole point about something that is working elsewhere is that it is working. Fiddling with it, 'making it your own' adds cost, delay and risk that it will not work.

Ultimately, no organization has all the good ideas, and there is always the possibility that the 'killer app' that changes the whole game will come from outside. Therefore people have to have the humility to be looking openly at what others are doing and thinking critically about the implications.

Observation 11

Define the line – and own it

Again, Formula One operates to different standards of governance to other businesses and even sports. No one should take the ethics of Formula One and apply them in business or government.

But the reverse is also true.

The point is to understand the governance of your activity, define the line clearly for everyone, and then operate up to that line. Not a millimetre beyond what is acceptable, but equally not a millimetre short either. The gap you create is like the one that Schumacher created for Barrichello: big enough to drive through. That gap is lost competitiveness and wasted opportunity.

What Ross demonstrates is that total competition means clarity in your own and your team's mind about where the line is. This side of the line there is innovation, creativity and opportunity, so it must be exploited and enjoyed. Ross's goal was to win World Championships. His line was not intentionally cheating. The rest is history.

This approach may be contrasted with the 'statesmanship' which we discussed in respect of both Ross himself and others. Back in 2008, Ross took the conscious decision to warn the other teams that the new aero rules for 2009 were not working. Sam Michael of Williams, at least, accurately interpreted what Ross was saying as a warning that Honda had found a loophole that would enable them to create much more downforce than everyone believed was possible under the new rules. Ross was lucky that his warning was not picked up, since it could have resulted in a quick rule change that might have left his team much less competitive than they proved in 2009. This was, on one view, a reckless and rare act of 'statesmanship' by Ross. It served no purpose and could have cost him everything that he went on to achieve in 2009. Others were not so fortunate. McLaren's gracious support of Brawn GP enabled the latter to obtain a Mercedes engine for the 2009 season. That led to a double title for Brawn and Mercedes leaving McLaren and acquiring Brawn. The consequences are still being felt today, although McLaren's securing of Honda as engine partner is a great achievement that could soon make up for the loss of Mercedes.

I appreciate that this attitude might be seen as unsporting – but my point is that, by definition, statesmanship benefits others, and there is a price to pay for this. Leaders need to make sure that they are being statesmen for the right reasons – such as that it is in everyone's longer-term interests – and not because of the vanity of occupying the moral high ground. Ross observes that there is a time for statesmanship – early on when it does not compromise your options and competitive position. This leads to a hypothesis that leaders should be able to be more statesmanlike on long-term issues, even while competing ruthlessly in the short-term.

Observation 12

Strive for simplicity, manage complexity

Complexity cannot be avoided, so it must be managed through – guess what – shared vision, clear accountability and the rhythms and routines described above. No one can manage everything.

But there must always be a bias towards simplicity. Simple solutions, where possible, bring less risk of unintended consequences. In Formula One, they tend also to offer larger performance gains, less weight penalty and greater reliability. But these kind of opportunities tend to come early in the life cycle of a set of rules, and taking advantage of them requires the step-back, project approach that Ross deployed so effectively.

Another dimension of simplicity is not to pursue quantity at the expense of quality. Scale creates additional challenges.

It is not just technical projects that require this approach. Sometimes Ross had to clear the decks and devote time to thought.

Observation 13

People innovate naturally

Formula One demonstrates that in the right environment and structure, people innovate naturally. It is astonishing how much they can achieve when their creativity is given the right conditions.

As a leader, you have to commit to creating these conditions, even though you cannot know what the results are going to be, and believing that people will come up with something. It is creative intellectual work that you can't really quantify and everyone has to know that you will stick with the commitments you have made to the project team.

Lack of confidence can mean that 'sometimes people try too hard, to make too big a jump.'

Perhaps a related point is that one should look at all situations as a chance to be innovative. Ross had the philosophy that adversity is an opportunity to gain competitive advantage. 'If you could deal with that sort of adversity better than another team, then you would come out on top.' He gave the example of Monaco – always a race that presented logistical and sporting challenges, but one that is quintessentially Formula One. He advised his team to enjoy what others find difficult. At the Monaco Grand Prix in 2016, Red Bull lost the lead to Mercedes because of just such a logistical challenge – in this case, the way the layout of the garage constrained communication and storage.

Observation 14

There is a place for data – and intuition

While Ross relentlessly pursued data, he also emphasized the place for judgement, intuition and surprise.

The example was the success he had with a three pit stop strategy. Race strategy is usually about calculating the fastest race, which dictated two stops. In this case, Ferrari opted for an extra stop, which was not the quickest, but gave the team control, enabled their drivers to race in 'free air' – i.e. out of the main body of cars. It had the additional, and perhaps less predictable, benefit of throwing McLaren off balance, and causing them to react in haste and compromise their own strategy.

Observation 15

Strategy can be studied and applied

Strategy is a process by which we overcome obstacles to achieve a goal. I emphasize, it is not a plan, it is a *process*. Furthermore, that process is subject to principles, perhaps rules even, that can be studied and applied.

Ross did not study strategy and he did not document or perhaps even articulate his approach until now. But when one reads his account, it is evident that the methodology he applied goes beyond a set of principles – these are *rules*. A person who took a different approach to Ross on each of these elements might still succeed – but they would reduce their prospects of success and they would have to over-compensate in other areas. So, Red Bull and Renault were not as effective as Mercedes in developing a competitive power unit under the new rules that came into force for the 2014 season. In

Ross's view, this was because they did not plan ahead and did not integrate their teams as well. However, as time has gone by, Renault has improved the performance of the power unit and Red Bull has done a great job on the chassis. The total package has become increasingly competitive and has already won a race in 2016 and come close to winning two others by mid-year. In order to do this, Red Bull and Renault have had to compensate for their relatively slow start.

There is a reason why these principles have the force of rules. Strategy is not a human construct – it is part of the human mind, indeed the human body. It is how human intelligence operates. As cognitive scientist Steven Pinker states, 'If we are intelligent then we must have goals.' He continues: 'Intelligence, then, is the ability to attain goals in the face of obstacles by means of decisions based on rational (truth-obeying) rules.' Intelligence is the ability to shape the world around us and strategy is how we go about it. Human intelligence has evolved (or was created) to exploit three things: (a) the natural resources around us; (b) the technical ability to order, shape, process and transform those resources; and (c) the resource represented by other people. This is why strategy has three dimensions (social, economic and technical); and this is why methods that extract the best from other people, make the most of the available resources and constantly improve technical capabilities are more successful. Formula One just happens to be an activity that perfectly and rapidly rewards those methods; and also requires proficiency in all three fields. To have sustained success as a competitor in Formula One, you have to get the politics, economics and technology right.

Total competition requires a complete, integrated and inclusive process.

SELECTED FURTHER READING

Strategy

Clausewitz, Carl von, *On War* (First published 1832; translation by J. J. Graham; revised By F. N. Maude; introduction by Louise Willmot) (Wordsworth, 1997)

Freedman, Lawrence, *Strategy: A History* (Oxford University Press, 2013)

Gat, Azar, *A History of Military Thought: From the Enlightenment to the Cold War* (Oxford University Press, 2001)

Handel, Michael I., *Masters of war: Classical strategic thought* (Routledge, 2005)

Heuser, Beatrice, *The Evolution of Strategy: Thinking War From Antiquity to the Present* (Cambridge University Press, 2010)

Luttwak, Edward, *Strategy: The logic of war and peace* (Bellknap Press, 2001)

Mead Earle, Edward (Ed.), *Makers of Modern Strategy: Military thought from Machiavelli to Hitler* (Princeton University Press 1973)

Murray, Williamson, MacGregor Knox and Alvin Bernstein (Eds), *The Making of Strategy: Rulers, states, and war* (Cambridge University Press, 1994)

Paret, Peter, *Makers of Modern Strategy* (Princeton University Press, 1986)

Zamoyski, Adam, *1812: Napoleon's fatal march on Moscow* (Harper Perennial, 2005)

Operational art

Harrison, Richard W., *The Russian Way of War: Operational Art, 1904–1940* (University Press of Kansas, 2001)

Isserson, Georgii Samoilovich, *The Evolution of Operational Art* (first published in 1937, translated by Bruce W. Schneider) (Combat Studies Institute Press US Army Combined Arms Center, Fort Leavenworth, Kansas

Krause, Michael D. and R. Cody Phillips (Eds), *Historical Perspectives of the Operational Art* (Center of Military History, United States Army, Washington, D.C., 2005)

McKercher, B. J. C. and Michael Hennessy (Eds), *The Operational Art: Developments in the Theories of War* (Praeger, 1996)

Olsen, John Andreas, and Martin Van Creveld (Eds), *The Evolution of Operational Art: from Napoleon to the Present* (Oxford University Press, 2010)

Simpkin, Richard E., and John Erickson, *Deep Battle: The Brainchild of Marshal Tukhachevskii* (Potomac Books Incorporated, 1987)

Svechin, Aleksandr A., *Strategy*: a translation of *Strategiia* (Moscow: Voennyi vestnik, 1927), edited by Kent D. Lee. (East View Publications, 1999)

The *Sunzi* and its setting

Ames, Roger T. (Tr), *Sun-tzu: The Art of Warfare* (Ballantine Books, 1993)

Graham, Angus C., *Disputers of the Tao* (Open Court, 1989)

Griffith, Samuel B. (Tr), *Sun Tzu: The Art of War* (Oxford University Press, 1971)

Hui, Victoria Tin-bor, *War and State Formation in Ancient China and Early Modern Europe* (Cambridge University Press, 2005)

Johnston, Alastair I., *Cultural Realism: Strategic Culture and Grand Strategy in Chinese History* (Princeton University Press, 1995)

Loewe, Michael and Edward L. Shaughnessy (Eds), *The Cambridge History of Ancient China: From the Origins of Civilization to 221 BC* (Cambridge University Press, 1999), notably: Hsu, Cho-yun, 'The Spring and Autumn Period,' pp. 545–86; and Lewis,

Mark Edward, 'Warring States Political History,' pp. 587–650.

Mair, Victor H. (Tr), *The Art of War: Sun Zi's Military Methods* (Columbia University Press, 2007)

Minford, John (Tr), *The Art of War* (Penguin, 2002)

Needham, Joseph, and Robin D. S. Yates, *Science and Civilisation in China. Vol. 5: Chemistry and Chemical Technology, pt. 7. Military Technology* (Cambridge University Press, 1986)

Pines, Yuri, *Foundations of Confucian Thought: Intellectual Life in the Chunqiu Period (722–453 B.C.E.)* (University of Hawaii Press, 2002)

——*The Everlasting Empire: The political culture of ancient China and its imperial legacy* (Princeton University Press, 2012)

Sawyer, Ralph D. and Mei-chün Sawyer (Trs), *The Seven Military Classics of Ancient China* (Westview Press, 1993)

Van der Ven, Hans J. (Ed.), *Warfare in Chinese History* (Brill, 2000)

Watson, Burton, *Basic Writings of Mo Tzu, Hsun Tzu and Han Fei Tzu* (Columbia University Press, 1967)

Wilkinson, Endymion, *Chinese History: A New Manual* (Harvard University Asia Center, 2013)

ACKNOWLEDGEMENTS

Ross Brawn:

I would like to thank Frank Williams and Patrick Head for giving me my first opportunity in Formula One. Luca di Montezemolo, Jean Todt and Nick Fry all played key parts in my career. Jackie Oliver for giving me my first car to design and Tom Walkinshaw for persuading me to go into Sports Cars. I enjoyed tremendous support from a huge number of other people in Formula One, but I would like especially to thank all the team members and drivers I worked with for showing such tremendous dedication and commitment.

Michael Schumacher is a very special person to me on a professional and human level. We pray for his recovery.

Most importantly, I must thank my wife, Jean, and my two daughters and the rest of my family for unconditional support and for keeping my feet on the ground – I couldn't have done it without you.

Adam Parr:

I would like to thank the inspiring and generous people who have helped me experience so much professionally and academically since I left Formula One. In particular – the late Professor Lisa Jardine; Dr Andrew Mackenzie; Kevin Kalkhoven; Sam Michael; Jeremy Palmer; Richard King; Hamish Forsythe; Robyn Scott; Paul James and Max Mosley.

And a special thanks to my boys, Felix and Louis.

We would both like to thank the following people who have helped us make this book: Geraldine Conneely; Phoebe Kennedy; Max Mosley; Sam Michael; David Godwin; and Ian Marshall, Jo Whitford and the team at Simon & Schuster.

PICTURE CREDITS

INDEX